Fairies

Fairies
A Dangerous History

RICHARD SUGG

REAKTION BOOKS

To the memory of Christopher Luckens (1944–2016),
healer, adventurer, and friend.

Published by Reaktion Books Ltd
Unit 32, Waterside
44–48 Wharf Road
London N1 7UX, UK

www.reaktionbooks.co.uk

First published 2018, reprinted 2019
Copyright © Richard Sugg 2018

Printed and bound in China by 1010 Printing International Ltd

A catalogue record for this book is available from the British Library

ISBN 978 1 78023 899 9

Contents

Introduction

A HOT OCTOBER NOON; black yew shadows; strong sunlight dappling the clay banks of a stream. Shooting by, something fast, there and gone, a bright vanishing flashes from shade to shade. I pause, pass on. A squirrel? A kingfisher? Surely nothing more exotic than the latter, for I am in the local park, thronged with people, bounded by traffic on either side. Yet just for a moment the thing in the hot shade, off that deserted back path, was more than animal and less than human. For half a second it was a nymph, felt rather than thought.

The fairies had got inside my head. Perhaps they were always there, buried deep in the caves of childhood, deeper still in the childhood of our species. But I had worked hard to get them to the surface, through weeks of listening to those who once believed in them – believed unshakably, and accordingly saw, felt, heard and suspected them everywhere, every day of their lives. It is my aim, here, to get you to see the world as they saw it. An aim, if we are to be fussily literal, which is of course impossible: it would involve amnesia, require robbing you of the ability to read and write, oblige me to take away your car keys and dissolve the solid streets around you into fairy hills and glades. Let us try, all the same. This is my dark and impious dream: to get fairies into your head, and to get you into the heads, behind the eyes, of people to whom fairies were terror and wonder, danger and glamour, and yet – unlike the angels and demons of educated Christianity – right *there*: romping and singing, fiddling and feasting in the turf which your nailed boots crushed day by day, on the glowing hearth where they warmed themselves as you slept.

Once, people really believed in fairies. By the close of Chapter Three you should be able to see why; and you should (I must warn you) then find that fairies never look the same to you again. But I take no offence if, at this point, you are unconvinced. Few beings of the supernatural world have suffered greater indignities than the fairy. Vampires and witches have been the victims of much distortion, and even ghosts rather belittled by their role in the jokey films of recent years. But fairies? Imagine that one day you are torn from the earth, scrubbed clean, hideously perfumed, shrunk down from four foot of sturdy muscle into a diaphanous five inches, showered in glitter and rainbow hues, and forced to wave a flimsy wand at small girls for the rest of your immortal life. Once, the fear of you moved people to murder, and scared some to death. Your pedigree stretched back to the edge of Time itself, and your powers ranged from the tiniest accidents of field and kitchen to the potential destruction of the world. Once, fairies were woven through the tree roots, bobbing on the tides and, on some enchanted island off the coast, living a life as intricate and complex as that of any human society. Let us meet them now, in two remarkable encounters.

'It was in the year 1757, in a summer's day, about noon, I, with three others, one of which was a sister of mine, and the other two were sisters.' Thus wrote the Reverend Edward Williams, in a letter dated 24 March 1772. Aged seven on that earlier summer day, he was playing with the girls in a field called Kae-kaled in Bodvary parish, Denbighshire, Wales, 'near the stile which is next Lanelwyd house', when suddenly

we perceived a company of dancers, in the middle of the field, about seventy yards from us. We could not tell their numbers, because of the swiftness of their motions, which seemed to be after the manner of Morris-dancers (something uncommonly wild in their motions) but after looking some time we came to guess that their number might be about fifteen or sixteen. They were clothed in red like soldiers, with red handkerchiefs spotted with yellow about their heads. They seemed to be a little bigger than we, but of a dwarfish appearance.

... Presently we saw one of them coming away from the company in a running pace; upon seeing this we began to be afraid and ran to the stile. Barbara Jones went over the stile first, next her sister, next to that my sister, and last of all myself: while I was creeping up the stile, my sister staying to help me, I looked back and saw him just by me; upon which I cried out, my sister also cried out, and took hold of me under her arm to draw me over; and when my feet had just come over, I still crying and looking back, we saw him reaching after me, leaning on the stile; but did not come over. Away we ran towards the house, called the people out, and went trembling towards the place; which might be about one hundred and fifty yards from the house: but though we came so soon to see, yet we could see nothing of them. He who came near us had a grim countenance, a wild and somewhat fierce look. He came towards us in a slow running pace, but with long steps for a little one. His complexion was copper-coloured, which might be significative of his disposition and condition; for they were not good, but therefore bad Spirits ... and he looked rather old than young.

Twenty-five years later, all this was still very real to Williams: so much so that reading the encounter now is rather like being there in real time, gasping from the terror of pursuit, yet seeing in detail numbers and colours, and even the peculiarly uncanny motion of the approaching fairy man. In the earlier stages of my quest through fairyland I would have felt that Williams's account, written down by an educated author, was rather atypical. In fact, there are actually scores of similar reports from educated men and women, running on well into the present day.

A second meeting brings the witness up closer still. The mound known as the Gump, at St Just in Cornwall, was a 'reputed playground of the Small People' – here termed spriggans. Climbing up there one night beneath a harvest moon, an old man in search of fairy treasure presently 'heard music of the most ravishing kind ... and on more than one occasion he was compelled to dance in obedience to the time'. Presently there was a great crash; the hill opened; myriad lights blazed. 'Out from the opening in the hill marched a host of spriggans,' followed by scores of musicians and soldiers,

> each troop bearing aloft their banner ... One thing was not at all to our friend's liking; several hundreds of the most grotesque of the spriggans placed themselves so as to enclose the spot on which he was standing. Yet, as they were none of them higher than his shoe-tic, he thought he could 'squash' them easily with his foot if they were up to any mischief.

Next, there 'came a crowd of servants bearing vessels of silver and ... gold, goblets cut out of diamonds, rubies, and other precious stones ... [and] laden ... with the richest meats, pastry, preserves, and fruits'. The lights grew still more dazzling: 'out of the hill were crowding thousands upon thousands of lovely ladies and gentlemen, arrayed in the most costly attire'. The old man was nearly over-powered by the scent of flowers, and by voices 'united in one gush of song, which was clear as silver bells'. This singing was directed towards a newly approaching company: children in white, scattering flowers which blossomed where they fell; boys playing shells strung like harps, and 'line upon line of little men clothed in green and gold'. Finally, 'carried upon a platform above the heads of the men, came a young prince and princess who blazed with beauty and jewels, as if they were suns amidst a skyey host of stars ... eventually the platform was placed upon a mound on the Gump, which was now transformed into a hillock of roses and lilies'.

With the feasting begun, the crafty old man thought he spied his chance. But, stealthily advancing on his belly, 'he never saw that thousands of spriggans had thrown little strings about him'. He was just about to clap his hat down over the royal table when his hand was fixed powerless in the air, and everything became dark around him. Whirr! whirr! whirr! as if a flight of bees were passing him, buzzed in his ears. Every limb, from head to foot, was as if stuck full of pins and pinched with tweezers ... he felt as if a number of insects were running over him, and by the light of the moon he saw standing on his nose one of the spriggans, who looked exceedingly like a small dragon-fly.

Stamping and jumping, the spriggan 'shouted, "Away, away, I smell the day!" ... At length the sun arose, and then he found that he had been tied to the ground by myriads of gossamer webs, which were now covered with dew, and glistened like diamonds in the sunshine.'

Just what do we make of this? In many ways – and especially by contrast with Williams's encounter – we seem now to be deep inside the realms of folklore. We have no date or name for the old man. While we certainly have a lot of detail, much of this can be accounted for by the probability that this tale was told and retold by numerous semi-professional storytellers: people who were deliberately seeking to amaze and beguile their fireside audiences. At the same time, this is not quite a purely disconnected wonderland. Notice, for example, how the pins and needles, paralysis and speech loss look remarkably like the symptoms of a minor stroke.

What did it feel like to hear this tale, to visualize it, perhaps as a child, in Cornwall two hundred years ago? Let us assume that the listeners were ordinary country people. Most of their lives were taken up with survival. Save on the very rare occasions when they travelled to a market town or rural fair, the brightest colours and most dazzling textures they saw were those of flowers, berries, grass, wings and sky. They could not read and had no coloured pictures of any kind. But if they could believe in what we have just read, they had a kind of riches now lost to us. If glamour is relative to your own material limits and poverty, then this was high glamour indeed.

And the fairies certainly had glamour. Indeed, they might be said to have patented it, if not invented it – for the word means magic, enchantment, a spell (and was once used verbally, in much the same way as 'enchant'). So recurrent and so potent is this darkling shimmer of fairyland, from Orkney and west to Aran, through Wales and southwest England, that at times it seems to give the fairies a status which fuses the capricious powers of Greek gods with the erotic charge of modern celebrity. They are like us, but hopelessly unlike us. They may look human, but . . .

In journeying from the fairy worlds of Homer and the fallen angels of the Old Testament we will see just how powerful this glamour was, and how much it has been reduced in the past two centuries. This journey takes us from a world in which it was danger-ous not to believe in fairies, into one where it was fun, sometimes even enchanting, to *try* and believe in fairies. But there is also another way of viewing this changing arc of belief. Probably the biggest and sharpest contrast involved in our story is this: once, it was dangerous not to believe in fairies. Later, it became dangerous to believe in fairies. The first was a supernatural peril, the second a social one. In the time of Shakespeare or Milton an educated person might well believe in fairies, and had far less mockery to fear if they said so. Through the nineteenth century the fairies became more and more the stuff of fancy, whimsy and childhood. And at some point in the twentieth we entered the attitude which predominates as I write. To actually believe in fairies is now the nadir of childish irrationality – signifi-cantly more absurd than to believe in ghosts or alien abductors, and perhaps (in an unadmitted but interesting way) more ridiculous than belief in vampires or witches, these other entities having at least a certain dark weight of supernatural gravity about them.

Without much thinking about it, we take it for granted that, in a kind of hierarchy of the irrational, fairies are the very lowest, most embarrassing level of all. If atheists or agnostics might at least bother to argue with Christians or Muslims or Jews about religion, they would probably only smile condescendingly at someone trying to draw them into a debate about fairies. Religion is for grown-ups; fairies are for children. Once we start to think about it, this hierarchy of the irrational becomes interesting in several ways. Do fairies have this lowly position because of the way they were remade into harmless, prettily feminine butterflies? Do they sit more or less outside rational debate just because all their millions of followers never had the chance to make a literate, educated case for them between the covers of books?

One Monday in 2009, the Irish story collector Eddie Lenihan was berated by a passing woman for broadcasting his beliefs about fairies, and thereby perpetuating stereotypes of the Irish as mystically backward or irrational. Lenihan's response was to gesture at the nearby cathedral and assert that everyone believed in God, although no one had ever seen him. Although Lenihan himself believes in fairies and in God (and argued to the woman that these were part of an interdependent unity), his response is intriguing if thrown into atheistical territory. Where – the atheist asks – is the empirical, physical evidence for God or Christianity? Very few people claim to see God or even Christ. But a startling number of people do claim to have seen fairies. I do not have any great hope of persuading Richard Dawkins to supplement his anti-religious activities with an impishly spirited campaign on behalf of oppressed fairy believers. But the point stands. If it is evidence you want, the fairy believers have much more than the Christians.

I quite understand if, on hearing this, you are scowling and swearing softly to yourself. It took me quite a long time to unearth some of the more arresting fairy sightings given in the following pages. And, quite frankly, I still do not know what to make of them. I will say just two more things on the subject before moving on. First: just as when I was researching vampires, discussion of fairies often prompts the plain question: are they real? Do they exist? If to some this question may seem naive, I for one find it useful and refreshing. I like real things. And I like people who are not too airily detached from the physical world to ask such questions. (The question 'are ghosts real?' is after all vastly more important than academic meanderings about the cultural meanings of ghost beliefs.) So

I think that such people deserve at very least an engagement with this question. Are fairies real? I would agree with the scholar Simon Young that if they are, it is hard to see why they should mean such very different things, and often look so very different, to a Celtic farmer of 1850 and a vegan ecologist of 2017. These differences do indeed look like the products of cultural change, moulding and remaking something which does not actually exist. But as you will soon see for yourself, a good number of recent sightings do not match the kind of stereotypes you might expect. In a small but significant batch of reports, the observers do not believe in fairies, and do not expect or want to see them. And in these cases it is hard not to feel that they really did see something.

Let us first turn, however, to the fairies of traditional belief. Where had these beings come from? Where did they live? And just what sort of creatures – physically, temperamentally, theologically – were they?

One

Origins, Appearance, Locations

ONCE UPON A TIME, the angels tumbled out of heaven:

The Proud Angel fomented a rebellion among the angels of heaven, where he had been a leading light. He declared that he would go and found a kingdom for himself. When going out at the door of heaven the Proud Angel brought prickly lightning and biting lightning out of the doorstep with his heels. Many angels followed him – so many that at last the Son called out, 'Father! Father! the city is being emptied!' whereupon the Father ordered that the gates of heaven and the gates of hell should be closed. This was instantly done. And those who were in were in, and those who were out were out; while the hosts who had left heaven and had not reached hell flew into the holes of the earth, like the stormy petrels. These are the Fairy Folk – ever since doomed to live under the ground, and only allowed to emerge where and when the King permits.

These words were spoken by a 92-year-old man, Roderick Macneill, on the Hebridean island of Miunghlaidh, Barra, in October 1871. He was echoed, come 1877, by Angus Macleod on Harris:

there is not a wave of prosperity upon the fairies of the knoll, no, not a wave. There is no growth nor increase, no death nor withering upon the fairies. Seed unfortunate they! They went away from the Paradise with the One of the Great Pride. When the Father commanded the doors closed down and up, the intermediate fairies had no alternative but to leap into the holes of the earth, where they are, and where they will be.

Had we been one of those stormy petrels, we could have drifted down to the Isle of Man, where just after Christmas 1909 William Cashen, Keeper of Peel Castle, explained:

> my father's and grandfather's idea was that the fairies tumbled out of the battlements of Heaven, falling earthward for three days and three nights as thick as hail; and that one third of them fell into the sea, one third on the land, and one third remained in the air, in which places they will remain till the Day of Judgement.

Winging south into Wales, or west to almost any part of Ireland, you could have heard the same beliefs expressed time and again – in certain places as late as the 1980s.

Despite the translation from Gaelic, it is impossible not to be struck by the forceful lyricism of Macleod, or the peculiar mixture of grandeur and homely precision heard from Macneill: heaven, in his mind, has a doorstep, and the fallen angels are as real as the stormy petrels he saw around him every day. Something of this purity and force is still evident in Cashen, even though he himself may not have believed in the old creeds he relates. Intriguingly, when I first read his words, that magnificent explosion of flailing wings ('as thick as hail') already seemed to have something of Milton about it. Only later did I learn that as a young boy Cashen went to help an elderly weaver woman, Paiee Cooil, and that as she worked she would recite to him *Pargys Cailt*, the Manx version of *Paradise Lost* – a poem which she knew, even though she was herself illiterate.

Although Cashen himself was not illiterate, Macleod and Macneill very possibly were, and much of our information on fairies comes from people who could not read or write. Think of this a moment. What would it be like to hear stories, poems and songs, to retell them and perhaps add to them, when the words on a page were, to you, far more remote and otherworldly than the fairies stalking around your cottage day and night? We might fairly guess that in part, your experience of literary art would resemble that of modern children, raised on songs and stories some time before they learn to read. This is by no means intended to be patronizing. But it should remind us how precious lyrical or poetic language could be to people who had to preserve it in their own heads. Something of this already comes across in the moments of biblical purity we have just heard – the phrases and rhythms of old men whose response to questions has far greater pith, grace and fluency than the extra-grammatical speech of so many modern graduates. What is stranger still is that somehow, these people handed a set of beliefs – arguably, a whole mythology – across the centuries without ever writing it down.

And this, indeed, brings us to the most extraordinary core of traditional fairy beliefs. They were heresy. A quiet heresy, and in fact a very pious one – but heresy, nonetheless. Somehow, these illiterate, politically powerless people had evolved and sustained their own largely independent cosmology: one arguably as robust, as dense, as complex and as beautiful as any Greek myth or monotheistic theology.

Occasionally, it is true, they were backed up by educated Christians. In the mid-seventeenth century, the geographer John Ogilby seemed to take seriously the idea that the less guilty of the fallen angels had been cast into earth, air and water as 'nymphs, fairies, goblins, satyrs' and fauns, and in 1691 the Puritan Richard Baxter admitted uncertainty as to whether 'these aerial regions have not a third sort of wights, that are neither angels (Good or Fallen) nor souls of men, but such as have been there placed as fishes in the sea, and men on earth; and whether those called fairies and goblins are not such'. Around two centuries later the men who questioned Macneill also heard that Barra's late reverend Donald MacDonald had believed in fairies, and had repeated the fallen angel theory to his sometime housekeeper.

Yet, while this kind of educated open-mindedness is interesting, it generally lacks the sensuous richness of popular belief. In the Highlands, for example, the tripartite division of angel–fairies covered the mermaids and blue men of the sea; the fairies on land; and the Merry Dancers of the upper air – these last being nothing less than the Northern Lights. On the remote island of Rathlin (the only inhabited island north of the Irish landmass, whose 2001 population ran to 75), one inhabitant had heard that after 'the rebellion in heaven, they were cast out, and some fell on the land, some fell in the sea, and the seal, he's the one that fell in the sea'. In Shetland, meanwhile, sea trolls or sea trows were fairies or elves of the sea; these included not only mermen, but those whales which broke fishing nets, while one old man spoke of 'a kind of sea trow in the form of a woman, who uttered wailing cries which were heard on the sea by fishermen'. This, like the Highland beliefs, seems to have been current with some in the early twentieth century, and our Rathlin islander was speaking around 1980. On Clare Island, the claim that fairies were 'the least guilty of the fallen angels condemned to wander on the earth until the day of judgement' is vividly coloured by the fact that here, in the spring of 1896, 'one John Needy saw about a hundred fairies in white running on the mountainside.'

These fragments of the great heresy of fairyland would have been wholly silent, rather than merely quiet, if they had not been actively hunted by folklorists such as Thomas Westropp (1860–1922) and W. Y. Evans-Wentz. Although both potentially outsiders, both of these men got close enough to the ordinary people of Ireland and Britain to learn things which would otherwise never have been committed to print. It is perhaps no accident that Westropp was in part an archaeologist, and therefore frequently out on foot in the Irish landscape. Evans-Wentz's closeness was rather different. Although wealthy, American and Oxford-educated, he felt passionately about his Celtic roots (his mother being Irish), and when talking to country-dwellers in Ireland and the Celtic fringe, gained their trust largely because he himself believed in fairies.

The elusiveness of these amazing beliefs, hiding so long in plain sight, comes across in another way in a court case of 1938 in Dundalk, County Louth, where various parties were debating the contested will of the recently deceased Margaret Carolan. Giving evidence on Margaret's state of mind, William Hynes recalled how he had seen her shortly before she died, in October 1937, at the age of 88. She had told Hynes that 'she would be alright only for the fairies in the marsh,' and asked him if he would go with her to see them. Impressively sturdy and fearless for a woman of her age, Margaret 'led the way through the white flowers and told me not to touch them, for they were fallen angels'. Hard as this woman's life may have been, it is difficult not to feel a gleam of envy for the world she looked on; and equally difficult not to feel that the body-count of centuries of religious war would have been very much lower had her beliefs replaced those of orthodox theology.

Had Margaret Carolan read Ovid's *Metamorphoses*? It seems unlikely. Indeed, given that she was born in 1849, when Ireland was still reeling from the effects of devastating famine, it is quite possible that she could not read at all. For her, as for so many fairy believers, earth and heaven flowed easily into one another. The mind and the senses were one. Carolan not only believed in fairies and fallen angels, but knew that they smelled like marsh-flowers and marsh-mud.

At the same time, this kind of earthy faith did not stop its adherents from being quite as thorough or questioning as educated theologians. Would the fairies be saved, for example? Time and again people had stated or implied that fairies were less guilty than Satan and those other rebel angels locked permanently into Hell. Ellen McKeever, daughter of a small farmer in Cavan, explained in 1894 that the guiltiest devils had committed active rebellion, and the intermediate air spirits sinned in word, while the fairies' sin was to have 'stood neutral in the contest' (perhaps explaining why they, like the Swiss, ended up in charge of so much gold). Yet despite this, McKeever seemed to think that the fairies could not be saved. For she also told a story of how, when the priest one morning broke his chalice while saying Mass, a little man in a red jacket came up to the altar, promising to mend the chalice if the priest could answer a question. Would they, the Good People, go to Heaven after the end of the world? The priest replied that they would if there was a writing pen full of blood among them. The key to this cryptic story was not the pen but the blood. In the 1980s Jenny McGlynn from County Laois repeated a slightly different version in which the priest responded by getting the questioning fairy to cut its finger. When it did so, and no blood came, the priest concluded, 'No, there's no redemption for you, because you are not a human being, you're a spirit.' As we will see, however, not everyone agreed with this; and it is interesting to note that when this latter fairy ran screaming in distress across the fields, he did so because he had piously hoped to be saved.

Where else might the fairies have come from? Other answers were no more orthodox. As that great pioneer of fairyland, Katharine Briggs, explained decades ago, one longstanding theory held them to be the hidden children of Eve. 'One day, God walking through the world, called on Eve and asked her to present her children to Him.' Having so many children that she was ashamed of them, 'Eve sent half of them to hide and brought out those she thought most presentable; but God was not deceived. "Let those who were hidden from me," He said, "be hidden from all Mankind." And this, Briggs concludes, 'was the beginning of the Huldre, "the Hidden People"'. In this version of the Scandinavian *huldre* myth we already have a typical mix of pious orthodoxy and homely adaptation. You cannot deceive God, and beneath the overt shame about the state of the children there probably also lies the basic shame of human lust and generation, linking this excessive number of offspring to the Fall itself. Yet, at the same time, both the quantity of children and the difficulty of caring for them all are of course reflective of ordinary human lives, filled with poverty and innumerable hungry mouths.

Moreover, when told by an elderly Welsh woman, Mrs Spurrell of Carmarthenshire, in 1909, the story grew yet more homely and still less orthodox.

> Our Lord, in the days when He walked the earth, chanced one day to approach a cottage in which lived a woman with twenty children. Feeling ashamed of the size of her family, she hid half of them from the sight of her divine visitor. On His departure she sought for the hidden children in vain; they had become fairies and had disappeared.

Here we have an exact number of children (probably double the size of the typical families among whom Mrs Spurrell grew up) and far less godly control. The Lord merely chances on the cottage, and does not detect the hidden children, who show typical fairy touchiness and independence, punishing their mother by running off for good. Although Eve has faded out of the tale, sex is clearly the central cause of shame, which springs not from shabby appearance but from sheer quantity of offspring. Given that this version was related by a woman, it is interesting to wonder if it also reveals a faintly touching maternal bias: offending one's children, ultimately, is more serious for a mother than offending God.

Spirits of the Dead

Were fairies ghosts? Until the end of the nineteenth century, many people in Ireland, Wales, Cornwall and the Isle of Man would have told you that they were. The link can still be seen in the word 'sprite', once just another form of 'spirit', and now more narrowly denoting some kind of elfin being. A song printed in the time of Charles 11 referred to 'Oberon in Fairy Land' not as the king of fairies, but as 'the King of Ghosts'.

Perhaps not surprisingly, this belief was especially strong in Ireland, a country whose Catholic theology actively promoted the presence and memory of the dead. One unnamed graduate of Dublin University asserted in 1908 that 'the old people in County Armagh seriously believe that the fairies are the spirits of the dead; and they say that if you have many friends deceased you have many friendly fairies, or if you have many enemies deceased you have many fairies looking out to do you harm.' Notice how this not only replaces guardian angels with guardian fairies but appears as much pragmatic as moralistic. Meanwhile, listening to the schoolmaster from Benbulbin who told Evans-Wentz that older locals considered the fairies to be 'the spirits of their departed relations and friends, who visit them in joy and in sorrow', and that 'they believe the spirits of their near relatives are present; they do not see them, but feel their presence', we hear one more version of the very porous Catholic divide between the living and the dead. Far less comforting was the Highland belief cited by Briggs that 'the sluagh or fairy Hosts are the evil dead' (offering us, also, a very early use of a phrase later made famous by zombie cinema).

With their tendency to mimic almost every aspect of human life, down to feasting and dancing, fairies clearly do not much resemble the more ethereal ghosts with which most of us are familiar. This may in part be explained by the fact that the ghost-fairy was only *one type* of fairy. And certainly the question of fairies as spirits of the dead is itself complex. For some, it was not just a matter of being dead, but of how, when or where you had died. Writing around 1780, the Welsh Independent minister Edmund Jones was quite certain that fairies were 'the disembodied spirits of men, who lived and died without the enjoyment of the means of grace and salvation, as pagans and others, and their condemnation therefore far less than those who have enjoyed the means of salvation.'

A different version of the problem of salvation was offered by those who had died before Christ. Writing on Cornish fairy beliefs around 1865, Robert Hunt explained how one type of local fairy, the Small People, was 'believed by some to be the spirits of the people who inhabited Cornwall many thousands of years ago – long,

long before the birth of Christ . . . they were not good enough to inherit the joys of heaven, but . . . they were too good to be condemned to eternal fires'. Intriguingly, this belief gave one more twist to the oft-debated question of fairy size. For, 'when they first came into this land, they were much larger than they are now, but ever since the birth of Christ they have been getting smaller and smaller. Eventually they will turn into muryans [ants], and at last be lost from the face of the earth'.

Another category of fairy dead was 'dead people whose time is not up'. Elderly Tara resident John Graham explained that 'people killed and murdered in war stay on earth till their time is up, and they are among the good people. The souls on this earth are as thick as the grass (running his walking-stick through a thick clump), and you can't see them; and evil spirits are just as thick, too, and people don't know it'. Graham's vivid sense of souls and demons thickly texturing the world was once relatively common among educated Christians: the great medical reformer Paracelsus, for example, said some time before 1541 that 'the earth is not so full of flies in summer, as it is at all times of invisible devils'. Not only that, but Paracelsus and his many followers also believed that all human beings had a foreordained lifespan. If they died young, by some violent, unnatural death, then their time was indeed 'not up'. For many early modern Christians this meant that you could actually extract the unspent life force from their corpse and use it as medicine.

The popular version of this belief held that those dying young, by violent deaths, were all too likely to return and haunt the living, whether in the form of ghosts or vampires. The fear of this was intense all across the vampire countries of central and eastern Europe, while in much of Russia these people were 'the unclean dead', luckless men or women who not only died before their time, but as a result had to be buried away from ordinary Christians, if indeed they were buried at all.

In the fairy versions of this belief there may be some sense of fairness involved. And there must often have been a comforting feeling of presence and earthly continuity for the bereaved. Perhaps less obvious, but no less powerful, was a very basic sense of *waste*. For us now, there is something simply *wrong* about the death of a young person – viscerally and even impersonally so in cases where we do not know them well. In western Ireland this feeling could harden into myth. One ancient tale described how the three drowned children of an Inishark chieftain had been 'spirited away to "Ladra" or some other undersea paradise, for children who die young are really alive in the fairy hills'. Hearing this in the early twentieth century, Westropp implied that the belief was still current – adding that 'women who die in childbirth are believed to have been carried off to fairyland'. And this strikingly pagan afterlife was by no means purely Irish. In Cornwall, seventy-year-old Henry Spragg recalled how, years ago, he had heard 'the old people say that the piskies [pixies] are the spirits of dead-born children'.

This refusal to accept the seeming waste of life must have had something quite primal about it for people who depended so intimately on the mysterious forces of fertility, and who at times seemed to be unconsciously recycling the human dead into a more impersonally vital Nature. It was possibly this impulse, and possibly again that sense of fairness to those beyond the reach of Christ's salvation, which prompted one more rewriting of orthodox theology: namely, that certain kinds of fairies were 'the lost souls of the people who died before the Flood'. So said the Manx seer and herb doctor John Davies, referring to fairies of human size which he had seen himself.

Fairy Dwellings

Where did fairies live? For those who believed in them, almost everywhere. They sifted through our world like beings of another dimension dropped clean into our own. But we can certainly be quite precise about particular locations. In keeping with that threefold split of the fallen angels, there were indeed fairies of the air, waters and earth.

The fairies of the air generally seem less tangible or visible than their peers. But we should not too easily assume that this made them less real. One Manxman stated simply of fairies: 'they throng the air, and darken Heaven, and rule this lower world.' Recalling the beliefs of his parents and grandparents, a Welsh Justice of the Peace, David Williams, explained that the king of the Welsh fairies had a 'residence ... among the stars ... called Caer Gwydion.' And this aerial court could also press closer to our own, condensing into a kind of everyday myth. For the fairy queen was called Gwenhidw, and (added Williams), 'I have heard my mother call the small fleece-like clouds which appear in fine weather the Sheep of Gwenhidw.' As so often with fairy belief, this zone could be coloured by the particular conditions and features of local landscape. Off the west of Ireland, Westropp had more than once seen (and drawn) extraordinarily detailed and convincing mirages of non-existent islands, with towers, smoke and cattle. Little wonder, then, that here 'fairy ships and boats sail in the air and are often seen over Inishturk.' Fairies seem only very rarely to have taken the form of birds (perhaps because one did not like to think of oneself eating fairy stew, or fairy pie?). But they undoubtedly had the ability to take many shapes besides the semi-human, and one among these was that of flies.

In lakes, streams, rivers and seas, meanwhile, fairies lurked in a bewildering range of types. There were mermen and mermaids, seals, naiads and the shy but dangerous kelpie of rushing Scottish burns and glens. On the Isle of Man the eighteenth-century antiquary George Waldron knew of a particular 'creek between two high rocks, which overlook the sea on this side of the Island', where 'they tell you ... mermen and mermaids have been frequently seen.' In Cornwall one mermaid, Selina, had a very long story of her own, and in all there were probably as many tales of these amphibious wonders as there were gnarled and lichened coves along the coasts of Scotland, Man, Wales, Ireland and southwest England. Although nominally of both sexes, on the whole these beings seem to have been gendered female, as the wilder and more potent sides of Nature so often were.

Mermaids or seal-women indeed acted like the sirens of the North, beautiful yet dangerous, alluring and elusive. Everyone knew a version of the story in which a human male could keep his seal-wife on land so long as he retained her oceanic skin in hiding somewhere. Among the many elements comprising this mythic waterworld, a specially powerful one must have been the sense of precarious dependence on the seas experienced by so many coastal dwellers. 'If you would know the age of the earth,' wrote Joseph Conrad, 'look upon the sea in a storm.' Abundantly fertile and abundantly savage, the oceans have a primal force exceeding anything else in nature, and this fecund otherness crystallizes into the forms of all those fleeting water-wives, held briefly before they plunged back beneath the waves.

Little wonder, then, that fishermen should be so notoriously superstitious, and keep their own special religion of the sea. In Cornwall a 'sea-strand pixy, called *Bucca*, had to be propitiated by a *cast* (three) of fish, to ensure the fishermen having a good *shot* (catch) of fish'; and in Brittany 'the *Fées des Houles* (Fairies of the Billows) . . . lived in natural caverns or grottoes in the sea-cliffs,' forming, for some scholars, a kind of rationalized sea-divinity.

Yet if the ocean presented to coastal dwellers the greatest extremes of life and death, fairies also resourcefully and colourfully filled all other watery spaces in a given landscape. Lough Gur in Limerick was an enchanted fairy lake, and 'once in seven years the spell passes off it, and it then appears like dry land to any one that is fortunate enough to behold it. At such a time of disenchantment a tree is seen growing up through the lake-bottom.' This 'is covered with a green cloth, and under it sits the lake's guardian, a woman knitting. The peasantry about Lough Gur', added Evans-Wentz about 1910, 'still believe that beneath its waters there is one of the chief entrances in Ireland to Tír-na-nog, the "Land of Youth", the Fairy Realm.' And, 'when a child is stolen by the Munster fairies, Lough

Gur is conjectured to be the place of its unearthly transmutation from the human to the fairy state.'

Meanwhile, in some uncertain space between air and water, between myths and maps, there lay the fairy islands of the Welsh and Irish coasts. Having just glimpsed the latter in those mirages noted by Westropp, we can screw the spyglass tighter on this hazy vision, hearing from him how 'I saw again on June 18 1918 the dark hills, the southern falling steeply to the sea, and three towers against the setting sun from Kilkee, County Clare. It was certainly a bank of cloud and lay on the sea, as in 1878 . . . but the illusion of a city was perfect. I especially noted the curls of smoke between the towers such as [Roderic] O'Flaherty saw at Skerd' in 1684. Given that the educated Westropp found such imaginary islands compelling enough to make sketches of them, we can begin to grasp how the whole western coast was haunted by these spectral lands, with Tir Hudi off Donegal, Ladra off Mayo, Skerd off Galway, Clare's Kilstuitheen and Kilstapheen, and 'the Island' opposite Ballyheigue in Kerry. Certain of these, though usually buried beneath the waves, could be clearly seen every seven years. Anyone visiting Galway, moreover, can actually set foot on a fairy island. The small inhabited isle of Inishbofin was believed to have been such, and therefore had floated unstably in the water until it was disenchanted and fixed in place by fishermen who dropped a live coal on it. Off Pembrokeshire similar enchanted islands lay in the Irish Sea, sometimes sighted by sailors, yet always vanishing on nearer approach. 'From a certain spot in Pembrokeshire', land-dwellers could also see them, if they were to stand 'on a turf taken from the yard of St David's Cathedral'.

Above all, though, fairies lived underground. Seen from a modern viewpoint, these creatures of the waters and the earth remind us how little use traditional fairies had for the wings now thought so integral to them. Their subterranean haunts, on the other hand, make a good deal more sense if we understand them as being, on the whole, that little bit closer to the underworld – and in particular the hell where the advance guard of the fallen angels had ended up.

The majority of the fairies we will meet in the following pages lived in caves, mines or tunnels, or under hills. In the first category we have Buman's Hole, near Saxon Blankenburg – a place where, around 1600, a young shepherd supposedly wandered for eight days, finally emerging with 'his hair … perfectly grey' and giving 'a relation of a great many odd kinds of spirits and apparitions'. Certain miners indeed claimed to have travelled twenty miles through this under-world, and many others (wrote Moses Pitt in 1680) had reported meeting 'with the like fairies' in its vaults. Rather less terrifying – and indeed popular with tourists come the later nineteenth century – was the Pixies' Cavern at Chudleigh, Devonshire, in a woodland cliff-face where a small waterfall had carved the rocks into striking forms. Researching the elfin creatures of Orkney and Shetland, Alan Bruford heard of how a fairy boy had allegedly 'jumped out of a crack in a peat bank and claimed he had a "run" from one end of the island [of Yell] to the other'; while the fairies dwelling in sea caves beneath a house on the Out Skerries 'could lift a flagstone in the floor to steal oatcakes'. Down on the Scottish mainland in Ayrshire, the caves under the Marquis of Ailsa's castle were still reputedly 'haunted by fairies' in the 1930s. Writing in 1890, an author told of how the forest of Maes Syward, near Pontyfon in Wales, 'is associated with a haunting Pwcca, who inhabited a deep pit, wherein is to be seen an excavated chamber'. This in turn led, via an underground passage, to some neighbouring ruins, and from here the Pwcca, 'clad in a red coat and cocked hat … would ride or walk forth, bent upon doing whatever evil or mischief came in his way'. So dreaded 'was he in the countryside that no one would approach the forest after dark'. No less memorably, an educated author writing around 1730 recalled being told by his grandmother that fairies lived underground 'and generally came out of a molehill'.

As for fairy hills? These abound across Britain and Ireland: Craig-y-Ddinas in South Wales, Elbolton Hill in Yorkshire, Stirlingshire's wooded Doon Hill, and Glastonbury Tor. Many fairy hills had previously been Iron Age hill forts, often featuring burial mounds and chambers. Fairy forts play a particularly central role in Ireland, and it is telling that the Irish phrase 'the sidhe' has come to mean both mounds and fairies. No less tellingly, some held that the fairies had indeed built these mounds themselves.

On closer inspection, the seemingly diverse homes of earth and water spirits have certain interesting things in common. First, all of these sites allow the fairies to be present yet hidden, suiting their shy and secretive nature. In the case of fairy hills they might often seem very immediately present – hidden, as we said, in plain sight. Second: because they are hidden, it is possible to imagine these fairy worlds as impressively complete in their own right – something very clear in that Boschian extravaganza beneath the moon on the St Just Gump, where the fairies not only mirror human society but effortlessly outstrip that of the homely yokel observer. A third feature may already have caught your attention in looking at the image of Craig-y-Ddinas. Fairy hills tend to be ones that look *unusual*. As Kai Roberts emphasizes, Elbolton and Doon share the same kind of domed shape, while Glastonbury's famous tor is easily identified scores of miles away. In the case of hill forts, it is now obvious to us

Henry Gastineau, *Craig y Ddinas, Breconshire, Wales*, 1835, print: one of many 'fairy hills' identified by traditional fairy believers across the British Isles and Ireland.

that they looked unusual because they were partly man-made; but geology alone can produce some striking rivals.

This third quality of fairy haunts weaves itself in diverse colours through the whole of our opening three chapters, whether in the shape of 'a weird looking hollow oak tree in Manau Park', Wales, 'known as the elf's hollow tree', or any of the numerous strange rock formations called fairy saddles or elf churches. Pausing for a moment here, we are reminded just how many remarkable landscape features are named after fairies, or the Devil himself. Casting our eyes over the Devil's Pulpit above Tintern Abbey, to the Devil's Cauldron in Lydford Gorge, and the unjustly more obscure Devil's Dyke (a Roman anti-chariot ditch in woods on the edge of St Albans where as children we romped and marauded like lawless fairies), it is hard not to be struck by what all these variously dark and pagan structures say about the popular mind through most of history. Once again, let the ministers prate as they like about the glory of God's creation; its more striking natural sites are viewed by the mass of the rural population in very different ways. God of course exists for them, but only distantly. Here on earth the creative forces and powers around you are darker and far more capricious – above all, far more real.

Another way of viewing this contrast, perhaps, is to say that all the emotional, mental and creative energies which educated Christians put into theology or evangelism were far more immediately and sensuously infused, by the rural masses, into the raw sap and mass of roots, leaves, earth and stone. This latter kind of worship was often no less pious or reverent. What we should also remind ourselves, again, is how distinctive it must have been for people who could not read or write.

The Fairies and Nature

We now have a good idea of where fairies lived. We can add that their presence within your local environment was held to be a highly active one, and that some thought them to relocate habitually from place to place. In one version this wandering appears haplessly nomadic, as when an old Cornish fisherman recalls his grandmother telling him: '*they* are a sort of people wandering about the world with no home or habitation, and ought to be given a little comfort.' In another it is a kind of lofty royal progress from one grand home to another: 'in Ireland, the gentry live inside the mountains in beautiful castles; and there are a good many branches of them in other countries. Like armies, they have various stations and move from one to another.'

In much of this book we will also be hiking across country, eyes peeled for the next fairy tree, fort or lake on our map. But the walking is the easy part. What is more difficult is to try and see this landscape as it was seen by true fairy believers. To begin even to attempt this we will need to try and grasp some strange and unexpected ideas about nature. 'Ideas', in fact, is perhaps too detached a term for the habits of mind we need to try and adopt – implying as it does that most ordinary people had any choice in the matter, or any self-conscious sense that their mode of seeing landscape and growth was in any way unusual.

One basic point is how intimately people knew the landscape around them. To some extent all of us can begin to appreciate this. As children, whether we grew up in town or country, or some area between, we had a very definite sense of the space around our home. We knew perhaps an acre of this space (beyond which there might lie town, school, relatives and so forth) very intimately indeed. We broke it down carefully and minutely into legitimate playing spaces; places to hide; places unknown to adults (or beyond their feeble climbing skills); places haunted by rough children; forbidden places; places to make camps or fires . . . To most adults these spaces have different meanings, if they even notice them at all. But for the child these unremarked or mundane areas and structures have a secrecy, a magic, a kind of exact excitement that in part echoes the fairy-haunted landscape of the past.

To fill out this partial resemblance, however, we must add the remarkable historical sense which fairy dwellers had. This was brilliantly captured by Eddie Lenihan during a 2009 interview – by which time he had been gathering stories for 33 years. Lenihan stated: 'people who know of big areas, they know it shallowly. But a person who knows a small area, they know in depth that can go back 300, or 400, or 500 years.' Illustrating this claim, Lenihan recalled recording the stories of an uneducated old man in around 2000. He was saying goodbye to the man when,

> at the door he just pointed out across the valley and said, 'Do you see those trees? . . . Just before the famine there used to be a house there.' Now here we were in 2000 or 2002, and the famine was 1845, 1847, and he named the girl who used to babysit in that house and told me a story about her. Now the house is gone. Only the trees are left . . . But he can still remember the girl's name who babysat at that house before the famine. And I said, 'What the hell? That *is* memory.'

An English example of this prodigious local memory concerns the man-made tumulus Willy Howe in Yorkshire. Passing this small, tree-covered mound a few yards off at the nearby lane, many walkers, cyclists or motorists might barely notice it. But to locals around a hundred years ago such ignorance was unthinkable. Back in the time of Henry I (d. 1135), a man walking past the mound one night heard a banquet within. Going inside, he was offered a drink. Like all his peers he knew the danger of being trapped by the fairies should he swallow any of their food or wine, and so emptied the goblet out on the ground before managing to escape with it in his grasp. Uncannily foreshadowing those alleged alien artefacts made from no earthly matter, this fairy goblet was said to be wrought of a material unknown to man, and was accordingly presented as a great rarity to the king himself. Originally, all this was written down around 1198 by William of Newburgh. And incredibly, almost seven hundred years later, a version of the story – preserved by purely oral transmission – was told by locals to historian Thomas Wright when he visited Willy Howe in around 1861. Now that, surely, is memory.

Even today, the tightly intertwined knots of belief and landscape are still to be found on maps from the north to the south of Britain and Ireland. The chances are, indeed, that most of you have cast your eyes or fingers over one of the innumerable fairy places of the British Isles when navigating a walk or a drive. At the more easily decodable level, Sussex boasts Puckscroft and Puckstye Farm, and Wiltshire Puck Pit and Pucklechurch, while more opaque forms include Cumberland's Scrat Gate ('goblin road') and Yorkshire's Hob Stones, along with multiple Hob Halls and Hob Lanes (hob being a byform of Rob, as in Robin, as in Robin Goodfellow). In Ireland, County Clare alone offers us Lisfarbegnagommaun, the 'fort of the little men playing at hurling', and Cahernanoorane, which takes its name from 'fairy melody'. In Scotland, Coire nan Uraisg and Argyll's Gleann Uraisg both recall a sinister Highland water fairy. Tellingly, these places range in size from villages down to fairy-spots as small as a gateway or a particular place in a field.

This, then, was a natural world with few, if any, blank or meaningless spaces – one where fairies and the stories about them were wriggling in every gap beneath the tree roots, hills, lakes and shores of the surrounding world. What other distinctive features did it have? Perhaps no less basic was the fact that you – the fairy believer – were in so many ways very *close* to nature all the time. It was not something you escaped to on special occasions, in order to get away from it all. You were there already, and may well die there. And journeys elsewhere were rare – often arduous, if not dangerous. For some, nature was the thing you *could not* get away from. You worked in it and walked through it, sailed on it or fished from it, all day and every day. Come the evening its stench might carry from the cesspool outside your door, or the sizeable manure heap inside your single-roomed cabin. And as you slept, there filtered into your dreams the smells and gruntings of the pig and cow who shared that room with you by night.

Focusing in a little more sharply on this kind of life, we need also to remind ourselves that being close to nature and being out in it for long hours had important implications for one's sense of the fairies. Let us imagine for argument's sake that fairies do exist, but only in the countryside. They are shy and not easily seen if they hear or spy human observers. This being the case, most of us have only the tiniest chance of ever seeing them by comparison with people who were constantly out on foot or horseback in hills or fields or coasts, and who indeed probably covered thousands of miles more country in this way than we today do across a lifetime. Across the 42 years in which he served the Gordon family of Fochabers, Scotland, James Gordon 'frequently performed 80 miles a day, over hill and dale' on foot and horseback and, aged 69 in 1827, was still managing fifty or sixty miles a day. It was calculated that he had 'travelled about 230,000 miles, or nine times the circumference of the globe'.

Abundant evidence shows that you did not need to actually see fairies to be continually aware of their presence. Here is just one example. In 1890 an elderly Lincolnshire woman recalled the fairy beings of her youth:

> the chief spirit of the bogs was Tiddy Mun, who was no bigger than a child of three; he dwelt in the water holes, down deep in the still green water. And he only came out at evenings when the mist rose. Then he came creeping out in the darklins, limpelty lobelty, because he was lame, he was like a dearie wee old grand-father with long white hair, and a long white beard ... gowned in grey, he could scarce be seen through the thick mist; and he came with the sound of running water and a sough of wind, laughing like a pyewipe screech [a lapwing]. He wasn't wicked ... [or] creepy ... but nevertheless it was sort of shivery-like, when set round the fire at night, to hear the screeching laugh out by the door, passing

in a skirl of wind and water; but folks only pulled in nearer together and whispered, with a keek over their shoulders, 'Hearken to Tiddy Mun!'

This memory seems to conflate seeing and hearing Tiddy Mun. But let us assume that, on some occasions at least, people saw those first images in their minds *because* they heard that ambient fusion of water, wind and the laughing screech of the lapwing. And let us indulge them by granting that, although what they *actually* heard was a lapwing's cry, what mattered was what they believed it to be. This fireside shiver of apprehension is vivid enough in itself. But what we might easily forget is that, living in the deepest countryside nowadays, many people would hear nothing at all from outside. The houses of the past, however, were permeable to outer sounds in ways that most modern ones are not. Sound whistled in through single glass panes and holes in the thatch, around ill-fitting doors. And when it reached you, it cut into a hush which was not screened or softened by television, radio or the background hum of any number of appliances, from computers to fan ovens.

However hard we try to be aware of these differences and changes, we can never fully lose them. We can never really imagine what it must have been like to live a Highland life so detached from nineteenth-century England that, on the day when Queen Victoria made a charitable visit to your cottage door, you could meet her and *not know who she was.* (This really happened.) Indeed, visiting Mull in the 1990s with friends, I took the five-minute rowing-boat ride to the tiny island of Ulva, learning only later of an old Ulva woman, still living, who had never been to Mull. Perhaps most of all, we can never fully inhabit the cold, hunger and fatigue that routinely dogged these ordinary country lives. Unconsciously selecting the beauty, the release, the catharsis or purity of nature as we read of these vanished worlds, we all too easily forget how harsh and precarious they could often be. Even in times when you were not hungry, sick or bereaved, you might well be anticipating any or all of these things. As we will see, you could blame the fairies for any of these problems – or, in some cases, be consoled to think that perhaps your dead child was now happier in fairyland.

Buried beneath these more obvious differences – of routine discomfort or uncertainty – was something related to them, as well as to the way that nature flowed through you day by day. This was fertility. Things grew and died – partly according to accepted rhythms, partly in ways you could neither predict nor control. For most people, across most of history, fertility has been a mystery deeper, richer, more frightening than any god or religion. What was it like to be so dependent on fertility when you lived before or outside science, and could not read or write? Though we can only sketch an answer, it probably has something of paradox about it. On one hand, you did not fully understand fertility, especially when it failed. On the other, you were not alienated from it, either by the sense that others (scientists) understood it *better* than you, or by language and associated concepts. Because of this, it flowed with a raw single force through the lives of your children, your animals, your crops and all the energies that nurtured or endangered them. Sketchy as this answer might be, we know it is broadly true because, when life was threatened, people tended to blame just one culprit for problems affecting humans, animals, crops or climate. Fertility was as single as the scapegoat which attacked it. That scapegoat might, depending on location, be a witch, a vampire or the fairies – but whichever it was, people all across Europe took this intensely seriously right through into the early twentieth century.

Nature, then, will be with us in many forms in this book – often sucking at our boots or soaking our rucksacks, sometimes apprehended at a more comfortably filtered distance. Its rawer side will return in our Conclusion, when we consider the curious relationship between fairies and ecology. Before we briefly move away from it, we can outline the broad arc of change occurring across the near three-thousand-year span between Homer and the present. Once, nature was on top of us. Now, in the developed world, we are on top of nature. The relationship between oppressor and underdog has flipped clean on its head. Nature, indeed, is already taking its revenge – but the broad difference holds good.

How to Spot a Fairy

Fairies, then, were creatures of nature. They had the power, the mystery and the capriciousness of nature itself. This association is one of their clearest identifying features – albeit one subject to a good deal of change by those privileged city dwellers for whom nature was prettily delicate, rather than rawly powerful. What else can we know about fairies? Their size, appearance, clothing, colours, society and temperaments? I will try to give some clear answers to these questions here, as people may rightly feel reluctant to tramp across country hunting for creatures which could look like anything at all. Taking the broadest known parameters, we find that size can range from fourteen feet high to a being small enough to sit on a cowslip. A majority of descriptions narrows the scale down to between eight inches and four feet. While anything under six inches can fairly be said to match the delicate miniature creatures of Victorian painting, we need to realize at once that most fairies were far from tiny.

Nor did they necessarily insist on wearing green. Red is almost at least as common. A good few wear brown or dark colours, while a number of quite exact descriptions have them wearing no clothes at all. This question is complicated further by the fact that fairies, like humans, may well dress in a variety of colours, sporting (say) blue caps, red jackets and green leggings. Scottish fairies tend to wear different colours to Irish ones. On the whole, traditional sightings are more likely to give the fairies exact and complete outfits, and in many cases their clothing looks rather old-fashioned by comparison with that of their observers. As we will see, however, many people were prepared to accept that fairies could look *exactly like us*. For some, this may have been quite simply because fairies – like witches or vampires, or that Prince of Lies, the Devil himself – could very easily change shape, size and form. Seals, flies and foxes were just some of the animal guises they could assume.

Very few traditional fairies ever had wings, and they were probably slightly more likely to be male than female. It is also rare for fairies to talk – at least in a way that humans can understand. If sounds other than music or singing are mentioned, they are often a kind of agitated twittering or whirring – perhaps roughly the kind of noise we would expect from a startled group of small birds.

We will meet an abundant range of very precisely described fairies in following pages. But even the brief artist's impression attempted here already points to one difficulty of fairy identity. To ask naively what fairies were like is in one way rather like asking what humans are like. For, to those who really believed in fairies, there were numerous types and ranks. Most modern children could probably tell you about dwarfs, gnomes, elves, pixies, goblins and leprechauns. And besides these we have numerous fairy trades, from the familiar shoemakers through gold- and silversmiths, blacksmiths, potters, tailors and miners. The brownie is well known for assisting with housework and farmwork, while dwarf women are adept at spinning. Even our brief glimpse at the dazzling miniature society swarming that night on the moonlit Gump has shown us what a precisely layered social hierarchy fairies could have.

And this point is in fact one of the most important and distinctive qualities of fairyland. Like no other supernatural being, they uncannily *mirror* the human world. On our quest for them we will meet fairy dances, fairy music, fairy funerals, hunts and battles, as well as fairy animals. Fairy transport has been claimed to include not just horses and boats, but even cars. Evans-Wentz heard from the Manx people that 'they have seen the fairies hunting with hounds and horses, and on the sea in ships, and . . . have heard their music. They consider the fairies a complete nation or world in themselves, distinct from our world, but having habits and instincts like ours.' Like humans, fairies have genders, while their habit of either stealing human children or requiring the services of human midwives indicates that they have families.

It cannot be emphasized too strongly that witches, ghosts or vampires achieve nothing like this completely mirroring society. The angels and the blessed souls of heaven, meanwhile, seem far too happy to fully replicate human life, and are in any case too vaguely distant for the ordinary Christian. What does this tell us about fairies and fairy beliefs? One of the most interesting implications again concerns the extraordinary heresy of this creed. Looking sideways at this complete alternative reality, we get the impression that the popular mind had effectively substituted the fairy world for both heaven and hell. It was far more real, more present, more likely to cut at any time into their own lives, than the alternative societies of orthodox Christianity. Remarkably, fairyland contained blisses as great as the Christian heaven, intermingled with much of the gloom and terror of hell, *in the same place*. And that place really could be a stone's throw from your kitchen door.

The fairies were exactly like us, and peculiarly unlike us. A second interesting point about this is, simply, that this kind of quality has been vital to so many of the stories beloved by children, from *Peter Pan* through to *The Wind in the Willows* and *Harry Potter*. Imagine, by contrast, that as a child you grew up with stories about fairies which were real, and dangerous – and would certainly steal you away if you should leave the house at night.

The Middle People

Uncannily similar, yet fundamentally different from humankind … time and again, accordingly, fairies were described or represented as the 'middle people' or 'middle kingdom'. Perhaps most obviously, they sat between us and God, his heaven and his angels. As one Irishman explained to Evans-Wentz, 'they are a distinct race between our own and that of spirits, as they have told me.' Yet this broadly intermediate quality was only one of many. They were fallen angels, stranded between heaven and hell; they were the 'illegitimate' (shameful) children of Eve. In one version of that story they were the children of Adam and his first (apocryphal) wife, Lilith. As we will see, certain Irish coastal dwellers insisted on a perhaps more remarkable degree of hybridity at the dawn of the twentieth century – believing not only that seals were fairies, but that some local families had interbred with seals.

For some educated Christians, this seemingly indeterminate nature was really just one more trick of the Devil, designed to lure in the unsuspecting. So the Puritan physician James Hart talked in 1633 of those 'white devils, the fairies', whose apparent harmlessness was 'a far more efficacious means to delude the simpler sort, and to lead them hood-wink'd into hell'; while Bunyan, in a poetic litany of temptations, warns: 'Here haunt the fairies with their chanting voices,/ Fiends like to angels, to bewitch our choices'. When discussing fairies in around 2015, *Spectator* writer Tim Stanley was told by a Catholic academic friend that they were demonic. 'The best thing you could do if you encounter a fairy is step on it,' he said, 'or lay down slug pellets.'

But the popular mind saw matters very differently. The most important thing about the fairies was that they were powerful. There is surely more envy than condemnation in the Welsh belief that the will o' the wisp was 'too bad to go into heaven and too clever to be taken into hell'. It is tempting to say that this kind of intermediate supernatural power looks very Catholic. But given its presence and status in Wales, Man, many parts of England and Protestant areas of Scotland, we might more accurately argue that in fact, for popular Christians, educated religious divisions mattered far less than simple *usefulness*. Twisting and turning between related but contrary statements, it is hard to be sure if fairy power resembles that of the Greek gods, the Catholic saints or the pagan deities. Count John de Salis, for example, concluded of the peasants around his ancestral home, Lough Gur: 'under ordinary circumstances . . . the old people will pray to the Saints, but if by any chance such prayers remain unanswered they then invoke other powers, the fairies, the goddesses Aine and Fennel, or other pagan deities, whom they seem to remember in a vague subconscious manner through tradition.' Meanwhile, an Irish fairy believer told Evans-Wentz that 'the gentry take a great interest in the affairs of men, and they always stand for justice and right. Any side they favour in our wars, that side wins. They favoured the Boers, and the Boers did get their rights. They told me they favoured the Japanese and not the Russians, because the Russians are tyrants.' It is hard to imagine a tighter fusion of the Christian God and the Greek gods than this.

We might add that, for many, the fairies were immortal – resembling in this not only the major Greek gods, but a nymph such as Calypso, a kind of fairy who was thought immortal, but who ate and drank, and had sex with her human captive, Odysseus. Recalling that others held fairies to be capable of salvation, some readers may irritably be wondering why fairy believers cannot get their story straight and clear. Mortal or immortal? Pagan deities or Greek gods? Tall or short? Red or green? Of God's party, or the Devil's? If so, I sympathize. And yet, pausing for a moment and probing deeper here, we might equally ask: is the clarity, the precision, the binary quality of written theology really that *honest?* Much of our life, of our feelings, is messy, fluid, contradictory. At times we may feel this way about our closest friends or family. Let me tell you the most important thing about life. I can do it in two words. Life *moves.* By contrast, educated theology often attempts to fix life into static truths which are neither realistic nor helpful.

If you were a hungry, uneducated peasant, rather than an old Etonian bishop, you had a far sharper sense of the uncertain movement of life – weather, sickness, death or crop failure – and you had far more important things to worry about than what was Right or True or Good. You were interested in religion for the same reasons that you were interested in the fairies: because it was powerful and useful. At times this kind of basic social pressure leaks out into nearly overt statements: surely it was no accident that the most revered and potent class of the Irish fairies was called 'the Gentry'? In the words of one Irishman in 1910:

> the folk are the grandest I have ever seen. They are far superior to us, and that is why they are called the gentry. They are not a working class, but a military-aristocratic class, tall and noble-appearing ... Their qualifications are tremendous. 'We could cut off half the human race, but would not,' they said, 'for we are expecting salvation.'

While this mingles fairy power and fairy glamour (for most peasants the most impressive things you typically saw were the gentry, soldiers, or the Gentry) the elderly John Graham of Tara gives them perhaps still more godlike powers: 'the good people can see everything, and you dare not meddle with them.' For most others, they could certainly hear everything. This was why they were so often referred to in speech as 'the Good People,' 'the Gentry,' 'the Fair Folk' and so forth. They could well have been listening, and it was best to compliment them if you could. Even this very brief survey of fairy power makes us wonder if such beliefs involved another form of heresy: not only that the fallen angels lived on, in our world, but that – to paraphrase Milton – they retained within them, like fading coals, a stubborn glow of numinous force. Tarnished, perhaps, but far greater than anything humankind could achieve.

Let us, then, be quite clear about this. Fairies were omniscient and omnipresent. They were arguably also omnipotent – at least to those who believed they could 'cut off half the human race' or destroy the world itself. This, and much more, was what the ordinary Christians of fairyland really believed. They believed so fervently in fairies that at times they would, like Abraham, be ready to sacrifice their own children for this belief. There is good reason to think that, if these people could have written down their beliefs, the result would have been very drastic indeed. Simply, it would have torn official Christian history to shreds. From Augustine down to Churchill, only the tiniest fragment of Christians fully adhered to orthodox theology. Underneath the false history and false continuity of the Christian churches there lay these dark, magical, largely unspoken beliefs. In the words of that old Lincolnshire woman who recalled the bird-screeches of Tiddy Mun:

> there were, so to say, two churches; the one wi' priests an' cannells and all that; t'other jist a lot o' aud ways, kep oop all unbeknown an hidd'n like, mid the folk therselves; and they thought a good deal more, ma gran'ther said, on the aud spells, than on the sarvice i' the church itself.

In a moment we will begin to trace the bare lines of this map of heresy through all its intricate paths, caves and crevices – to give it colour and to feel the wind snapping it against our fingers. One more word, however, about these Middle People before we make ready for that journey. We should not want, catching our breath on some rugged Celtic summit, to stumble on these beings and show insufficient sympathy for their devilish powers. What, then, of fairy temperament? If pushed to say just one thing about it, it would be this. Fairies embody a kind of raw pleasure principle. True, they may help humans in various ways. But ethically they so often seem to be amoral, irresponsible – at times, indeed, barely more than sheer energy, finding outlets and expressions in wild motion and wilder magic. Borrowing from Freud, we might say that they look like a sheer and unrestrained id, far closer to the boisterous selfishness of children than the dutiful laws of the adult world. But perhaps a more accurate way of viewing this hedonistic fairy energy is simply this: fairies were just what you – the cold, hungry, overworked Celtic peasant – *would* have been, if only you could. The fairies were the impossibly beglamoured celebrities about whom you were always hearing stories, those beings with human form and godlike powers.

Two
Sightings, Meetings, Signs

CROSSING A WELL-KNOWN FIELD early one morning with a basket of eggs, you suddenly start and skid to a halt, tumbling over and hurling eggs into the air. Sitting up, you breathe a mighty sigh of relief. Sure enough, most of the eggs are broken. But you managed, crucially, not to step into the fairy ring which had sprung up in the field overnight.

Botanical science has now established that fairy rings are caused by one of many possible fungi in the soil, catalysing chemical changes and releasing nitrogen. Results vary. You may see a small ring of mushrooms or toadstools, occasionally very brightly coloured. You may see a circle of vivid grass, or a brown or withered one. And, given that some fairy rings have been as large as several hundred feet in diameter, you may well have recklessly picnicked in one, never suspecting the danger. We also now know that some modern ones are many hundreds of years old.

For people who paid very careful attention to all the details and changes of nature around them, fairy rings were things of wonder and power. Mushrooms (possibly edible ones representing a great windfall of food to anyone daring enough to pick them) had sprung up in just one night. The grass was printed with a newly vivid colour, taking that oldest magical shape of all, the circle. This must mean something. Perhaps most obviously it meant that the fairies had been dancing there. It probably also struck some observers that this was one more typical instance of the fairies' link with fertility. More precisely, the magic power of these rings meant that, in Wales, Scotland or Ireland, anyone with the nerve to sleep inside one on Midsummer's Night could gain the second sight. In certain regions they may be held to mark the site of buried fairy treasure. Usually, however, such power was darker. Countless children must have grown up in terror of ever stepping into a fairy circle, lest the fairies snatch them away. Meanwhile, as late as the 1930s, there were remoter parts of France where 'nothing will induce peasants to put foot in or on a fairy circle for fear of monster toads of Satanic ugliness.'

In the early eighteenth century, prior to the fungal theory, the educated were already trying to rationalize the circles away, as formations produced by lightning or the activities of ants. We now also know that roe deer can stamp rings into grass or earth, sometimes (to add an extra twist of wonder) even in a figure of eight. Needless to say, none of this rational botany would have made the slightest impact on you as you trudged home to your parents, armed with a bulletproof excuse about the eggs. And on returning to the spot, where all this high-energy food had now been gobbled by birds, rabbits and foxes, it would of course be perfectly obvious just *who* had taken the bounty.

Numerous other unusual substances and objects from the natural world surrounded and interlocked with those magical circles of grass. Unexplained lights were 'fairy balls' or 'fairy sparks'. In the Western Hebrides lichens which under frost turned yellowish-red, before producing a bright red spreading moisture during thaw, were known to be (what else?) 'the blood of the fairies after one of their battles' – events which occurred especially on Halloween, although presumably also in other frost-bound periods. Edging out to the water spirits associated with fairies in Ireland, we hear of the mermaid's blood sometimes seen in Lake Killone, County Clare – this having various origins, including the belief that the mermaid had been stabbed by a butler of Newhall Manor, for swimming under its cellars to steal wine. More prosaically, we learn from Westropp that the water here naturally 'turns red at times from iron scum and red clay after a dry summer'.

Elsewhere the sharp watchful eye of the fairy-fearing man or woman decoded the very particular local signs of a given landscape. Seeds which had drifted from the West Indies to the shores of the Faroe Islands were in fact fairies' kidneys – and held, accordingly, capable of generating another seed if kept long enough. In Monmouthshire the brownie could take the form of a handful of dried grass rolling before the wind, commonly seen on the moors. Over in Lincolnshire those distinctive 'Tiddy People' of the Ancholme river valley ('no more than a span high, with arms and legs as thin as thread, but great big feet and hands') were also known as the Strangers. Not only were the large flat stones on which they danced under the moonlight called Strangers' Stones, but – according to oral history – at some earlier time people had smeared these stones with blood and lit fires on them. Here as elsewhere, fairy customs slide into some of the rawer habits of our pagan ancestors.

In order to sustain all their dancing and fighting the fairies of course needed to eat well. No wonder, then, that in many places you could see fairy butter – not only in fields and woodlands, but even stuck on your house or barn. For Yorkshire fairies were known to fling their butter at your doors, gates and windowframes, where it would stick and rot the wood. The last part of this is true. The culprit was a fungus known as *Exidia glandulosa*, which does indeed rot wood, both wild and carpentered. It is found in the north especially; is held by some to be made in the night by fairies; and in Sweden was known as 'troll's butter'. Be warned, however, that although after heavy rainfall it has a buttery consistency, and is (allegedly) edible, what the fairies might offer you at their tea-party would be black in colour. If found inside your cowhouse door in Leinster, fairy butter also meant that your household would have no butter for a year. Here the alleged human culprit who had smeared it would instead get what was due to you.

When we hear, meanwhile, that in the late eighteenth century an old Borders woman, Nanzy, not only often saw processions of fairies, but occasionally found 'very nice rolls of fairy butter' on the grass, we seem to have strayed back into the mists of folklore. These mists clear a little when we learn that our educated author ('E') knew Nanzy, and that, though Nanzy was 'too good a Christian' to eat such dubious fare, she certainly 'applied it without hesitation to other household purposes'.

We also know that Irish fairy butter was very real, as in 1849 the Botanical Society of London was speculating about the commercial production of candles from this 'fatty matter' of Irish peat moss. Interestingly, this utilitarian stance ran directly counter to local peasant belief. For when you, the true fairy believer, saw 'a little well ... of 6 to 7 inches in diameter, containing the matter pure, and about the colour of butter' there in the peat, you knew it was for fairy consumption, and accordingly to be 'treated with great reverence'.

Fairy Senses

Like some strange hallucinatory chemical, the fairies in your head filtered all your senses. When you were not seeing them or their works around you, you were feeling, hearing and even smelling these uncanny beings. On the Isle of Man, for example, 'the fairies were most frequently to be seen, heard and smelt ("a stale, sour smell") in the lonely upper parts of glens, where the bright slender rivers tumble swiftly and musically from pool to pool and only a narrow strip of sky shines down between the high green banks.' Sniffing out fairies may have been a peculiarly Manx skill. Around 1882 a prosperous and pious Manx farmer, insisting to the Kirk Malew vicar that fairies lived in his home glen, asserted that, though he had never seen one, 'I've smelt them often enough.'

Back in Lincolnshire, boatmen on the River Trent told of a sharp turn between Wildsworth and Owston Ferry where strange things occurred, and where 'a pygmy man with long hair and the face of a seal, crosses the river from east to west in a small craft resembling a pie-dish, which he propels rapidly with a pair of oars the size of tea-spoons.' When not actually visible, the 'Jenny on Boggard' of the Trent was often still present. 'Old keelmen would tell weird tales of feeling bumps at the side of their keels', and never anchored at the bend if they could possibly avoid it. On Inishbofin – some time after 1876, and possibly as late as the First World War – the English Catholic landowner Cyril Allies ran a quarry where on one occasion 'his quarrymen stopped work because the rock was getting very hot from all the "good people" inside it'. While the status of this sometime enchanted island may have sharpened local sensitivity to fairy presence, everyone knew that fairies, of course, lived mainly underground.

Above all, though, fairies were heard. Sometimes the sounds were sharp and alarming. Around 1800 a Welshman, Thomas Andrews, was walking home one night when he heard the notorious 'Sky Dogs' of the Fairy Hunt, creatures whose uncanny qualities were attested by the way that their barking grew quieter with proximity, and louder farther off. In Yorkshire a noted fairy dog rejoiced in several aliases, including the barghest, padfoot and capelthwaite. This large, shaggy black animal had 'heavy footsteps, which are heard when the spectre is not seen'. Most memorably of all, in 1882 a woman called Betsy recalled the barghest's uncanny barking, echoing from her (perhaps not entirely happy) childhood. Betsy's father, irked by her sceptical modern disbelief in the animal, would come to her bed at night to draw her attention to the occasional cacophony of village dogs. When one beast in particular gave three unearthly yowls he would announce warningly, 'that's the barghest', leaving young Betsy awake with her flesh creeping, listening to the ordinary village dogs raging at this one sinister interloper.

Moving on swiftly from this not wholly enlightened mode of parenting, we can now cleanse our ears with the ambient music of fairyland. As we saw in that Lincolnshire cottage, country people once heard a good deal, even from inside their houses. And they were also, like Andrews, far more likely to be out on foot, day or night. What might they hear of the fairies? Compare this. Many years ago three friends and I spent Christmas in a cottage on the north of Skye. Venturing out towards the nearby cliffs one night, we were drawn on by the strangest music in the darkness just ahead. I can still see us exchanging silent glances of bewilderment at this sound – uncanny, ambient and yet almost vocal. At the cliff edge, we found its source. A small set of railings fixed there was being played by the wind like an aeolian harp. Even with this explanation before us, the sound remained distinctly haunting.

Hearing something like this in fairy country, you were perhaps unlikely to venture too close, and so not learn of any such mundane solution. All across the Celtic lands, magic elfin winds strummed such chords through the fairy-struck minds of men, women and children. On Harris, for example, fairy music could be heard from 'the hill of the pipers'. Raised on the island, the Scottish academic and ecological activist Alastair Mcintosh recalled in the 1990s how 'at certain times one could lie on the hill' and supposedly 'hear the music of piping deep within'. He went on to explain that 'in recent years a new mains sewage system was being installed . . . and the digger broke through into a multi-chambered souterrain buried under the hill. One of the passages ran down to the sea and . . . on stormy days the crashing of boulders on the beach was commu-nicated through the chamber to create a "tinkelling" [sic] sound.' Those who claim to have heard fairy music on other parts of the island should be warned, however, that Mcintosh would 'frequently delight in playing my penny whistle in remote locations outside and often muse as to the extent to which distant walkers will take it as evidence that the faeries are still alive and well'.

In Cornwall, locals heard the sounds of fairies knocking in the Ransome Mine, and in a well at Towednack, where the noise of their picks and shovels ceased only on certain religious holidays. In more boisterous mode, the fairies of Inishbofin could be heard 'romping and carousing inside' the island's hills. Off the coast of Aberdovey, a whole sunken kingdom was believed to lie beneath the waters of Cardigan Bay. Cantre'r Gwaelod, the Lowland Hundred or 'Welsh

Atlantis', reportedly included a church whose bells could still be heard ringing, on occasion, from the depths. Around 1890 a vicar's wife, Mrs Powell, recalled visiting the area at age seven in 1852 and that she 'used to lie awake trying, but in vain, to catch the echoes of the chime'. Mrs Powell, however, may merely have mistimed her visit, for the Victorian scholar Sir John Rhys adds that at a certain phase of its tide the waves at the river Dovey's mouth would move pebbles with a bell-like tinkling – a sound which no doubt evoked glittering images of the subaqueous fairy kingdom in certain minds, childish and adult.

We have no such source for the alleged chimes heard in Crymlyn Lake (between Briton Ferry and Swansea), where another legendary sunken town had been converted by the fairies into an underwater palace. But all across these vanished fairy lands, the music of nature must have often produced precise and haunting cadences, whether plucked by wind from railings and wires, or (in the experience of Lincoln College fellow Owen Edwards) brushed by a southwesterly across the metallic broken ice of Lake Bala in Gwynedd. Perhaps most memorably of all,

> on Dalby Mountain, this side of Cronk-yn-Irree-Laa the old Manx people used to put their ears to the earth to hear the Sounds of Infinity (Sheean-ny-Feaynid), which were sounds like murmurs. They thought these sounds came from beings in space; for in their belief all space is filled with invisible beings.

No matter that these (as even the fairy-struck Evans-Wentz concedes) were probably just the sound of waves 'washing over shifting masses of pebbles on the rock-bound shore'. Listen again. Stop your ears, if you can, to the smudge of nearby traffic, the intermittent trilling of telephones and text-message alerts, the robot barking of vans turning left or coming north, even the hiss of radiators or muted boiler roar . . . and try, if you can, to catch the *Sounds of Infinity*.

Few, if any of us, still can. We have lost something. It is one of those things whose loss itself is all too easily forgotten. Amid a babel of instantly accessible and portable music, staccato and mundane, we can no longer ever hope to tune our ears to the Sounds of Infinity, to the faint sighings of that now closed dimension, the forbidden frequency of wonder.

And would we, if we now visited the very exact Manx territory described by W. W. Gill, a remote fairy-haunted triangle of hills and river valley, be able to hear that unearthly 'singing, as of human voices in distant unison, exhaled mysteriously on still evenings out of a certain steep piece of ground on the opposite bank, called the Granane, where long mossy stones lie half hidden under bushes and briars, and lights tremble along the rugged surface after night-fall'? Perhaps, if we could find that pebble on which one Manxman was said to have transcribed the sounds, we could try to get them performed . . . All we know for certain now, however, is that local 'villagers and farmpeople used to come to their own bank of the river to listen to this singing', a free and impromptu recital by nature's middle kingdom.

If this claim seems as bewildering as it does enchanting, readers might be interested to know that in fact fairy music has been transcribed and performed. In 1922 the composer and sometime Oxford fellow Dr Thomas Wood was holidaying with friends on Dartmoor when he heard

music in the air! It was overhead, faint as a breath. It died away, came back louder, over me, swaying like a censer that dips. It lasted 20 minutes. Portable wireless sets were unknown in 1922. My field glasses assured me no picnickers were in sight. It was not a gramo-phone nor was it an illusory noise in my ears. This music was essentially harmonic, not a melody nor an air. It sounded like the weaving together of tenuous fairy sounds. I listened with every faculty drawn out to an intensity . . . I am prepared to say on oath that what I wrote down is so close to the original that the authors themselves would not know the difference . . . The music drifted into silence. No more came, then or since. I was reasonably certain that I had been deliberately encouraged to listen to the supernatural.

Wood was not the only Oxbridge lecturer prepared to 'swear on oath' to the truth of a fairy experience. Although he does not seem to have recorded the music himself, recently the American author Chris Woodyard did so, via a transcription for electronic organ. Readers can listen for themselves at her website; and anyone who wants to achieve another musical first could also arrange a performance of Wood's original score for two violins.

Fairy Animals

Fairy signs which were actually real (though usually misread) are in one sense the most interesting of all. They remind us that the seemingly mundane world around us is sometimes shaped out of our heads, with surprising degrees of subjectivity and creativity. At one level, this could be true of real animals, birds or insects which were understood to be fairies.

From Ireland's County Cavan, we hear of 'an invisible fairy path' which 'ran from Moneygashel down to Gowlan Cross . . . The fairies came down to the crossroads in the form of foxes, and a man living at Gowlan had his chickens killed by them. He went up to Moneygashel and found a hole and smoked them out.' After this, 'the fairy foxes were never seen again.' More dramatically, by a ruined abbey in County Mayo, an epic fairy battle took place, lasting a day and night. Though no eyewitness accounts of the conflict survive, hundreds of corpses were seen at its close, for 'one could have filled baskets with the dead flies which floated down the river.'

In County Clare in 1910, Westropp heard of how, 'early this year a clever intelligent man, near Ennis, went with a boy and a ferret to shoot rabbits from a fort. Three ran out and were shot at and missed. The man then called the boy to come at once, and ran off in great excitement and fear, saying the rabbits were fairies.' In the same area, perhaps twenty or more years before, Mrs MacDonnell of Newhall told Westropp that, 'when a girl, she took up a small and very tame white rabbit in the glen at Edenvale, and immediately afterwards found that she had lost a ring. The people who helped in the search, and her father's gamekeeper, were convinced that the rabbit was a fairy and had taken the ring with it.'

Here the case of the fairy foxes shows how the most utterly ordinary incident can be explained in a supernatural way. While both the rabbit tales display a high proportion of superstition to a small grain of the unusual, it is worth recalling the immense amount of superstition generated around magical and witch rabbits elsewhere. In nineteenth-century Yorkshire, for example, a grown man who saw what he believed to be a magical white rabbit went to bed and literally died of fear. When we hear, meanwhile, that 'a Highland name for the cuckoo was eusz-sidhe, fairy-bird', we can fairly guess that the very distinctive sound of this bird, and probably its nesting habits, had something to do with that name.

Other fairy creatures slip further along the scale of the mythic or folkloric, once again typifying the fairies' tendency to mirror the human world at so many points. Manx fairies, explains Gill, 'keep all the domestic animals except cats and fowls, and cats they steal, in Denmark'. More on cats in a moment. As we have seen, one reason that fairies needed both horses and dogs was their fondness for fairy hunts. Waldron found it a fixed and very general Manx belief that 'these huntings are frequent in the island, and that these little gentry being too proud to ride on Manx horses . . . make use of the English and Irish ones, which are brought over and kept by gentlemen'. Once again, there was evidence for this belief. For it was all too common 'to find these poor beasts in a morning, all over in a sweat and foam, and tired almost to death, when their owners have believed they have never been out of the stable'. This, as readers may know, does actually happen to horses, and has been variously attributed to fairies, ghosts, poltergeists and vampires. The tangled manes associated with this condition were often held to have been impishly plaited by fairy grooms – hence the term 'elf locks'.

Rather harder to explain was the fairy gymkhana which a man allegedly saw during a moonlit cart journey at Bunnahow, County Clare, some time before 1916. Our witness told Lady Gregory of seeing little men in red clothes and jockey caps, using a screen of bushes to jump their horses. 'Some of the horses', he added with eerie precision, 'would jump over it, and more of them would baulk.' Although it is not made explicit, these fairy horses were presumably scaled-down animals, perhaps like the dog-sized ones we will meet below.

Fairy dogs are arguably the biggest, most varied category of fairy animal, and probably the one sighted the most. These elfin hounds have an impressively long reign, with their paw prints stretching from the *Mabinogion* of the fourteenth century down to the twentieth, and from the Hebrides to the Chilterns. They are not easy to categorize. Here I will split them into ghost dogs and dogs more definitely belonging to the fairies.

We have already glimpsed the supernatural dogs of Yorkshire. But such animals were not limited to that region. Sightings of spectral dogs, sometimes the size of a calf, sometimes with eyes of fire, are legion across Britain. Some cases were doubtless pure folklore. But others are not so easy to dismiss. Westropp gives a very precise account of how his brother, mother and two servants saw a black dog floating beside their coach in the Cratloe hills in February 1869. In Lincolnshire, where spectral black dogs were always benign (and sometimes protected late-walking women), people claimed to have heard these animals brushing leaves or breaking twigs as they passed. Down in Lyme Regis, one 'goblin dog' was said to lie by the fire in a very ordinary and contented way, night after night in a farmer's house – also being, as the farmer remarked, admirably cheap to feed.

Should we attempt to track all of these spectral hounds, we would ultimately be led too far out of fairy territory. But we do need briefly to examine the *mauthe doog*, or black dog, of Peel Castle. Evans-Wentz considered this a fairy dog, and sightings of it were so numerous, indeed habitual, in one era to make one wonder if it was in fact the ghost of a real dog. In about 1726 Waldron spoke to an old soldier of the castle who had seen it 'oftener than he had then hairs on his head', the height of its fame being around sixty years before this conversation. Every night the dog would enter the castle by a certain passage and lie down by the fire, leaving again at dawn. Modern readers may not find the animal entirely bloodcurdling on learning that it 'took the shape of a large black spaniel with curled shaggy hair'. But the soldiers, although grown used to it, were sufficiently awed by its nature and demonic potential as to 'forbear swearing and all profane discourse while in its company'. Nor would anyone ever be left alone with it, the soldiers deliberately going in pairs for certain duties at this time. One memorable night, however, a soldier emboldened by drink went off alone, boasting that if he met the animal, he would 'try whether it were dog or devil'. A great noise was heard; the soldier returned speechless and, taking to his bed utterly dumb, died in three days' time. After this no one would ever venture into the haunted passage, which was presently sealed up.

Although the drunkenness and the moralistic element of the non-swearing soldiers may be in part folkloric creations, the soldier's symptoms look strikingly like those of conversion disorder and voodoo death. In the first case people have, for purely psychosomatic reasons, been rendered mute, blind or paralysed, and there are numerous cases of death through fear, including many caused by encounters with ghosts. Tellingly, three days is very often the outer time-limit for voodoo deaths. There are also many reports of ghostly dogs, often pets of the home's owners, and almost always benign. Notably, these are often taken for real, living dogs, and in one memorable case they were said to play with the live dogs of the house in question.

Ghost dogs, then, may not be pure folklore. What we do know is that, with a few exceptions, the phantom dogs of popular lore were usually black. Dogs belonging to the fairies, by contrast, were very often white – sometimes strikingly so. In the *Mabinogion* the Prince, Pwyll, meets a fairy hunt whose dogs are 'exceptionally white and glittering' with red ears. This kind of beast had a genealogy worthy of the Kennel Club, with Mona Douglas writing in 1970 of the Manx 'coo ny Helg or fairy hound, sometimes seen running across the fields at twilight, a big white dog with red ears and paws, which it is lucky to see'. In Galway, Steven Ruan told Evans-Wentz: 'I saw a dog with a white ring around his neck by that hill there, and the oldest men round Galway have seen him, too, for he has been here for one hundred years or more. He is a dog of the good people, and only appears at certain hours of the night.' Here the animal was presumably dark in colour, for the ring to be noticeable.

On the whole fairy dogs of this type seem not to be as terrifying as 'black dogs' (although the Scottish fairy dog 'cu sith' was sometimes said to have the evil eye). There again, these animals certainly commanded respect and obedience in the Isle of Man. Having fought his way through snowdrifts to the farmhouse of the Leece family, Evans-Wentz heard from Mrs Leece a tale of her grandfather, John Watterson, dating back around a century:

> all the family were sometimes sitting in the house of a cold winter night, and my great grandmother and her daughters at their wheels spinning, when a little white dog would suddenly appear in the room. Then every one there would have to drop their work and prepare for the company to come in: they would put down a fire and leave fresh water for them, and hurry off upstairs to bed. They could hear them come, but could never see them, only the dog. The dog was a fairy dog, and a sure sign of their coming.

We can see that this broadly matches the folklore tradition of bribing the fairies with nightly food and drink. But it is also a significant step on to have them send a special dog to announce a kind of fairy curfew. In a perfect world we would be able to show how some especially shrewd Manx dog had learned that, by poking its snout in someone's door at night, it would secure for itself free bed and board (and had perhaps passed the trick on to its pups).

And this possibility brings us, finally, to the question of fairy dogs which were actually real animals – albeit not, in fact, dogs. Let me explain. Writing in 1926 of his Bedfordshire home near the Chiltern hills, the veteran naturalist Oliver Pike spoke of local 'farm labourers who will tell you that fairy dogs still hunt the meadows at night'. Pike went on to assert that, 'remarkable as it may seem our meadows are hunted by night by packs of small but desperate robbers.' What awe-struck viewers had not realized, however, was that 'these miniature hounds' were actually weasels – creatures which at certain times of year will hunt in packs of up to forty. Tales to give one pause, if ever we heard them.

Back on the more typical fairy island of Man, we hear Gill considering the belief that fairy dogs wore red hats (rather than having red ears), with the same fashion accessory being reported also on fairy pigs and fairy lambs. These last were held lucky if seen among one's flock, to which they would bring extra fertility. Much as this might seem to denote merely a lamb with a partially red fleece, around 1900 one Manx woman swore to having seen a lamb with a red saddle and bridle. Her experience, which seems to have been traumatic and which may even have caused her death, implies that these animals, like so much else in popular magic, were better viewed as 'powerful' rather than simply good or bad.

Cats also seem to have had some status beyond the purely fluffy. On Man some held the cat to be a special 'friend of the fairies', and indeed 'the only member of the family whose presence was tolerated by the fairies when they came into the kitchen at night'. Others went so far as to credit 'a king of the cats, which during the day lives the life of an ordinary domesticated cat, but at night roams in regal state and is all-powerful'. Perhaps of equally royal blood was the fairy cat which guarded treasure at the fairy fort in County Louth, and which could be lured from its post only by a trail of lamb's blood at midnight.

Fairy Islands

In the time of Pepys a sea captain, John Nesbit, sailed regularly from Donegal to trade with France. Out at sea on 2 March 1675, he had a particularly memorable voyage, for he and his crew found themselves in a dense fog off an unknown island. Nesbit and eight other mariners saw it, and presently he and three officers landed, and beheld woods, horses, cattle, sheep and black rabbits. The travellers came to a castle, but no person answered them from it. They returned to the shore and lit a fire, the evening being cold. At this a hideous noise ensued, and they took their boat and fled to the ship. Next day they saw a gentleman and his servants on the shore and brought them off. These men explained that they had long been imprisoned in the castle by an enchanter, but the lighting of a fire by Christians had wrecked the main tower and broken the spell. Nesbit brought them back to his home port of Killybegs, where many believed their story on seeing their old coins and hearing their out-of-date language and ideas.

Confronted with a tale such as this, we find ourselves in a peculiarly disorienting zone. Dropping anchor and splashing up through the shingle, from the unstable waters of myth to the dry land of charted fact, we suddenly realize that the island itself is floating on the tides of legend. Is this peasant folklore or the business-like truth of the captain's log? In fact, not quite one or the other. Around 1915 Westropp related this story with an open-mindedness which may have given some readers the impression that the report was factual. Whatever Westropp's own view, he seems not to have been aware that the tale in fact derived from one Richard Head, an opportunistic character writing for a living in the time of Charles II. In his 1675 *O Brazile, or The Enchanted Island*, Head deviously presented the above tale in a soberly realistic form in a supposed letter of March 1674, penned by the real-life William Hamilton, MP for Londonderry. To complicate matters a little further, Hamilton himself had allegedly claimed that many had seen such an island from the coast of Ulster. Indeed, he knew of a man who, under Charles I, had taken out a patent to hold the island. Meanwhile, a little further digging shows that Nesbet too was real, being mentioned in an Act of Parliament, and associated with Donegal and Killibegs. In 1684 the Irish historian Roderic O'Flaherty talked of personally seeing O Brasile much further south, off Aran, and of spectral cities, towers, flames, smoke and people running.

All down this Atlantic coast, from Donegal to Kerry, fairy islands slipped in and out of view, perhaps visible just once in seven years, perhaps sailed from place to place by the Gentry to keep them out of mortal sight. Indeed, in this region the fairies themselves might look comparatively tame or homely. Once, this was the edge of the world. Standing long enough on wind-scuffed cliffs the clear-sighted might spy, in a fleeting shift of light, the Isle of the Blessed or the Isle of Youth. You might even descry Ladra, the mythic island named after the man who in 2348 BC, just before the Deluge, escorted Noah's niece, Cesair, to Ireland, later dying and becoming the first person ever buried on the Emerald Isle. Poor and illiterate though you were, you knew all this, and knew too that once every seven years Ladra could be seen, covered in houses and churches.

It was perhaps not so surprising that O Brasile had such a status in this period, featuring on most maps at the end of the seventeenth century, and lingering on some as late as 1865. In the Restoration, after all, the Americas were still a relatively recent, unexpected find, further out across these waters, and were by no means fully known or mapped, almost two centuries after Columbus. Three centuries back, then, open-mindedness about uncharted lands was a rational attitude. And yet, even as we drop this coal of stabilizing fire at our feet, we find the picture freshly complicated when we recall those eerily exact mirages seen and sketched by Westropp, across the decades between 1872 and 1921. Meanwhile, in 1859 an educated Ulsterman quoted a peasant woman who told of how,

> not long ago, my brother saw their ships one day as he was sittin' on the ould castle hill at Red Bay, sailin' in the air, and some on the sea with sails set, and thousands of the Gentry, visible at times and then disappearing, on the decks and about the masts and riggin'. He watched them comin' in nearer and nearer, till they sailed in at the far side of Red Bay, past Galbally Point, and then the mist came on, and they wint up Glenariff in it . . .

If the fairies had islands, and if the fairies had horses, castles, courts and virtually every other human invention, then why not ships?

Lest we think this female informant wildly fanciful, we should hear too from the unnamed writer who took down her story. For he, looking off Antrim's Galbally Point in autumn 1857, saw, at about four o'clock, following a thunderstorm, 'seven yachts, masts, and white sails, with what appeared to be a confused mass of other vessels behind them', become 'suddenly and distinctly visible off the point . . . So perfect was the appearance' that he asked a nearby person 'if there was a regatta at Larne or Glenarm'. He then 'went into his house for a telescope, but before he returned, yachts and all had disappeared. A heavy mass of black clouds on the verge of the horizon had in the meantime assumed the appearance of stupendous ruins, irregular in outline, but the angles of the walls sharp and clearly defined.' Seconds later, all this solid masonry melted in the blue air.

Reports such as this suggest that the special atmospheric conditions of western Ireland at times gave particularly vivid shape to the fairies already rooted in your head. But clearly there was much more to fairy islands than this. Although the Isle of Man does not seem to have been ringed by them, it had once been a fairy island in its own right. In the nineteenth century people would tell how the fairies had been its first inhabitants. And, like the fairy isles, it had in its mythic past been shrouded in enchanted mists – until the day when a sailor, landing by chance, struck a flame and 'drove the gloomy mists up into the mountains and exposed the seaboard to the human race'. Much later this story had reshaped itself into the belief (still held in Waldron's time) that 'if the island should ever be wholly without a fire for even the briefest moment it would vanish again into its primeval mystery.'

Leaving Man from Douglas in the south, we have a good chance of stowing away on a fairy boat headed for the coasts of Pembroke and Carmarthen in Wales. As we saw, Evans-Wentz heard of Welsh fairy islands as a living reality around 1909. Like those of Ireland, they floated in spaces between outright myth and the most mundane reality. The fairy archipelago off Carmarthen Bay might be seen 'rising up from the sea – islands so beautiful, and so covered with glittering palaces and lovely flowers, that the eye which is once permitted to look upon one of them, can never recognise any beauty in anything else, and pines away from an intense longing to visit such wondrous regions'. Here our fairy danger is of a special kind – a perilous siren magic of the eye, a visual drug which turns all else sour grey by comparison. And like their Greek counterpart, these isles were also full of melody. For sometimes they would 'float close to the mainland, so close that strains of glorious music come stealing over the waves'.

And indeed, these aqueous fairies were known to get much closer still. At perhaps the most mundane end of the spectrum, these dwellers of the enchanted islands would sometimes 'come to shore and attend both Laugharne and Milford markets, carrying off their favourite joints, and leaving the just price upon the scale in the shape of silver pennies'. Now this, surely, is proof. If you, on your shift at the supermarket till, had seen fairies queuing up with their Five Fairy Items, and had later cashed up a number of fairy coins . . .

At which point, of course, we want to know who had seen these fairies shopping at the markets of Laugharne and Milford. Well, many would certainly tell you the fairies had been there. They paid without speaking and were usually invisible. But the very sharp-eyed sometimes saw them, while it was well known that at Cardigan and Fishguard markets the fairies paid in such good coin that they cleared all stock and raised the price of grain. We hear too of how 'the Tylwyth Teg [literally, 'Fair Family'] formerly used to frequent the markets at Bala' in Gwynedd, where they would 'swell the noise in the market-place without anybody being able to see them'. And of course this, as any shrewd housewife knew, 'was a sign that prices were going to rise.'

Stepping back, shifting our angle of vision (and hearing), we might wonder if markets really *did* get more boisterously noisy just when prices were about to rise. Or, we might recall that for those who fervently believed in them, fairies could often look just like you or me. At least, *almost* like you or me . . . For yes, some Welsh market-goers really had *seen* the fairies queuing with their baskets. Shifting onto the mainland to investigate these sightings, we learn of the mythical descendants of Rhys Ddwfn, or Rhys the Deep, 'a handsome race enough, but remarkably small in size'. In a twist on the invisibility of fairy islands, these Children of Rhys Ddwfn had in their lands 'certain herbs of a strange nature . . . so that they were able to keep their country from being seen'. This domain lay somewhere between Cemmaes, in Powys, and Aberdaron in Lleyn, and we further learn that these herbs grew on just one square yard of mortal soil, in 'a certain part of Cemmaes'. Anyone standing alone on this spot 'beheld the whole of the territory of Plant Rhys Ddwfn; but the moment he moved he would lose sight of it altogether'. And what would you see, in that magical instant, from that magical yard? In one more version of fairy glamour, you would find that, amid miles of open country, the Rhysians *lived in towns*. Because of their lack of farmland,

> they were wont in former times to come to market to Cardigan, and to raise the prices of things terribly. They were seen of no

one coming or going, but only seen there in the market. When prices happened to be high, and the corn all sold, however much there might have been there in the morning, the poor used to say to one another on the way home, 'Oh! they were there to-day,' meaning Plant Rhys Ddwfn.

So here we have fairies that are both seen and inferred (by their effect on prices). But, in a kind of poetic justice, the fairies themselves were ultimately forced away by this inflation, after which (stated one nineteenth-century informant), 'the old people used to think that they now went to Fishguard market, as very strange people were wont to be seen there.'

At this point our fairies jump into unexpectedly sharp focus. For they are indeed real people. Echoing what we established in Chapter One, they are very like you, and yet, not *quite* like you. They are strangers. At first glance this tale looks sadly like all our own modern scapegoating of immigrants for social and economic problems. And yet . . . I dream, as I have said, of getting fairies into your head. To do that, no cunning sociological explanation is so effective as the plain words of a Fishguard woman, speaking around 1896: 'there are fairies,' she asserted, 'for they came to Ha'rordwest market to buy things, so there must be.' Opaque? Perhaps. Neatly circular? Perchance. And unshakably persuasive, to her and most of her peers? Quite definitely.

Adding up these different pieces of the coastal jigsaw, we find the fairies typically filling all the space between their enchanted islands and the marketplaces of Fishguard and Haverfordwest. Some lurked in *Gwerddonnau Llion*, the 'green meadows of the sea'. And, while the Irish fairies might sail to your shores, those inhabiting the 'green Fairy Islands' off Milford Haven were known to go 'to and fro between the islands and the shore, through a subterranean gallery under the bottom of the sea'. In at least one case, moreover, they appear to have lived almost on the seashore itself. In 1890, 'upon a large barren plain of sand, down upon the seacoast of Glamorganshire' there still stood 'a lonely ruined castle', allegedly 'built by the fairies in one night' and known occasionally to rise 'in all its former magnificence, watch-towers, battlements, and turrets complete, while at others it disappears altogether . . . no one will approach it after dark under any pretext whatever'.

Fairy Artefacts

Glimpses of fairy castles and cities have already shown us that fairies could make things. Smaller, portable fairy artefacts also had the distinction of sometimes entering the human realm, and being kept there. In Herefordshire into the 1920s the small clay pipes people found when digging gardens were called 'fairy pipes'; while the Roman coins unearthed at Bolitree were 'fairies' money'. Westropp, meanwhile, tells of a Connacht man who, after finding and using a fairy razor, later suffered a disfiguring skin disease. (We can reasonably guess that he thought this an ordinary razor until afflicted, only then imposing the perilous fairy character upon it.)

Some of the most famous fairy artefacts were certainly powerful, and some at least potentially dangerous. The MacLeods of Dunvegan had a fairy flag thought to have twice saved the clan in battle, and another prized fairy banner belonged to the MacDonalds. In Cumbria, a glass beaker owned by the Musgrave family, near Penrith, was known as the Luck of Edenhall – reputedly because when fairies, surprised by the family butler, dropped it, their parting words were: 'If this cup should break or fall,/ Farewell the luck of Eden Hall.' Similarly, when the Manx Fairy Cup of Ballafletcher was ceremonially drained at Christmas 'in honour of the good fairy', the Fletchers were aware that the beautiful but perilous female spirit the Lhiannan-shee would haunt anyone who shattered it, and destroy the family fortunes.

While we should not underestimate the power of the stories attached to these vessels, it is easy to forget that part of their status derived from their sheer physical glamour. The Luck of Edenhall, now in the Victoria & Albert Museum, must to many who first saw it have looked not only beautiful but exotic, deriving as it does from fourteenth-century Syria or Egypt. Equally, the ornate glass Luck of Skirsgill, belonging to the Cumbrian Whelpdale family, was valuable enough to be auctioned at Sotheby's in 1968. The Ballafletcher cup, now in the Manx Museum, is a slightly decorated glass tumbler which looks humble by comparison. But we should note that, in the nineteenth century, even a brass dish belonging to a farmer could be graced with the title the 'Luck of Burrell Green'.

In some ways the most intriguing of these fairy talismans is the cup a farmer, Tom Kewley, was supposed to have stolen from a Manx fairy banquet near Mount Murray. This was allegedly made of silver, and when Kewley showed it to the vicar of Kirk Malew, this minister, declaring it to be of demonic craftsmanship, shrewdly concluded that the only safe place for it would be in his church. Among the many transgressions of nominally Christian fairy believers, the use of a fairy cup to take communion (for this was its new role) surely stands high. And whatever the cup's origin, it may well have actually existed. Trying to track it down around 1882, Edward Callow found that it had disappeared, reportedly because an unusually high number of communicants had gone mad after drinking from it. If the vessel had been of lead, or lead alloy, this fairy cup may well have been both real and chemically dangerous.

Through all of these fairy artefacts there runs one buried thread. Once, there were far fewer man-made *things* in the world, and for many people any single one of these, from pipe to razor, could have value and glamour. This was certainly the case for the Irish labourer Thomas Conway when on 16 March 1852 he found a strange-looking urn while digging a potato trench in Columbkill, Kilkenny. 'Overjoyed at the discovery, supposing it to be a "crock of gold"', Conway 'watched over the urn for the night, sacrificing a black cat, according to the ritual recommended by the most esteemed "fairy doctors", to propitiate the spirit supposed to guard the treasure'. Finding no fairy treasure come cock-crow, Conway in disappointment broke what was in fact a burial urn, scattering ashes and fragments about – somewhat to the disgust of the Kilkenny archaeologist who later recounted the incident.

Fairy Men and Women

Who were these 'fairy doctors' so esteemed by Conway? Closing in now a little more tightly upon our elfin quarry, we come to those men and women who gained various sorts of power from their special association with the fairies. Many of them claimed to have met the fairies or to have been to fairyland itself, and some that medicines were given to them by fairies. Others claimed actually to be fairies. On the whole, the first group were more likely to be genuine amateur healers, of people and/or animals. Hence the term 'fairy doctor' often applied to them. Viewed more broadly, this class were also 'cunning folk' – people now largely forgotten, who were once found in all rural districts, where they were the first and last resort for numerous of the problems afflicting ordinary men and women, both natural and supposedly supernatural. Those claiming to be (say) the queen of the fairies, and to promise their dupes great wealth, were usually con artists. As we will see, in between these two types there fall a few more ambiguous cases. The fraudsters, incidentally, can now seem relatively more numerous than the genuine fairy doctors, when in fact they probably were not. Surviving data on them is greater just because their exploits sometimes landed them in court, whereas fairy doctors carried out a great deal of their work under the official radar.

Fairy Fraudsters

On 14 February 1594 one Judith Philips was whipped through the streets of London for various offences, including an episode occurring a few miles from Winchester, probably in late 1593. Though married to a man called Pope, Philips, unhappy with her humble life, had left him and now wandered southwest England. At a place called Upsburne in Hampshire she heard of a wealthy Mr X, and began to con him and his wife by first burying some money under a tree near their house, this 'secret treasure' presently being used as evidence of her power to bring them still greater wealth. Persuaded by this (and by her witty assertion, sworn on the Bible, that she came lately from the Pope – true, as far as her husband went), Mr X gave her the very considerable sum of £14, and on her instructions put out five candlesticks, with a gold coin under each. Philips then put a saddle and bridle on Mr X and rode him three times around the garden, next explaining that she had to go inside to meet the queen of the fairies. While she did this Mr and Mrs X were to stay outside, 'grovelling on your bellies', under a tree. Philips returned presently, disguised in a white smock and some kind of white headgear and carrying a stick, in which state-of-the-art costume she persuaded the awestruck pair that she herself was the queen of the fairies. She then – our narrator rather vaguely states – seemed to disappear in some magical fashion. After what appears to have been at least three hours in the winter cold, with Mr X still sporting his saddle and bridle, the husband went indoors to find Philips had vanished with his gold and finest linens.

Now, there are a lot of things from this period I'd give five gold coins to see on film, but this, surely, ranks high among them. One can certainly understand why our narrator did not disclose the dupes' names. How did Philips pull this off? On one side we have, of course, the credulity of two people of considerable wealth (albeit perhaps not education) who believed not only in the promised treasure, but that the queen of the fairies had stood before them. This is interesting in itself, given how unlikely such a pair would be to fall for a fairy fraud in (say) 1793 or 1893.

But perhaps most intriguing of all is Philips herself. In a period when women of almost all ranks suffered degrees of misogyny, inequality and abuse now almost impossible to imagine (and when even clergymen wondered if women had souls), Philips had the ambition, nerve and bravura acting skills of a modern media celebrity, even perhaps an elite career woman. Brief as the surviving account is, it is clear that Philips's desire to humiliate the horsey-husband most thoroughly of all must have reflected her experiences of patriarchal misogyny, and her refusal to bow to it.

A slightly later affair involved a husband-and-wife team, John and Alice West, who in 1613 were convicted of defrauding Thomas Moore and his wife of £80. The Wests were more elaborate in their tricks than Philips, at one point showing Moore and his wife not only the king and queen of fairies, but some 'little elves and goblings' attending on their fairy Majesties, and at another parading the royal pair before the Moores' maidservant. Fairy glamour was again evoked, with Moore persuaded to put out a lavish fairy banquet, and secrecy was preserved by instilling fear of the fairies into all three dupes. Thomas Moore's personal fear was so great that he suffered some kind of paralysis during the affair, which was attributed to the fairies. While this may have been a minor stroke, it is also possible that it was one more instance of conversion disorder induced by supernatural fears. What we do know for certain is that Moore was ready to part with the then enormous sum of £80 because of promised fairy treasure, totalling 'seventeen hundred thousand pound' (which, in 1613 valuation, was a *lot* of fairy glamour).

The Wests seem to have been career con artists, with a more impressive resumé than Philips. Both episodes call to mind all those modern con artists of recent times in the realm of fine art or high finance, who seem not only to have flair and nerve, but to actually *enjoy* what they do. In those older cases we have the dazzle of fairyland and some perhaps fairly simple costumes. In the modern ones we have the reified glamour of art or business, and sometimes little more than one sharp suit for the occasion.

A brief sample of nineteenth-century fairy frauds shows us that some two centuries later, these incidents were by no means always confined to lowly countryfolk. In summer 1818, for example, a fortune teller, Elizabeth Hay, was charged with fraud at Marlborough Street police office by a London servant, Mary Woodward. Two years back Hay had approached Woodward in Foley Street, gone back to the nearby house of Woodward's mistress, and persuaded Woodward and the house's young lady (that is, a daughter of some status) that the house was 'built on fairies' land'. By dropping blue and red drops from two magic phials in the yard at 4 p.m. every day, they would ultimately gain £600 in buried fairy treasure. After taking £10 from the young lady on this first visit, Hay managed to con her out of money and clothing every day for a further three weeks. She presently escaped when her dupes grew suspicious, and was only spotted by chance in Marylebone Street two years later – showing us, again, how close this story came to being lost to us.

Back in more typical fairy territory, we hear from Ireland in December 1846 of an inquest on the body of one Denis Roche of Knockrow. Last seen with his week's wages going off for a drink, Roche was found after a fortnight drowned in a bog. During this uncertain period, though already suspecting him dead, Roche's family travelled from Knockrow to Enniscorthy to see an unnamed fairy woman, whom they paid £1 for details on Roche's presumed death. After two days' consultation with the fairies, the fairy woman stated that 'she had seen [the] deceased herself', and that he had been 'murdered by two men, one of whom had deceived a fair haired girl in the neighbourhood'. This was almost certainly incorrect, and probably deliberately fraudulent too, given the sum which the woman requested.

But what is most interesting here is what the case says about belief in fairies, and the status of fairy men and women. First, the woman acted as a kind of unofficial police officer or detective – something which cunning folk in general did surprisingly often. Second, it seems unlikely that the Roches were well-off, given that Denis was employed on the public works. This means that, as the worst famine in Irish history ground on, through one of the very worst winters, the Roches, having just lost a breadwinner, travelled around twenty miles across a county border and paid to the fairy woman a sum which (at a day rate of 6–8 pence) it would have taken a works' labourer around ten weeks to earn. At this time, Irish people were literally starving to death. Such was the status of fairies and fairy women.

Come August 1862, witnesses in Cork Police Court were convulsed with laughter as they heard evidence of an alleged fraud committed by Mary Colbert, 'the fairy', against a sick girl, Hannah Sullivan. Sullivan had asked for Colbert's help when she met her 'doctoring' another local woman. At one point in the cure, Colbert had left the house where Sullivan worked, only to return presently, saying that she had met the fairies in the alley and been asked by them to go back and cure Hannah. It is not quite clear if Colbert intended fraud. Although she asked for a total of 27 shillings (a sum Sullivan could not easily raise) she stated in evidence that her cures were done 'with God's help', and may have believed in them, just as her neighbours generally believed in the curse supposedly placed on Sullivan. The fact that Colbert was called 'the fairy' is also intriguing, given that a small number of adults, around this time, were believed to be fairy changelings who had grown to maturity.

Away with the Fairies

Like so much else from fairyland, the above phrase has survived in a very dilute form, now often meaning little more than a moment's absent daydreaming. By contrast, it was once understood literally, and at times accorded such elite travellers a kind of shamanistic status. An early example is that of Morogh O'Ley, the Irishman who claimed to have been abducted from Connemara and taken to the enchanted fairy island O Brasile. After two days there he returned with a medical manuscript, later known as the Book of the O'Lees and now preserved in Dublin's Royal Irish Academy. Around 1675 O'Ley began practising medicine and surgery, despite having never done so previously. His success was allegedly due to this magical volume, which he had not opened until seven years after the abduction, in obedience to instructions given on the island.

O'Ley probably did not need to emphasize his or the book's fairy credentials to those he treated in Galway. What is especially interesting about this case is that O'Ley chose to use a fairy island as his shamanic claim to medical authority. For not only could O'Ley read Latin, but his ancestors had in fact been 'hereditary physicians' in western Connacht (the book itself is now suspected to have been merely a family heirloom). Despite this status, it was the fairies to whom O'Ley turned when he made his apparently pragmatic side-step into medicine.

Come autumn 1878, another version of this was offered to the reading public by the dilettante writer Letitia McLintock, who claimed to have met an ancient fairy doctor, Dan Gow, outside her rented country home in County Cavan. After some vacuous whimsy about Oberon and Titania and the 'delightful' fairies, McLintock has a long conversation with Gow about a local woman stolen by the fairies some years back, and presently explains to her readers that Gow 'firmly believes himself to be a particular friend and protégé of the gentle race . . . he is a famous cow doctor, and the neighbours for miles round have the firmest faith in his supernatural lore'. This seems to have been at least partly because, after going missing a few years back (for so long that his cat and pig were nearly starved to death when anxious neighbours broke into his cabin), Gow returned, 'saying he had been underground with the good people . . . He had been fêted, had eaten, drunk, and lodged magnificently; and had played the fiddle for the elves to dance to.' Since then, the peasants believed that Gow continued to hold 'mysterious intercourse with his fairy friends', and his status had risen accordingly.

It is hard to be sure if Dan Gow really existed, as McLintock was also a novelist and could perhaps have invented many of the realistic details in her account. But, although no other references to him appear to have survived, there must certainly have been at least one cow doctor in the area, and any fictionalizing done by McLintock was probably based on local fact. While O'Ley happened to have a book which he could pass off as a fairy gift, Gow seemingly needed only to be entertained by the fairies for people to assume that he was a radically changed man on his return. In each case, there is something of the shamanistic rite of passage undergone by so many charismatic figures, famed or obscure. An early example was of course Christ, whose status as a healer seems to have depended in part on his changed nature after his forty days in the wilderness. Later, Merlin was said to have experienced a long period of shamanic retreat on a wild mountain top, where he communed with nature as thorns and hazels clustered around him in the early spring. Other fairy doctors may, a little ironically, have gained fairy status through personal illnesses of various kinds, thus somehow travelling without leaving their beds. As Evans-Wentz explains, 'persons in a short trance-state of two or three days' duration are said to be away with the fairies enjoying a festival.'

Fairy Doctors

Back in the mists of medieval Wales, the Carmarthenshire 'physicians of Myddfai' were reputed to have gained their healing powers from a fairy woman who emerged from the lake known as Llyn y Fan Fach. Later, at Dun Lean in Munster, a strange white cloud one day fell in a pasture, where it settled like foam before being licked up by a cow. After drinking milk from this animal, one Maurice Griffin began to both foretell the future and to cure people. So great was his fame that he was denounced from the pulpit by the local priest, until he essentially tamed the minister by telling him private details of the priest's life, seemingly known to no one else. Did 'Maurice Griffin the Fairy' really exist? The story about the strange cloud and cow is itself certainly folklore, once found in over 150 versions in numerous parts of Ireland. But this may not mean that the entire story is purely fictitious. It may rather be that

Griffin had genuine powers so mysterious that the folklore was superimposed on them as the most plausible explanation.

In 1677, 'a Yorkshire white witch supplied the sick with a white powder which effected wondrous cures and which he alleged was periodically given him by fairies.' If this healer used the fairies as a kind of personal validation, in one other notable case fairy power may again have been projected onto successful healers by their wondering neighbours. On the Isle of Man, the Teare family of Ballawhane in Andreas were reputed for their healing powers over several generations. W. W. Gill, suspecting that these skills dated back into the eighteenth century, agrees with others that the most eminent herbalist of all was Charles Teare. Many detailed stories of Teare's cures in the earlier nineteenth century imply that he had genuine skill with herbs, while like Griffin he was also credited with foreknowledge. Like O'Ley, Teare was thought to possess a medical book, given in gratitude to his father or grandfather after their family rescued shipwrecked French mariners one stormy night. So potent were the herbs of this 'fairy doctor' held to be that local fishermen allegedly came in secret at night to roll themselves on his 'fairy garden' before taking to their boats for the day's catch.

If this seems to indicate a somewhat hazy notion of herbal medicines, it was in reality probably inspired by a magical sense of the power radiating from Charles Teare and anything closely associated with him. In this sense he was treated like Christ and other New Testament healers, held able to cure by touch alone, or even through anything which had touched them, such as Christ's robe or handkerchief passed on by St Paul. Since we also know that Teare routinely 'doctored' fishing boats with herbs as protection, the night-rolling men may have been seeking to evade the payment required for official treatments. After one such case, the fishermen found that Teare had accidentally left his net purse in their boat. This was cut up and boiled with tea, and the whole mixture drunk before the remaining dregs were thrown over the nets. It is thought that any money in the purse was returned to Teare: the purse itself was more valuable, merely for having touched him.

It seems likely that many other things associated with the Teares were similarly prized and revered. Anyone visiting the island's museum can still see one of these today: a horse's skull displayed there was not only associated with the Teare family, but also known as that of 'the Fairy Horse'. Like other fairy doctors, Teare could 'cure the "fairy stroke"' – an affliction we will hear more about later.

Sightings

We are now about to move much closer to the heart of the fairies' world. Perhaps, indeed, we are not, as we assume, the hunters, but the prey, and the fairies are closing us into a web of strangeness from which we will never escape. This may be a good point, then, to breathe a moment and allow any more fearful readers to retrace their steps while they still can. What follows are the smallest handful of available sightings and meetings, selected with difficulty from among literally hundreds of printed accounts.

I have separated fairy encounters into two broad groups. Those below are either from popular culture, from typical fairy territory, or from educated witnesses living in pre-modern Britain. Those in Chapter Five come mainly from educated people, in the twentieth century, and from outside fairy territory. Arguably, this split does risk putting too much weight on the gap between these two classes. Should we trust educated men and women more than non-literate, unschooled ones? In defence of the decision, it probably is important to know whether an encounter happens among people who *all believe* in fairies, expect such things and are happy to speak of them – or the reverse. After all, if someone who doesn't believe in ghosts tells you they have just seen one . . .

One other tricky decision concerns the question of just when the educated themselves changed their attitude to fairies. Sadly, no committee ever met to decree an official switch of policy, and here we do not have the legal changes which give us a broad timeline for educated witch beliefs. It seems likely, however, that the majority of educated Britons had come to see disbelief in fairies as a marker of acceptable social status by about 1750 – which brings us, now, to our first witness for the defence, on the Isle of Man.

Waldron, who seems to have arrived there about 1710, tells us: 'at my first coming into the island', and hearing stories of changelings and fairies, 'I imputed . . . them merely to the simplicity of the poor creatures who related them; but was strangely surprised when I heard other narratives of this kind, and altogether as absurd, attested by men who passed for persons of sound judgement.' (I must at this point confess to a similar feeling during my time upon the enchanted island of fairy belief.) Waldron explains how 'a gentleman my near neighbour' was at first 'entirely averse to the belief that any such beings were permitted to wander', but became 'at last convinced by the appearance of several little figures playing and leaping over some stones in a field' a few yards away. Thinking them schoolboys, he approached, intending to reprimand them for playing truant, it being somewhere between 3 and 4 p.m. But, having got to within twenty paces, he found that 'they all immediately disappeared, though he had never taken his eyes off them . . . nor was there any place where they could so suddenly retreat, it being an open field without hedge or bush'.

This, then, seems indeed to be a case of the sceptic converted. But we should bear in mind that it occurred at a time when witches could still legally be executed in Britain, and that the little phrase 'permitted to wander' hints at a greater willingness to believe in the supernatural, so long as it is all held under God's proper authority.

We next enter Dryburgh church, just inside the Scottish border, around 1720. The church is being used as a temporary school while the latter building undergoes repair.

One fine summer evening . . . while the setting sun was shining bright and beautiful through the large western window, a shrill whistle on a sudden shook the casement, and instantly a myriad of tiny figures, dressed in green, rushed in through the window, passed in a train along the gallery, 'fistle, fistle, fistling' . . . and dancing over the pews with much agility and apparent merriment, and again as suddenly disappeared at the opposite end of the edifice.

Our educated author of 1817 (being again the figure modestly denoted as 'E') had this story from his grandfather, whose account is paraphrased here and who insisted that this otherworldly invasion 'was also seen by the other scholars and their astonished pedagogue'.

Just around two years before E published this report, William Butterfield, the attendant of the Ilkley Wells baths on the slope of the famous Yorks moor, arrived to open the building on a beautiful midsummer morning. His key behaved oddly in the lock, causing him to check that it was the right one. He next managed to push the door slightly ajar, only to have it shoved closed. Finally, Butterfield heaved it open with a bang, when:

> whirr whirr whirr! such a noise and sight! all over the water and dipping into it was a lot of little creatures, dressed in green from head to foot, none of them more than eighteen inches high, and making a chatter and a jabber thoroughly unintelligible. They seemed to be taking a bath, only they bathed with all their clothes on. Soon, however, one or two of them began to make off, bounding over the walls like squirrels

and, with the astonished Butterfield now shouting at the top of his voice, all raced off head over heels, making a noise like 'a disturbed nest of young partridges'.

The folklorist Charles C. Smith heard this story from an Ilkley man and close friend, John Dobson, some time before 1879. Butterfield, who died aged 69 in July 1844, was around forty when he had this encounter, in 'about 1815'. What do we make of it? Both the bird-like jabber and fluster, and the group acrobatics, look strikingly like the scene in Dryburgh church a century before. Additionally, the bathing fairies once more curiously mirror – or imitate? – the human world. Smith's report shows that Butterfield lived among people who still believed in witches, and he very possibly believed in them himself. We should also note that Butterfield was superstitious enough to fear that his sighting was an omen of misfortune to his family. There again, he was so genuinely bewildered by the experience that it was a long time before it leaked out – allegedly because, after he told his wife, she told other wives, and so on.

Let us assume for a moment that the echoing bird-like chatter of the fairies here (described in many other reports) is an apparently realistic detail which is actually folklore. But what of the door? If the problems with the key were pure coincidence, who was pushing the door shut? That detail does not look like folklore. Very similar reports in fact come from poltergeist cases. Smith himself seems open-minded as to the status of the account, while Dobson emphasizes that Butterfield was 'honest, truthful, steady' and respectable. Anyone who wants to see the site for themselves can do so, whether to use the surviving plunge pool, or chew over the problem of Butterworth's experience with a mouthful of cake. The buildings now feature a café, as my girlfriend and I found with surprised gratitude during a cold walk some 25 years ago.

Travelling southwest into the more typical fairy country of the Anglo-Welsh borders, we find ourselves alongside the curate Francis Kilvert, on 8 December 1870, as he pays a visit to the elderly David Price:

> Speaking of the fairies [Price] said, 'We don't see them now because we have more faith in the Lord Jesus and don't think of them. But I believe the fairies travel yet. My sister's son, who works at the colleries in Monmouthshire, once told me he saw the fairies dancing to beautiful music, sweet music, in a Monmouthshire field. Then they all came over a stile close by him. They were very yellow in the face, between yellow and red, and dressed almost all in red.

He did not like to see them. He fully believes he saw them and so do I. He said they were about the size of that girl,' said he, calling to a child of 11 who was blowing up the fire to stand up.

This encounter sounds much like that of Williams, in our Introduction, albeit lacking quite the terror of that incident. The yellow-red faces, in particular, look strikingly like the copper-coloured ones seen by Williams – a complexion noted by others, such as Hilda Scott, from her very urban bedroom window in Essex, in her childhood around 1913. Here in Kilvert country – the border territory of Radnorshire and Herefordshire – we are certainly among fairy believers, and the same was probably true of Monmouthshire. Interestingly, however, neither David Price nor his nephew liked the idea or the sight of fairies. They may have expected to see them, but clearly did not want to. Nor did the nephew report the tiny beings of Victorian art and poetry: the girl pointed to by Price implies a height of around four feet.

The Oxford-educated Kilvert, meanwhile, seems ambivalent on this subject. He does not – even in the privacy of his diary – deride Price's claims, and when visiting Rhos Goch Mill, near Painscastle, on 26 March 1870, seems pleased to have seen 'the place . . . where the old miller sleeping in the mill trough used to see the fairies dancing of nights upon the mill floor'.

Our final sighting comes from an educated witness who, at age ten, 'was standing on the side of an old fort called Lemon's Rock, near Newtownstewart, County Tyrone', looking down at a fairy thorn tree in a nearby field.

It was about 8 o'clock on a bright evening in July, and as she stood gazing she saw a number of little folk dancing in a circle around the tree . . . dressed in different colours . . . she watched them and heard the sound of singing and sweet music for about fifteen minutes, until a horse and cart came along the road and the fairies disappeared. Our witness, Mrs Andrew Crawford Fields, certainly believed in fairies at age ten, as she and other children 'were warned . . . not to go inside this ring lest the little folk should take us'. Others around her also believed in them. Yet, while the neighbouring Lemon family 'saw them dancing many times . . . I saw them only on this occasion'. Like our other sightings, this occurs in clear daylight, and is impressively lengthy in duration. It seems to have occurred some way into the twentieth century, although probably not later than 1920. Sceptics might point out that Crawford was heavily conditioned to expect fairies just here, and they have a point. It would also be nice to know *how* the fairies disappeared: like ordinary people running out of sight, or like ghosts, vanishing on the spot? For all that, the singleness of this sighting makes us pause, and the adult Crawford was clearly not ready to write it off as childish imagination.

This small sample offers us two indoor sightings; a mix of adult and child witnesses (with Price's nephew possibly being either); and a range of sizes, from 'tiny' fairies to the height of an older child. The Irish ones were probably smaller than the ten-year-old Crawford, but it is interesting to note that 'little', when used by the Manx gentleman, corresponds roughly with the size of schoolchildren. All are groups, and – with the possible exception of the Dryburgh group – all seem aware of human beings, via their reactions to them. And, once again, all are active, marked by a kind of energetic delight which seems almost to laugh at the more stolid human worlds through which it erupts.

Meetings

We begin on water. Voyaging from the Shetlands, past Rathlin and the Isle of Man, between Wales and Ireland, and on back up the western coasts of the Emerald Isle, even the hardiest sailor must be cowed – if not by hazards of wave and weather, then by these bewilderingly protean creatures which roll and tumble about our craft. Fish or fairies? Mermaids or seal-women? As these uncanny hybrids slither and slide through our fingers (a flash of human eyes, twist of scaly tail) we can console ourselves with an origin which seems to precede all problems of earthly categorization. The fallen angels, as our Rathlin islander explained, fell onto both land and sea, 'and the seal, he's the one that fell in the sea'. No less haunting than this epic genealogy was the Irish belief that 'seals embody the souls of those lost in the Deluge, doomed to bear this purgation til the world is burned, when they shall be purged and fit for heaven.' In this heretical cosmology, with its extraordinary stretch of time, we find not only greater justice than that offered by orthodox theology, but again that ability of the sea to somehow recycle or shelter the dead.

As if spun into some mythic whirlpool, we also recall the eerie legend of the 'soul cages'; in one local Irish version, the Coomara or sea-dog had a house under the sea off Killard, where he kept 'the souls of drowned sailors in magic lobster-pots'. Following a different stream out of the vortex, we find too that these strangely hybrid seals have another potent link with humanity. As we heard, seal-women were known to come ashore and, if their water-skins were hidden, would be obliged to remain as the wives of mortal men. In such tales they would always, perhaps after many years, eventually regain the skin and escape back into the depths. Utterly folkloric as this seems, seals were still held to be disguised human beings by dwellers of the Kilkee coast around 1870, and as late as 1910 the Kinealys dwelling between Connemara and Mayo were 'reputed to be descended from a beautiful seal woman'. As with the Kirwans of Castle Hackett – claiming 'descent from a beautiful fairy, whose loveliness is sometimes renewed in the family' – this may well have been a source of pride. Gill, similarly, had heard of White Ladies coming out of the sea to marry two Manx farmers. Glancing briefly outward, here, we realize that the seal-wife is one facet of a powerful, perhaps universal myth of marriage or union between men and seals, swans and other birds of various sorts. As Barbara Fass Leavy has shown, the swan maiden motif spans numerous cultures, from folklore through to Tchaikovsky's famous ballet.

The sense that seal-wives can never be permanently tamed implies the basic otherness of the oceans, an alien quality echoing that of fairyland itself. But there is also something else going on here. If you have ever seen a seal close up, then you have probably been struck by something just a little uncanny. The eyes, the attentiveness, the strangely dog-like head . . . seals, even to the coldest rationalist, can look eerily human, or at least hybrid. Perhaps little wonder, then, that they were held especially liable to reassume their human form at dusk or night, when light played extra tricks with their curiously anthropoid qualities. One other thing impossible to forget, once you have heard it, is seal song. In my head I can still hear it now, as I did on the Welsh coast some years ago, and to say that it is haunting, plaintive, oddly intentive, all seems hopelessly feeble by comparison with the reality. We can only begin to guess how it sounded to Shetland fishermen whose ears were caught by the 'wailing cries' of seal-women or sea trows, decades ago.

If seal-wives have been perhaps the most potent and enduring feature in meetings between humans and water fairies, one Irish encounter with a mermaid was just a few weeks old when Westropp heard of it. At the end of April 1910, 'several people, including Martin Griffin, my informant, saw . . . a mer-woman in a cove a little to the north of Spanish Point, near Milltown, Malbay. She was white-skinned, and had well-shaped white hands. The party tried to make friends with her, giving her bread, which she ate. Then a Quilty fisherman got frightened, said she was "something bad", and threw a pebble at her, on which she plunged into the sea and disappeared.'

Like so much else we see in the hills, coasts and valleys of fairyland, this appears both impossible and arrestingly realistic. As we move back now into the Middle Ages, another key encounter on land is perhaps still more so – not least because of the educated witness involved. In what seems to have been the late eleventh or very early twelfth century, a twelve-year-old boy, Elidyr, ran away from his oppressive school near Swansea and hid in a riverbank hollow. After two days there, with nothing to eat, he saw two tiny pygmy men and accepted their invitation to visit 'a land where all is playtime and pleasure'. A dark underground tunnel led to beautiful, though sunless, rivers, meadows, woodlands and plains, where a miniature king and his court all seemed as astonished by Elidyr as he by them. 'They had horses of a size which suited them, almost as big as greyhounds. They never ate meat or fish. They lived on various milk dishes, made up into junkets flavoured with saffron.' They hated lies, and 'whenever they came back from the upper world they would speak contemptuously of our own ambitions, infidelities and inconstancies.' For some time Elidyr switched between his home and this fairy underworld, finally being banished from the latter when he was persuaded by his mother to try and steal a golden fairy ball.

So far, all this seems a fusion of childish fantasy and fairy myth, the child's escape from adult cruelty moving neatly through a kind of fairy utopia to a sort of Fall, which blends his own imminent maturity with the adult greed of his mother. We could also reasonably imagine that two days without food might well help catalyse such visions. But . . . not only was this Elidyr later to become an educated priest; not only was his story repeated by Gerald of Wales shortly after 1188; but the young Elidyr allegedly spent 'nearly a year' vainly searching 'the overhanging banks of the river for the fairy tunnel', and remained so haunted by the experience that, even as an old man, when telling the story to David FitzGerald, Bishop of St David's (c. 1147–76), 'he would burst into tears' as he did so. He also repeated to FitzGerald certain words of the fairy court's language ('water', 'salt'), which seemed to be a hybrid of Welsh and Greek.

Time and again fairy encounters wriggle in this unsettling way across the borders of folklore and reality. Mingling qualities of either, they refuse to sit still in one stable category. Jumping, now, into the nineteenth and twentieth centuries, we find this peculiar hybridity in several cases – ordered here not by date but by the increasing closeness of the fairies in each. Around 1910 one Friday morning, the two boys, aged seven and ten, of fisherman Sandy MacDonald were hunting for driftwood on a shore of the Isle of Muck in the Inner Hebrides. They were just about to break open a tin they had found when two tiny boys in green vests appeared and asked them what they were doing, and about their home and family. They spoke English, but could also speak Gaelic. Next, the MacDonald children saw just offshore

> a tiny boat with a beautiful cabin aft. In the doorway of the cabin stood a wee woman. By her side barked a fully-grown dog, about the size of a rat. MacDonald's boys also noticed that the cabin contained a number of pots and pans and other kitchen utensils.

When the children nervously declined her invitation to take tea in the cabin, the woman 'gave them loaves of bread, as big as a walnut, which they ate and enjoyed'. Just before they left, the fairy boys told the MacDonalds: 'We will not be coming back here any more; but others of our race will be coming.' Presently the boys' older sister found them both sitting in a kind of trance, 'awfully happy', as they said, until she jolted them from it, when they grew fearful.

Did this actually happen? On one hand, we might respond that children can prefer make-believe to the dullness of reality, and that, besides the mirroring quality of these fairies, at least two elements seem potentially folkloric. First, there is the tin, possibly having some uncertain role as a catalyst. Second, we have the perhaps ominous statement about further visits from 'others of our race'. To us, this does sound rather like the fairy version of an alien encounter: one more curious foreshadowing of the 'little green men' who later came from far more advanced kinds of ship to deliver similarly prophetic words.

But on the whole this tale seems more realistic than archetypal. The tin appeared to be an ordinary paint tin; the day was Friday;

and although the story was about 25 years old when Alasdair Alpin MacGregor published it, it was originally related by a fisherman named Campbell to Alexander Fraser, the island's minister, just days after the boys' experience. Here the boys did not (as in so much folklore) refuse fairy food, and yet did not suffer for eating it. Even the mirror-like qualities of boat, cabin, utensils, dog and fairy bread could be taken as that bit too precise for the folkloric mirroring met with in fairy courts and banquets. We are also told that across the next few years the lads narrated this experience to their parents and to neighbours, 'without any variation'.

Edging a little closer still, we meet an elderly Shetland woman of the 1880s who regularly went to stay in a fairy household. The scholar James Barron knew this woman's daughter during his Shetland boyhood, and heard of the old lady's visits to a fairy trio: two men, named Canon Sultie and Horn Davie, and a woman, Eppie Sheeks. Eppie and the old lady did not get on, but the latter was very friendly with Horn Davie, the two sharing both food and recipes. The visits ended when one day the old lady broke a kettle, was warned by Davie of the great anger and potential violence of Sultie and Sheeks on their return, and departed, never visiting again.

The detail of the broken fairy object is certainly folkloric. Yet, when Barron asks, 'Where did this woman go when absent from home for days at a time? No satisfactory explanation apart from her own has ever been given,' he seems to have a point. Forced to make a guess, one would have to assume that the old lady actually went on a genuine visit, perhaps to some people who seemed strange enough to inspire a belief in their fairy origins. As Barron also notes, the story is remarkable for the three fairies being so definitely named.

Shooting down the length of Britain to Cornwall's Penberth Cove we find a bedridden old lady daily entertained by tiny creatures who visited her room. The men, mainly 'dressed in green, with a red or blue cap', looked, she said, 'for all the world like little sodgers [soldiers]', while the women were bedecked in elaborate petticoats and trains, with feathers and fans. Apparently as tiny as the Cornish spriggans, these fairies amused her day and night by 'dancing over the rafters and key-beams, swinging by the cobwebs like rope-dancers, catching the mice and riding them in and out through the holes in the thatch'. Here fairy glamour and the impish energies of the race mingle with an evident kindness towards an old lady whose life would otherwise have been drab and almost entirely solitary. Fantastic as all this sounds, it is interesting how distinctive a form of escapism it is for someone who probably could not read, and whose life preceded the later escapes of radio, television or the Internet by so many decades.

No less up close, and perhaps still more personal, was the fairy boy who lived for years in a Highland family's house. The anthropologist Andrew Lang had heard from a clergyman of a woman who died at the age of over a hundred in around 1894.

> There had been a fairy in her family. He came to the house one night, looking like a poor wandering boy. He was taken in, and lived with the household. Every night he went into a dusky corner, and vanished. He had much to tell of fairies. Their chief habitation in Scotland, he said, was under the pier of Leith.

Assuming that this was neither pure fiction nor pure folklore (and that 'vanished' meant something like 'kept to himself'), we seem here to meet one more example of a culture where anything or anyone strange instantly becomes part of fairyland. For this was a world where wanderers and orphans genuinely were taken in to become part of the family. The boy, then, was probably real. We can only guess now how much his fairy status was imposed by himself or his hosts. If he had a past he preferred forgotten, fairy origins may have seemed a useful substitute.

We have already seen that an extended stay in fairyland could give shamanistic status to fairy doctors. Similarly, Evans-Wentz heard of an old piper called Flannery who lived in Oranmore, County Galway. I imagine he was one of the old generation. And one time the good people took him to Fairyland to learn his profession. He studied music with them for a long time, and when he returned he was as great a piper as any in Ireland. But he died young, for the good people wanted him to play for them.

Some readers may have noticed that the broad outlines of this closely foreshadow one of the legends attached to Robert Johnson (1911–1938), the seminal blues guitarist whose extraordinary talents and early death have both been attributed to a pact with His Satanic Majesty. While this parallel seems to further emphasize the folkloric character of virtuosic fairy musicians, it is interesting that Flannery appears to have been a real person, not a folkloric myth. His talents were evidently so great that they became reified into things of supernatural origin.

In one twist on this narrative, a South Uist man was at first the clumsiest, least talented member of his highly musical family. But after an encounter in fairyland, his misery ceased, and he was now admired as easily the greatest piper in his large family of six elder brothers. Unnamed as this man was, he did exist. The story comes from Frederick Rea, an English outsider appointed schoolmaster on the island in 1889. Stressing that others 'seemed to listen to him in awe' when the man played the pibroch, Rea also stated that he 'was a peculiar-looking man with almost lint-white hair, smooth hairless face' and squat figure. Again, it seems possible that both the status of a 'seventh son' and these physical oddities attracted fairy associations.

Meet the Leprechauns

Early autumn in West Limerick, not far from the fairy hill of Knockfierna. A schoolboy named John Keely has just hurtled across country to the house of the Mulqueens, and is breathlessly insisting that he has seen a fairy. The Mulqueens send him back to interrogate it. 'I am', the fairy responds,

> 'from the mountains and it is all equal to you what my business is.' Next day two fairies appeared at the cross-roads between Ballingarry and Kilfinney, six miles from Rathkeale, in daylight, with skipping ropes, and 'they could leap the height of a man' according to Robert and John Mulligan and other eye-witnesses. The little people allowed Keely to approach them and he actually took one of them by the hand and 'set off along the road with him'. When the fairies spotted the others lying in wait in the nearby bushes, they took fright and 'away they went like the wind', with the Mulqueens, Keely and others in hot pursuit.

As far as we can tell, those lurking out of sight were adults. For we hear that 'boys and men had chased the fairies, who "jumped the ditches as fast as a greyhound"'. Soon crowds were assembling at the crossroads, with people coming from all over Limerick to see the leprechauns. Those who had spotted them asserted that they were

> about two feet in height and had 'hard, hairy faces like men and no ears'. They were dressed in red, with one sporting a white cape, and they wore knee-breeches and 'vamps' instead of shoes. Several who claim to have chased the 'little people' say that 'though they passed through hedges, ditches, and marshes they appeared clean and neat all the time'.

A suggestion 'that the fairies may in fact be human "midgets" brought from England by an Englishwoman' was 'contradicted by her'.

This leprechaun hunt seems to have occurred about the very end of August or start of September. The year was 1938. Where to begin? Although we are certainly deep in traditional fairy country here, what we have just heard implies that people no longer expected to see fairies or leprechauns – with some going out of their way to find a mundane, midget-based explanation. While sparked off by children, the affair presently involves adult witnesses too.

There again, once convinced that they have seen the leprechauns, locals know their fairylore well enough to act appropriately. They chase them. Why? Well, because leprechauns have treasure, and if you can catch one you can get it. Diarmuid Ó Giolláin, a recent authority on these creatures, confirms that red is their favourite colour, being mentioned three times as often as its nearest rival, green. He adds that they can be two feet or more in height, or very much smaller, and that they are often old and withered. He also cites many examples of their notorious trickiness. They are very hard to catch, and even if you do, you may need to keep yours in a box for a year and a day before it will reveal the location of its treasure. (Any thoughts from Health and Safety are welcomed here.)

Like fairies in general, our leprechauns were vigorously energetic, being smaller than children yet able to leap the height of a man. Unlike many fairies, leprechauns were also noted for being solitary, which fits the first sighting, if not the next one. Despite the initial frenzy of local interest, these encounters seem to have ended after the day of the chase. (Did the leprechauns drop their skipping ropes? Does anyone still have them?) In a nearly coincidental reference to the hunt, a newspaper article of 24 August cited Edward Plunkett, owner of Dunsany Castle in Meath. When he asked a local man about leprechauns and was told, 'ah sure, they are all nonsense,' Dunsany felt that this hasty response was disingenuous. Ó Giolláin, meanwhile, cites an undated conversation with an Antrim man who had spoken to a leprechaun. The creature, sounding more like a typical brownie, told the man it had been guarding local farms for around five hundred years, being sometimes rewarded with old clothes by the farmers. Meanwhile, very soon after the account of the leprechaun hunt appeared in *The Times* of 6 September, a County Monaghan resident, the Irish nationalist, old Etonian and graduate of Cambridge Sir John Randolph Leslie, wrote to the paper to assert that evidence for the existence of fairies was good enough for 'Courts of Law' – adding that he had three times 'taken down evidence . . . which showed that sane, humble people (to whom a lie is a sin unless it is for political purposes) believed they had seen supernatural beings' similar to those of the Keely incidents.

Holding the hand of a leprechaun might seem about as close as one can get to the fairies (short of having a seal-woman bear one's children, perhaps). But our next and final encounter shows that one could get closer still, and that, when people claimed to have seen a very small and strange-looking man in the Irish countryside, they were not always lying. In late April 1908 British newspapers reported that hundreds in Killough, County Westmeath, were hunting a leprechaun and his gold. It had already been 'seen by several people', and on 12 May a follow-up told of how 'some children saw the fairy dwarf under a hedge playing on a harp' before following it to 'an old moat beside the graveyard, where it disappeared'.

Readers were perhaps initially sceptical. But matters changed dramatically come 13 August, when it was stated that the leprechaun had been captured by the police and was now in Mullingar work-house. On this day he was interviewed by at least two journalists. Though generally replying only with 'strange jabbering sounds', he said enough to imply that he was from County Down. He had 'a very knowing expression of face, sometimes grave, and sometimes lighted up with a grin', and was no more than four foot tall. 'His most striking characteristic', we hear, 'is the avidity with which he eats and drinks. He also smokes a pipe.' Scenting journalistic gold here (and perhaps dispensing some to relevant officials), a *Daily Mail* reporter was led past crowds of clamorous children and through 'the gates of the workhouse', where he found the leprechaun

seated on a bench near a fire . . . 'He took my proffered hand', writes our correspondent, 'and shook it lightly between his thin fingers. He appears between thirty and forty years of age. Continuous conversation was impossible with him, as after a few words he broke into gibberish, ejaculating the sounds "Me me me. On on on." One minute his face was all smiles, the next his expression was ludicrously solemn. Asked if he knew where the gold was hidden, he answered with the ejaculations above referred to.'

As readers may have gathered, the leprechaun clearly suffered from some kind of mental and physical disability. As we will see in the next chapter, one possibility is the genetic disorder known as PKU, given his voracious appetite. It being now realized that he fitted the description of a County Clare man named Hough, missing for some time, his father was presently brought to the workhouse. Come 20 August – by which time the *Mail* was running a cartoon series on the leprechaun –

> the representative of an American museum and theatre of varieties in Glasgow [had] visited Mullingar, and arrived at an agreement with the supposed leprechaun, who, with his father, and the representative of the theatre, left by the midday train. His departure was the cause of much interest at the railway station, and the small subject was in the best possible spirits.

We can only hope that this was true. In the long and often horrifying history of disability and the supernatural, Hough's fate was probably a mild one, whatever he actually thought of it. And it may well have been easier than roaming the woods and fields as he had been doing for some weeks – perhaps as early as mid-April, if not earlier. Neither this brief history nor his father's deal with the impresario suggest that his family was very keen to hang on to him. There is clearly a chance that his voracious appetite in the workhouse was due to his being half starved when brought there.

Among the clamouring children at its gates that August, were there some who, as old men or women at the close of the twentieth century, still believed they had seen a leprechaun? There were probably many adults who thought they had in Glasgow in autumn 1908. Witness, for example, our impresario's bold advertising stunt on 1 September:

> for distribution among local charities if anyone can prove that the leprechaun is 'not genuine', the proprietor of the Noah's Ark, Glasgow, where the recently captured Irish leprechaun is being exhibited, has handed £1000 to the editor of the Glasgow *Daily Record and Mail*.

It has been noted by one recent commentator that the encounter of 1938 could well have been construed as an alien sighting just a few years later. With this in mind, it is intriguing to see how the differing attitudes to the Mullingar leprechaun partly mirror the split captured in Steven Spielberg's film E.T. *the Extra-terrestrial*. On the one hand there is the ferociously controlling adult, military and scientific stance; on the other a pack of excited racing children, one of whom touches the strange and lonely creature by the hand. In defiance of all the official power and paranoia, we have a small boy whose message seems to be: 'I have met you; I have touched you – and so, goodbye.' Wouldn't most of us rather be the child who spoke to the leprechaun, held his hand, and let him go?

Three

Fairy Dangers

'KILLER FAIRIES CAUSED FOUR deaths.' So ran a headline in *The Sun* on 30 November 2006. It was true: they had – not, admittedly, in 2006, but some time between 1656 and 1663, in Lamplugh, Cumbria, where archivist Anne Rowe had recently unearthed a list of deaths and their causes. As Lesley Park, at the Whitehaven Archive, kindly confirmed for me, this list included an entry reading, 'Frighted to death by fairies . . . 4'. With no more detail than this, we can already infer that fairies, in this context, were sinister enough to be blamed for mysterious deaths. We can also add that, well into the nineteenth century, many Britons died of their fear of ghosts, while across the world the fear of vampires, witches or black magic has quite literally scared innumerable people to death.

Come 2006, Rowe's find shot into the mainstream press precisely because the idea was so delightfully ludicrous. Who, after all, could possibly be scared of fairies? The answer, for most of history, was in fact: almost anyone. Fairies were dangerous. Not to believe in them was dangerous. Not to respect them or take them seriously was dangerous – hence all the carefully euphemistic or indirect names one used in speaking of them, from 'the Gentry' to 'the Good People', 'Themselves', 'the fair folk' and 'the people of peace' through to the charming Welsh phrase *bendith û mamme*, or 'such as have deserved their mother's blessing'. Fairies stole your children. They made you or your animals sick, sometimes unto death. They could draw the life, or essence, out of anything, from milk or butter through to people. Their powers, as we have seen, were almost limitless, not only demonic but even godlike in scale and scope.

Fairies and Witches

While ordinary people still believed this less than a century ago, the educated had also believed it in the era of the witch persecutions. Witches did these kinds of thing, and fairies or fairyland were quite often referenced in their trials. Although Joan of Arc was tried as a heretic, rather than a witch, the latter association naturally clung to such an unusual woman, and it is notable that in 1431 her interrogators took an interest in the 'fairy tree' around which Joan had played in her childhood in Domrémy. In the Protestant camp, Calvin later emphasized how 'the Devil works strange illusions by fairies and satyrs'. In early modern Sicily one distinct type of witch was the female 'fairy doctor', the phrase *donna di fuori* ('woman from outside') meaning either 'fairy' or 'fairy doctor'. Here Inquisitors encouraged people, including suspected witches, to equate fairy and witch beliefs. In 1587 they were especially interested in one Laura di Pavia, a poor fisherman's wife who claimed to have flown to fairyland in Benevento, Kingdom of Naples.

In many cases, educated witch-believers saw fairies and fairyland as sources of dark power for witches. Lizanne Henderson lists 38 Scottish witch trials (1572–1716) featuring references to fairy beliefs, including that of Isobel Strathaquin (Aberdeen, 1597), accused of using skills which she 'learnt . . . of an elf-man who lay with her'. At the 1616 trial of Katherine Caray the accused spoke of meeting not only 'a great number of fairy men' on the Caithness hills at sunset, but 'a master man' – a figure which in this context could have been seen as 'the King of the Fairies' or 'the Prince of Darkness'. After a Scottish girl, Christian Shaw, suffered hysterical fits in 1696, the ensuing trial featured a veritable cauldron of lurid evidence, from a mysterious black man with cold hands through to the eating of 'a piece of unchristened child's liver', and a charm of blood and stones used by one Margaret Fulton, a reputed witch whose 'husband had brought her back from the fairies'.

One particular case of demonized fairies is so intriguing that it merits a little space to itself. Its protagonist was Ann Jefferies, a maidservant of the Pitt family at St Teath, Cornwall. In 1645, aged nineteen, Ann was 'one day knitting in an arbour in our garden' when 'there came over the garden hedge to her six persons of a small stature, all clothed in green, which she called fairies: upon which she was so frighted, that she fell into a kind of a convulsion-fit.' So related the bookseller and printer Moses Pitt fifty years later, having been six at the time of Ann's encounter.

What followed looks in many ways like the career of a fairy doctor. Ann seemed to suffer some kind of neurosis about food and allegedly took none from the family for several months, claiming that the fairies themselves fed her. Ann presently cured Mrs Pitt's leg after a bad fall merely by stroking it, and soon became so famous that numerous people flocked to the house for cures from as far south as Land's End, and as far north as London. All cures seemed to be done purely by touch, without medicines. Ann showed psychic ability, knowing of her visitors before they arrived. Moses himself never saw the fairies but his mother and sister both did.

This case is already interesting for the way that it echoes those of other fairy doctors, despite the Pitt family (and other affluent patients from London) having no concept of such figures. The element of danger initially seems brief, being limited to Ann's fear at the first encounter. But presently local ministers began to insist that the fairies were 'evil spirits' and that the whole affair was 'a delusion of the Devil'. A warrant appeared; Pitt's family and Ann were questioned by local authorities; and magistrate John Tregeagle had Ann locked up – first in Bodmin Jail, and next in his own house, where he kept her without food. Although witchcraft was not explicitly mentioned, it is hard not to suspect that this was on people's minds. The instability of the Civil War may have further aggravated such fears: the female prophet Anna Trapnel had sparked controversy in January 1645, and Sarah Wight had a similar effect in the weeks after February 1647.

Like witches, fairies were powerful, uncanny and unpredictable. And like witches, or vampires, or any of the world's numerous magical figures, fairies were scapegoats. They could be blamed for almost anything, from human deaths through to mass famine. In one sense, the fairy as scapegoat was potentially a good thing. For fairies, real or not, could not be harmed. Women taken for witches certainly could be, and were – and after official persecution ended there were hundreds of serious vigilante assaults on them through- out Britain, right through to the end of the nineteenth century. In reality, however, fairy scapegoats did produce a great deal of human suffering. The problem, here, was what people did to real human beings who were believed to be fairy changelings.

Changelings

In August 1909 an old woman of Donegal, Annie McIntire, applied for a pension. She told the Pension Committee that although 'she did not know the number of her years', she 'remembered being stolen by the "wee people" (fairies) on Halloween Night, 1839'. Was she certain of this?

'Yes, by good luck my brother happened to be coming home from Carndonagh that night, and heard the fairies singing and saw them dancing round me in the wood at Carrowkeel. He had a book with him, and he threw it in among them. They then ran away.' The applicant added that the people celebrated the event by great feast- ing and drinking. The committee decided to grant her a pension.

Whatever actually happened that Halloween night, McIntire clearly believed her version until the end of her days. So, too, would many of those around her, young or old. For everyone knew that fairies stole children.

More broadly, fairies again resembled vampires or witches in that all three, very basically, *attacked life*. The latter pair could suck out your blood, soul or breath, or extract the essence from food. Much later, that iconic Other of our own times, the alien abductor, updated this basic assault with clinical probings or the removal of human eggs or sperm. In the pre-scientific cultures of the fairy or the witch, however, the most potent emblem of life was simply one's own baby or child.

One ironic result of this was that, for most of history, no child was delighted by fairies. Old people in Cornwall told Evans-Wentz:

> if we as children did anything wrong, the old folks would say to us, 'The piskies will carry you away if you do that again.' . . . In Tintagel I used to sit round the fire at night and hear old women tell so much about piskies and ghosts that I was then afraid to go out of doors after darkness had fallen.

At Cwmcastellfach farm in Wales a seventy-year-old man told Evans-Wentz that 'in his childhood days a great dread of the fairies occupied the heart of every child. They were considered to be evil spirits who visited our world at night.' Even in the less typically fairy-haunted flats of Norfolk, young children growing up around the First World War were told, 'if naughty . . . that the "hightie sprite" was at the bottom of the garden and would get them'. On the whole, this distinctive East Anglian spirit evoked far less terror than Celtic fairies. There again, one 1980s informant recalled it as 'a black bat-like figure, man-size, hovering silently in the twilight, waiting to snatch away disobedient children'. While many boys and girls were being enchanted by Rose Fyleman's 'fairies at the bottom of our garden', others still feared vampiric kidnappers at the bottom of theirs.

Writing in 1960, the Dutch scholar Jacoba Hooykaas found child-stealing fairy or elf types were feared in Britain, Germany, France, the Netherlands, Moravia, Greece, Lithuania, Bohemia and Hungary, with a modern-day variant in Bali. In Celtic territories, fairies stole babies and children – especially boys, and especially those with blue eyes and fair hair – leaving fairy substitutes in their place. Having identified such a switch, people did everything they could to make the fairies reverse it. To the end of the nineteenth century, and probably later, such children were ritually abused by their own parents to this end. Immersed in rivers or placed at the margin of coastal tides, stood on hot coals or hung over fires, exposed in freezing weather, bathed in poisonous foxglove essence, beaten, threatened and subjected to forms of exorcism, these babies and children sometimes survived, sometimes not. Ironically, part of the logic of this treatment was the sense that the fairies cared enough about their offspring to rescue them from such abuses and restore one's child in the process. Even as they tormented these supposed changelings, parents were projecting their own familial love onto fairyland.

Let us imagine a large rural family in which an initially normal, healthy new baby presently begins to seem suspect. He cries almost incessantly, fails to grow, walk or talk, has oddly wizened features and is constantly hungry. At one very basic level, a child continually crying and demanding food, and unable to work like its six- or seven-year-old peers, is a liability in such circumstances. But these problems almost certainly took second place to the real and frightening belief that it was *not yours*, and that your child had been stolen. Hard as it now is to credit, parents in such cases very probably felt just as distraught as the modern mothers and fathers making television appeals about their missing or abducted children.

While it was clear to educated Victorians that many change-lings were disabled children, much more precise clinical parallels were detailed in 1988 by the interdisciplinary scholar Susan Schoon Eberly. The case given above would fit especially well with a genetic disorder affecting metabolism, phenylketonuria (PKU). This and other similar conditions predominate among male children of Irish and English descent. Even brief references from fairy believers give clues to these disorders, talking of children like 'old men', perhaps suffering from progeria. Obvious physical deformity, such as the oversized heads of hydrocephalus, or 'water on the brain', would be singled out; yet so too might the pretty, blue-eyed, snub-nosed, 'elfin' children afflicted with Williams syndrome. Here, as in every magical culture the world over, it was never a good idea to stand out. Eberly also adds that certain of these conditions only manifested some time after birth. This, surely, was the smoking fairy gun: you had *known* your own baby, and this, now, was *not him*. All of this painstaking detective work can, in one sense, be collapsed into three letters: 'oaf', a word broadly cognate with 'elf', once meant not a clumsy or stupid person, but, literally, a changeling.

Plain and axiomatic as the real medical causes now seem to us, the majority view, from the ancient Romans to the Edwardian Celts, was intensely superstitious. When Martin Luther recommended drowning a changeling, it was because the child's appearance showed it to have no soul. In the seventeenth century, even the most rational Christians used 'changeling' as a loose synonym for the mentally disabled, with dramatist Elkanah Settle echoing Luther when he talked, in 1694, of 'some coarse half-souled fairy changeling'. The relatively enlightened physician and philosopher John Locke probably did not believe in fairies, yet did speculate at great length on the souls of the mentally disabled, and whether or not they should be classed as a different species.

With these kinds of attitudes lodged at the heart of Christian and proto-scientific elites in the early modern period, what could changelings expect from true fairy believers? In all households, there were routine precautions aimed to prevent child theft. A very common one involved putting fire tongs over a cradle, because of the fairies' well-known antipathy to iron. As in McIntire's case, books also had power over them, and religious ones especially – hence the placing of a Bible or prayer book under a child's pillow. In Ireland into the 1930s, babies were not believed safe from fairies until they (the babies) had sneezed, so that many infants had pepper thrust under their noses minutes after birth. In Connemara at the same time people still dressed boys and girls alike in red flannel petticoats until the age of twelve, a disguise used to trick those fairies who liked to steal boys in particular.

If such measures failed, the changeling met with violence – this often being advised or performed by the local fairy doctor. In some cases, such rituals were used on actual sick children thought to be 'fairy-struck' – though, as we will see, they too could be seen as in danger of abduction. Carole Silver cites changelings killed by fox-glove baths in Wales in 1857, and in Donegal in the 1870s and 1890s. Eberly tells of a Scottish case, in Caerlaverock, where the ceaselessly yelling and ill-tempered baby was thrown onto hot coals. In 1952 the Australian-born classical scholar Gilbert Murray (1866–1957) recalled how,

> in Ireland, in my own lifetime, a child, who was for some reason reputed to be a changeling, was beaten and burned with irons, the mother being locked out of the room while the invading fairy was exorcised, though unfortunately the child died in the process.

This killing does not seem to have been prosecuted, and many of those which escaped public or legal notice must now have been lost to us. This was nearly the case after the tragic death of a nine-year-old boy, son of Kilkenny labourer Patrick Kearns. Late at night on 7 April 1856, a police patrol met the Kearnses taking their son's body to an unused burial ground, and insisted on examining him. Thus, instead of an unknown secret burial, there came to light the tale of how the child, confined to bed for three weeks past, was judged to be suffering from a 'fairy-blast'. Although he was not himself a changeling, it was said that he was 'being gradually carried off by the fairies'; if he had died naturally it may have been believed that They had taken him. Versions of this affair vary. But it seems that a man called Thomas Donovan, assisted by Patrick Murphy, attempted a ritual test, giving the boy water and getting him to cough. When the boy could not cough, he was dragged violently out of the house and around the yard, strangled and badly beaten. He died early the next morning from his injuries.

Some accounts have Donovan as the 'fairy doctor' making the initial diagnosis; others mention an unnamed 'wise woman' as doing so. Although one report has Patrick Kearns apparently trying to rescue his son from Donovan, the versions which claim the parents to have agreed with the procedure, even after the boy's death, match other known cases better. Interestingly, during the trial, the judge briefly mentioned delusions about fairies, emphasizing that these could in no way absolve Donovan (Murphy having by now fled to America). A QC, meanwhile, could see no motive for the crime, and wrongly inferred that perhaps there had been some delusion about the boy being 'possessed by the Devil'. This already shows the gulf between educated and popular perceptions of fairies. Moreover, we also learn that the Kearnses resorted to the fairy rituals *despite* their son having previously been under the care of two licensed doctors – one of whom confirmed after autopsy that the boy, though killed by Donovan, would have died of a tumour and water on the brain within a week. Donovan was sentenced to a year's hard labour.

A few years before, the parents of six-year-old Mary Anne Kelly, allegedly 'in a dying state' for six months prior to September 1850, turned from the dispensary physician to a Roscrea 'fairy doctress' named Bridget Peters. Peters seems at one point to have declared Mary Anne 'fairy struck', and at another that the child *was* a fairy. She gave the girl verbena and foxglove, and ordered that she be exposed naked outdoors for three nights on a shovel. This was done, despite Mary Anne's cries being audible in the house. On the third night she died.

Here again fairy ritual took on demonic overtones. One report claimed that a prayer had to be said over the girl 'in the name of the devil', and several carried the headline 'Witchcraft'. In this instance the mother, Mary Kelly, seems to have been unusually complicit (and was initially tried along with Peters). If uneducated, the Kellys were by no means desperately poor. A key witness in the trial was their servant, Mary Maher, who was sacked after refusing to put Mary Anne out on the shovel, and who may have been the only reason the crime came to light. Mary Kelly seems ultimately to have been acquitted. Peters, described as 'respectable looking' and evidently literate, was found guilty.

Cases such as these now seem so extraordinary as to be almost unreal to us. Eberly has argued convincingly that modern-day responses of parents to disabled children still sometimes mingle anger and guilt, and that such emotions could well have fed into the violence directed at changelings. Silver has suggested that one benefit of the changeling belief was the way it shifted blame for the child's condition into a thoroughly separate, supernatural realm, beyond human control. With these points in mind, it bears emphasizing that Mary Anne had from birth been blind, brain-damaged and partially paralysed. Having said all this, we need to grasp that such modern rationalizations were largely alien from the fairy cultures in which changelings suffered or died. Most parents really, unshakably believed that this was a dangerous, uncanny fairy creature, and very possibly feared it too.

In some cases, this level of terror was also apparent in the 'fairy child'. In April 1840 James Mahony, a man living on the country estate of Charles Riall, at Heywood, County Tipperary, was influenced by his neighbours into the belief that his son, John (aged six or seven), was a fairy. This was partly due to a curvature of the spine which had kept the boy in bed two years, and partly to his being a suspiciously 'intellectual child'. On the night of Tuesday, 14 April, Mahony, with the connivance of neighbours, held the near-naked boy over a hot shovel, threatening to put him on it, and dragged him halfway to the water pump, proposing to drown him under it if he did not reveal the whereabouts of Mahony's true son. John seems to have become so terrified by this that he presently 'told them that he was a fairy, and that he would send back the real John Mahony the next evening, if they gave him that night's lodging' – even going so far as to specify that the real John was in a farmer's house, wearing corduroys and a green cap. Next morning, John was found dead in his bed. Although a doctor decided that this had resulted from the boy's spinal condition, this fatality looks as though it may have been caused by sheer terror. We have seen that voodoo death can occur in such cases in around one to three days, while vagal inhibition can kill in seconds or minutes, when shock affects the vagus nerve, the autonomic nervous system, and ultimately the heart. We have to wonder, here, if John's parents ever doubted the child's terrified 'confession'. Did they remain convinced that they had actually killed a *fairy*?

Similarly, Westropp remembered from his boyhood, in 1869, 'a very old woman, Kate Molony', from Maryfort, County Clare, who, many years before, being anxious about her daughter's failing health, 'went to a "wise woman", who assured her that the child was "changed". She spoke of this on her return, and unfortunately the patient was old enough to understand the fearful decision. The poor child turned over on the bed with a groan, and was a little later found to be dead.' This sounds unmistakably like vagal inhibition. If so, the child must have died either because of her sheer terror of her own fairy status (in which she apparently believed) or because of the ensuing tortures which she knew this diagnosis would bring.

Such dangers were not entirely confined to the uneducated inhabitants of the Celtic countryside. Writing around 1865 about the fairies of Cornwall, Robert Hunt had recently heard from a friend of how, 'the other day . . . an Irishwoman . . . was brought before the magistrates, in New York, for causing the death of a child by making it stand on hot coals, to try if it were her own truly-begotten child, or a changeling.' Meanwhile, Westropp's family – affluent landowners at Patrickswell, Limerick, since the sixteenth century – had a much closer brush with changeling superstitions than the one recalled above. For Westropp's 'second sister, whose delicacy, when an infant, excited remark, was, about 1842, taken out by a servant to be exposed on a shovel on the doorstep at Carnelly. The angry and hasty intervention of another servant saved the child, but the would be "exposer" was convinced' of the rightness of her attempt to "'get back the child" from the fairies'.

This incident partly echoes the 1884 case of three-year-old Philip Dillon of Clonmel, severely burned after two neighbours put him to a changeling test in his mother's absence. In such contexts, 'changelings' were at risk from others besides their parents, with these people very possibly acting 'for the good of the community'.

It is easy to forget, looking back from a thoroughly medicalized world, how profoundly extra-scientific these people's lives were. The disabilities and illnesses of these children perhaps seemed just as fundamentally wrong as the youthful deaths we considered earlier. Changeling beliefs therefore offered two important benefits. First, they allowed people to shift from being helpless victims to active combatants of the perceived problem. Second, and probably more importantly, they gave an otherwise frighteningly arbitrary condition a *meaning* – a known and accepted place within a shared framework of explanation.

Yet, if this helps us make some sense of the majority of popular changeling cases, it fails to shed any light on the abuse suffered by Walter Trevelyan of Penzance. On Monday, 10 July 1843, local magistrates and residents heard of how the upper-middle-class Trevelyans had routinely tortured Walter, now aged two years and nine months, for at least a year at their grand Georgian house, The Orchard. Servants and visitors testified that Walter had been kept without food or water for hours, had been left outside in a tree during winter, been made to lie face down on the gravel walk, kicked over a slope in his baby carriage by his father, and tied upside down in a tree until he was black in the face. After the miseries of the day Walter was put to bed on a mattress filled with corks, lest he should gain any comfort in the few exhausted hours of night.

Some of this was specifically ordered by Mrs Trevelyan, and all of it seems to have been the sole responsibility of Walter's parents. Indeed, although the hearing was catalysed by local vicar Reverend Le Grice, all of the evidence was supplied by working-class servants or visitors, with gardener Francis Dale stating that Walter's cries were so heart-rending as to force him to move away to another part of the garden, where he could not hear them.

Was all this really inspired by the belief that Walter had been 'changed by the nurse'? Simon Young, to whom I am indebted for answering various queries on the original newspaper reports of the case, thinks not. He suspects that this phrase refers not to fairy changelings, but to the belief that a child's nurse might change her affluent charge with her own baby, so that the latter could have the benefits of an elite upbringing. He adds that servants may have heard the parents remark facetiously that they thought the naughty Walter to have been 'changed at nurse' (that is, so naughty that he could not be their natural child). They then took this literally, as partial explanation for the cruelties inflicted on him.

For educated parents to act on fairy beliefs in this way would be very unusual. We can further add that not all of the abuse looks precisely ritual – as, for example, John Trevelyan kicking Walter over the slope. But much of it, though different from popular habits in detail, does seem to fit the same broad logic: treat the child so badly that its fairy parents will reverse the switch. Ultimately, this case seems to me too unclear to permit a decisive judgement on its origins. One reason for this is that, bizarrely, the Trevelyans themselves seem to have given no evidence at the hearing. We therefore have not a word from them on why Walter was treated in this way. The impression that local magistrates essentially connived to spare the powerful family is grimly reinforced by the final verdict: 'we are unanimous in the opinion that the child has been most cruelly and shamefully treated, but there is not sufficient evidence to connect Mr Trevelyan with the ill-usage, for us to send the case to a higher tribunal.' If ever there was an instance of the Victorian elite shamefully closing ranks, then clearly this was it.

If we accept, hypothetically, that the parents' cruelty was purely mundane, we are left with some curious ironies. Was it worse for people like the Trevelyans to torture their child than for fairy believers to do so, actuated by supernatural terrors? I would say yes. Second, we have the reaction of the household servants. It is not quite clear if they understood Walter to have been a human change-ling or a fairy one. Given the popular fairy beliefs then prevalent in Cornwall, the latter notion would be plausible. In this case, we would have to assume that the mundane sadism of upper-middle-class parents was so appalling to ordinary people as to persuade them that it *must* have a supernatural origin.

Whatever Walter suffered in adult life (and fighting in the Afghan War, as he later did, was probably a walk in the park by com-parison with childhood), we can assume that he did not find people around him looking askance and muttering 'changeling' whenever he passed by. But this was the fate of a handful of mentally or physically disabled adults – people who were held by their neigh-bours, even parents, literally to be 'fairies' throughout their lives. John Rhys heard in the late nineteenth century of a woman called Nani Fach at Llanover, Wales, supposed to be one of the fairies' off-spring, and also, more specifically, of a farmer's son called Elis Bach at Nant Gwrtheyrn, northwest Wales. All of the large Bach family were quite ordinary, save for Elis, whose legs were

> so short that his body seemed only a few inches from the ground when he walked. His voice was also small and squeaky. However, he was very sharp, and could find his way among the rocks pretty well when he went in quest of his father's sheep and goats . . . Everybody believed Elis to have been a changeling.

Meanwhile, in Yorkshire in 1884 Mr J. Cocksedge recalled how, as a child, he had often looked in wonder at hat-maker Fanny Bradley, the tiniest woman he had ever seen. Fanny's brother Tom was of similar stature, and it was said that when they

> were infants their mother took them with her to a field adjoining Almscliff Crag, where she had occasion to go to shear or reap

some corn . . . While this woman was busy at work these fairies came and stole her children. When she found that her children had gone she cried and was so much troubled that the fairies brought them back, and placed them where they found them. And they said that that was the reason Fanny and her brother were so little.

Other writers, including a niece or nephew of Fanny, stated that she was so small as to have once stood in a man's pocket when measuring him for a hat. Whatever the exact size of Fanny and Tom, their quasi-changeling status (the fairies *did something* to them, before handing them back) seems to have been reinforced by the fact that they and one other Bradley child had this appearance, while all the others were quite normal. We can only guess how such people made it into adulthood at all. Perhaps their parents were too kind-hearted to subject them to potentially fatal changeling tests; perhaps they underwent them but survived. Such cases also raise the question of when parents stopped trying to get their real child back, and what it felt like to accept that you would live with a fairy for the rest of your life.

Adult Abduction

Once, fairies stole children. Later, children stole the fairies. These dangerous beings of angelic pedigree became, for nineteenth-century elites, the stuff of childish whimsy, delight and poetical enchantment. But between a Victorian mother in Chelsea and a Celtic peasant woman of that era, there remained an insurpassable gulf of meaning when either said, 'the fairies have enchanted my child.' A similar gulf also lay between the supernatural beliefs of two groups of educated Christians: namely, those of Shakespeare's or Milton's time, and their peers in and after the eighteenth century.

Take, for example, an alleged case of fairy abduction from Dromgreagh in County Wicklow. In autumn 1678 one Dr Moore arrived here with two friends, Richard Uniack and Laughlin Moore (apparently no relation). A discussion followed. Dr Moore recalled how, during his Wicklow childhood over 34 years before, he was said to have been routinely abducted by the fairies. Though no harm came to him during these absences, his frightened mother would consult a local wise woman (possibly a fairy doctor), who used magic to secure his return. Just as Uniack was trying to dissuade Moore from such beliefs, the latter felt himself called away, and began to rise off the floor of the inn where they were staying.

In a scene which now looks like a bizarrely comic anticipation of Ian McEwan's opener to *Enduring Love*, both Uniack and Laughlin seized Moore firmly from either side. Yet the two men could not stop Moore rising into the air. Laughlin let go first, and Uniack, after being lifted more than a yard off the ground, 'was compelled [by some unperceived force] to quit'. Moore now disappeared. In their terror Uniack and Laughlin could not recall if he had vanished through door or window. The innkeeper, seeming 'not ... much terrified thereat, as if such disasters were common thereabouts', directed them to a local wise woman, who outlined where Moore was and where he would be during that night, using various spells to prevent him from accepting any fairy food while there.

Returning hungry and thirsty at six the next morning, Moore told his friends that he had been carried from the inn by around twenty men, on horse and foot, and that during his adventures in a wood and at a fort, food or drink had been somehow struck from his hand whenever he tried to take it. A company of around three hundred men and women (of ordinary size) had feasted and danced, and at one point Moore had led a dance, whose tune he still remembered. Despite his previous scepticism, Uniack was sufficiently impressed to travel seven miles with Moore to the fort, where they found the grass as heavily trampled as if hundreds had recently been there.

It is certainly striking how thoroughly Uniack reversed his position, going on to relate the story in the presence of a Dr Murphy and a High Court clerk in Dublin. Equally, John Cother, the man who published this after receiving it in letter form, does not seem to have made a habit of trying to sell fantasy, as no other work by him has survived. It has been stressed many times that educated early modern Christians were doubly hostile to lying, both through their piety and their reputation as gentlemen.

Did this actually happen? Did *something* actually happen? Levitation, often involuntary, has certainly been reported many times, especially among Catholic saints and mystics. St Teresa of Ávila (1515–1582) implied that, like Moore, she sensed it seconds before it happened. In Iceland in 1907 the medium Inðridi Indriðason was lifted up despite the efforts of a grown man to hold him down, this being witnessed by one Reverend Niellson, professor of theology at Reykjavík University. Perhaps most impressively, when a group of sceptical debunkers invited the famous Victorian medium D. D. Home to Amsterdam in 1858, they saw him levitate a mahogany table in a lighted room, despite several of them sitting on it to pin it down.

Our second educated witness for the fairy defence is the Scots minister Robert Kirk (1644–1692). During his lifetime the intensely pious Kirk was known as the minister of Balquhidder and Aberfoyle in Perthshire, and for producing the first Christian Bible in Gaelic. After conversations about Highland beliefs with Edward Stillingfleet, Bishop of Worcester, Kirk wrote down a very detailed account of the fairies, which was later published as *The Secret Commonwealth of Elves and Fairies*. On 14 May 1692, Kirk was found dead at the fairy hill near his manse, having apparently wandered out in his nightshirt to take the air just before bed. In 1812 Patrick Graham reported that Kirk was said to have appeared, shortly after death, as a ghost to one of his relatives. He told them that he was not dead, but a prisoner in fairyland. He would next appear (he went on) at the christening of his posthumous child, where, if his cousin Graham of Duchray could throw a dagger over his (Kirk's) head, he would be released. Graham seems to have tried to do this.

But when Kirk's ghost appeared he was so astonished that he failed, at which Kirk vanished.

This remarkable story, rather like some intricately chambered fairy hill, might be entered and explored on many different levels. For me, what is most compelling about it is the reactions it has produced. A short book could easily be written on Kirk's Fairy After-life and what this says about the modern danger of believing in fairies. First, we have those who believed in it. It was common knowledge among most locals that Kirk was not in his coffin, which was in reality filled with rocks. When Evans-Wentz visited the area in 1909, Margaret MacGregor doubted the story, but still believed that 'the *good people* took Kirk's spirit'. This belief – which could not be disproved by merely opening Kirk's coffin – is again utterly heretical. Going back to the educated relative of the 1690s, we find that he at very least believed himself to have seen a ghost. For anyone who does not know Kirk's *Secret Commonwealth*, I should stress that it reads like the work of someone who is reporting fact, not folklore. In October 1689, after arguing with the sceptical Stillingfleet about fairy beliefs, Kirk was sufficiently animated to defend in his diary the existence of 'an invisible polity' of 'people to us invisible' – insisting that, after 1492, the first discovery of America was 'looked on as a fairy tale, and the reporters hooted at as inventors of ridiculous Utopias'.

Now, compare this to the words of Kirk's recent biographers. In 1964 Stewart Sanderson felt that there was 'something apt yet faintly ludicrous about the translation of this Scottish clergyman to the fairy realms ... in which he so firmly believed', adding with seeming bafflement: 'yet ... Kirk was not a ludicrous figure ... He was, in the truest sense, a scholar, a gentleman, and a Christian.' Already, here, we find Kirk curiously remade by Sanderson's implicit hierarchy of the improbable. One can be a serious scholar and gentleman if one believes that one knows, solely on the evidence of a book assembled between 900 BC and AD 150, the greatest cosmic truths about Creation and the afterlife, namely, the entire span of past, present and eternity as related to the entire universe. By contrast, to believe in fairies, which are perhaps purely local to this earth, is ludicrous. Moreover, belief in witches is also implicitly less ludicrous, despite the suffering this caused, and its equally magical basis. For Kirk, like his peers, certainly believed in them.

Yet matters only get stranger when we come to Kirk's most recent and authoritative biographer, Louis Stott. Having related Kirk's 'keen interest in fairy superstitions', Stott goes on to lament that the long-running interest in Kirk's alleged fairy translation 'has meant that the importance of [his] work, as the scholar who was among the first to record highland folk-beliefs as well as to make the Bible accessible to highlanders, has sometimes been under-estimated'. Anyone coming to Kirk for the first time via this biopic would be very hard pressed to realize that these were Kirk's *own* beliefs, not merely those of 'superstitious' Highland peasants. A description which implied that Kirk was 'keenly interested' in Christian beliefs as a detached subject of study would be only a little more misleading.

A less famous tale than Kirk's is no less intriguing. Telling of the splendid fairy court held to exist on Bofin Island, off Connacht, Westropp reported the case of a young man who 'incautiously slept under a rick on a Friday night and was carried off to the palace and told to help the cook. To his horror he saw that the fairies were preparing as meat for the feast an old woman, whom they were skinning as she hung from a hook. He was told she was a miser and had a bitter tongue, hence her fate.' Though he refused this well-matured steak, the young man rashly took some fairy wine and, after waking back under the rick, pined away and died.

What to make of this, the only instance of fairies actually eating humans which I have so far encountered? The best guess is that it was a nightmare, fuelled by existing local fears. Yet there is also a good chance that the young man did *die* of this fear – that this was one more voodoo death among so many caused by terror of ghosts, witches, vampires and fairies. Also striking is the fairy morality on display here. The old woman's punishment resembles many other popular tortures designed for sinners in Hell, with the fairies here standing in as Judicial Devils.

Bridget Cleary

In late March 1895 English newspaper readers were taking a strong interest in any reports on Ireland, with the highly charged question of Home Rule still in the air, and a newly progressive Land Bill having been recently passed by the Liberal MP John Morley. What they were probably not expecting as they sipped tea or chocolate in the high-windowed rooms of Belgravia or Bristol was the column which appeared in *The Times* on 26 March:

> A shocking occurrence, recalling the barbarities practised in the Middle Ages upon prisoners charged with witchcraft, has taken place at Baltyvadhen ... Two men and are a woman are charged with causing the death of a woman 27 years of age, named Bridget Cleary, wife of a cooper, by forcing her, as she lay ill of influenza, to drink noxious potions ... and then seizing her and roasting her on a fire under the supposition that she was a witch.

The writer went on to explain that these 'savage orgies' were motivated by the belief that the woman in the house that night was not Bridget but a fairy changeling, who must be ritually assaulted to gain the return of the real woman.

No matter that the atrocities inflicted on innocent women by powerful and educated men during the witch hunts occurred largely in the sixteenth and seventeenth centuries (or that the hamlet was Ballyvadlea, and Bridget 26). These were emotive times, and with headlines in Scottish and English papers all screaming of the murdered witch and her burning, this case offered right-wing Unionists further proof that the Irish – often likened to the Hottentots or the savages of Dahomey – were not fit to govern themselves. In fact,

England and Scotland had far more cases of violent assault and even murder against supposed witches. Far from medieval, one involved a man cutting his own mother's arms in Lincolnshire in 1842, and another the death of an elderly Frenchman in Essex in 1863. The one thing *The Times* had got right was the belief about the fairies. So convinced was Bridget's husband, Michael Cleary, that he spent the three nights following her death at the fairy fort of Kylenagranagh, a mile from their house, waiting to snatch Bridget from the fairies as they rode by.

For the fullest, most sensitively presented version of this story we are now indebted to Angela Bourke, whose 1999 book *The Burning of Bridget Cleary* is strongly recommended. Carefully drawing out the complex social tensions which fed into Bridget's tragic death, Bourke stresses that Bridget (maiden name Boland) and Michael Cleary were by no means the kind of backward Irish peasants certain Unionists would have liked to imagine. Both were literate, relatively affluent and forward looking, housed in a newly built brick cottage whose windows and slate roof offered comparative luxury, given the number of Irish still living in windowless, mud-walled, thatched dwellings at this time. Bridget in particular, with her gold earrings and a certain flair for dress, was evidently thought of as unusual or superior by some of those around her.

Contrasting starkly with this relatively progressive culture was their 'fairy-ridden' neighbour Jack Dunne. Able to read but not to write, Dunne was steeped in tales of magic and fairy danger, and – as Bourke emphasizes – enjoyed some authority and status through these associations and his role as an old-fashioned *shanachie* or story-teller. It may have been a sense that this authority was being eroded which prompted the 55-year-old Dunne to play such a central part in identifying Bridget as a changeling. Bridget had caught a chill when out walking on Monday, 4 March, and from the 5th was confined to bed. When Dunne came to visit on the 13th, he pronounced dramatically, 'That is not Bridgie Boland.' While Bourke admits that this may just have been a euphemism alluding to how ill Bridget looked, Dunne certainly seemed convinced of her fairy status by the following night, when he advised that she be held before the fire as one of various fairy tests. On the night of Friday 15th, moments after killing Bridget, Michael Cleary exclaimed, 'God knows I would never do it but for Jack Dunne . . . It was he who told me my wife was a fairy.'

We will never know just what went through Cleary's head in the days following 4 March. After the initial fairy tests of Thursday night, he certainly seems to have been one of the few of the assembled group still convinced that Bridget was a fairy. Yet he had also gone to a good deal of trouble to get her medical assistance as she lay sick, walking four miles to Fethard for a doctor on 11 March, and starting out again at 5 a.m. for the same reason on Wednesday 13th. Bourke thinks that Cleary had not meant to kill his wife, and this view is plausible. In a highly overwrought state, he was threatening Bridget with a hot stick from the hearth when her clothes caught fire. Bourke also believes that what pushed Cleary over the edge was a remark made by Bridget earlier that night: 'Your mother was going with the fairies . . . she said she [spent] two days with them.' This may have implied to Cleary that he himself was potentially of fairy blood, if 'going with' denoted sexual intercourse. At any rate, Bourke suspects that this severely damaged the newly modern, progressive self Cleary prized, causing him finally to snap. Having apparently killed Bridget when her clothes caught fire, he now seized lamp oil and threw this over her. She blazed up. He shrank back, and threw more – apparently three times in all.

Did Bridget believe what she said to her husband? It is certainly possible. At very least, she probably knew that Cleary's fairy beliefs were strong enough for this retort to wound him badly. She had been publicly abused by him two nights running: stripped, manhandled, threatened, more or less force-fed, and had a chamber pot flung over her by her husband. A proud woman, she chose an insult which had force to it – something which Cleary might well believe. And his beliefs seem to have had a degree of supernatural terror to them. He may at one point have called Bridget a witch (though those listening through a closed door at the time could have misheard the word 'bitch'); he referred to driving out 'the Devil' just after her death; and when Bourke sees his flinging of the lamp oil as 'almost a hygienic impulse, a necessarily violent way of driving out a sickening pollution', she rightly implies the kind of cathartic purification so often resorted to by those in the grip of darkly magical terrors. So thorough was the apparent transformation of Bridget to her husband that, waiting for her return at the fort, he would tell Dunne: 'She was not my wife. She was too fine to be my wife; she was two inches taller than my wife!'

At the subsequent trial, the judge's attitude to a magically inspired crime was one of typical educated bafflement. When Cleary's lawyer, Dr Falconer, was seeking to gain more information about the fairies of Kylenagranagh fort, he was cut short by the judge: 'I will not allow a question as to where fairies are supposed to be . . . We are not here acting a play, but to inquire into *matters of fact!*' (italics mine). Yet the jury may have felt differently. Whatever they themselves believed, they seem to have accepted that Cleary himself had acted with a certain twisted good faith. He had genuinely believed the assault could bring the 'real Bridget' back to him. Accordingly, they agreed on a verdict of manslaughter, and Cleary was sentenced to twenty years in jail, not to death. As Bourke points out, the apparent feelings of the jury were explicitly voiced in England by Andrew Lang and the novelist E. F. Benson, the latter stressing that Bridget's attackers had 'acted . . . honestly, and, as they undoubtedly appear to have believed, for the best'.

Readers may now still be wondering just why Bridget was held, by Dunne and Cleary and others, to be a fairy. Although physical illness could, as we have seen, prompt such beliefs from relatives, Bridget's case was different. At one level, she seems to have suffered from some kind of nervous disorder across these ten days. Recalling a visit to her on that last Friday morning, local priest Father Ryan spoke of her 'wild and excited looks', though also stressing that her conversation was 'coherent and intelligent'. A neighbour, Thomas Smyth, similarly found her on this day to be 'very excited' and apparently not 'right in her mind'. Already, on the Thursday night, she seemed to suffer some delusion about police officers being in the house, and the kitchen being filled with smoke. How might this have acted on Michael? We have seen that even positive mental states, such as the Mahony child's being 'too intelligent', could rouse suspicion if considered atypical.

And it is telling that Lang, suspecting Bridget to have suffered 'some hysterical change', compared the case to popular Chinese beliefs about 'demon possession'. For the sad fact is that, for much of history, mental illness of various kinds attracted supernatural interpretations and corresponding violence. Crossing back into vampire country a moment, let us consider the Russian *erestun*, or 'living vampire'. Felix Oinas cites the belief that certain of these *erestuny* could '"transform themselves", i.e. acquire another person's face and endeavour to sneak into their own or into another family'. It took me some time to make sense of that opaque transformation. What could it mean to steal someone's face? Suddenly, it hit me. The person you have known for so long looks broadly the same on the surface, and *yet* . . . This, again, was a transformation due to mental illness. The result? 'In order to destroy the transformed sorcerer, it is necessary to take the whip used for a heavily-loaded horse and give him a thorough thrashing. Then he will fall down and give up his ghost.' Even once dead, this demon must suffer the usual vampire treatment, being staked between the shoulders to prevent his return. From Russia to China, from Europe to Ireland, from vampires through demons, fairies and witches, mental illness was just one more dangerous way to attract attention in the magical cultures of the world.

The hissing, yelling crowds who greeted the prisoners' first arrival at court on 25 March show that such belief was far from universal in Tipperary. The case may indeed have acted to some extent as a check on fairy violence among existing believers. The

Clearys' cottage would stand empty, a grimly desolate reminder, for years to come. We do not know what kind of reputation Michael Cleary received when he emigrated to Canada in June 1910, having been released that April after fifteen years imprisonment. But the story was certainly a sensation in the North American press in 1895, as it was in Australia. In Ireland memories were naturally darker and longer-lasting. Bourke found, researching her book in the 1990s, that there was still some reluctance to speak of the affair, a full century later. And, echoing eerily from the mouths of children in South Tipperary at this time, one could yet hear, now and then, a well-known rhyme:

> Are you a witch or are you a fairy,
> Or are you the wife of Michael Cleary?

Fairies and the Dead

On 8 September 1843 there appeared in the Irish press a reprint of an anonymous article from the *Waterford Chronicle*, apparently written a few days before:

A tailor named Thomas Keevan in Carrickbeg, has for some time past laboured under paralysis, and is thereby quite feeble, reduced to a skeleton, and is at this moment 'waking and laid out' in his house as a dead corpse, with candles lighting at each side of him, in shroud and ribbons since last night; and is to continue in that state til twelve o'clock this night, when he is to be interred, and a few shovels of clay thrown on his coffin; and to be then left in the churchyard alone. The sorcerer, or fairy man, who gave directions to Keevan's wife and himself in this business, says, that the true Keevan will be at home in Carrickbeg, sitting at the fire, on her return from the churchyard, after his returning from the 'fairies', as by his doing the above the spell will be broken, and in the coffin there will be found only a broom instead of the fairy buried.

It is clear enough that this ritual matches the broad logic of the changeling cases seen above. And yet, even as we thereby manage to keep one foot planted in familiar terrain, we seem with the other to be stepping off the very edges of our fairy map, beyond even those uncertain cartographic borders marked *terra incognita*. What on earth went through Keevan's head in these hours as he lay shrouded and coffined, first in the candlelit hush and then in the cemetery itself? Sombre as his reflections doubtless were, we can assume that they were scarcely less strange than his state of mind when he, seemingly, *agreed* to the whole proceeding ('directions to Keevan's wife and himself'). Although the trail of this story goes cold after that single report, it seems almost certain that Keevan suffocated to death in his coffin.

In part, the link between fairies and the dead dates back to ancient traditions of a pagan afterlife. Proserpine had been potentially able to return from Hades, and we will in Chapter Four see similarly porous boundaries when considering medieval fairy beliefs. By the nineteenth century, however, the place where the dead strayed back and forth across metaphysical borders (aided by the fairies) was almost always Ireland. Clearly Catholicism, with its intermediate zone of Purgatory and its potent links between dead and living, had much to do with this. Alice Cunningham of Dromintee, County Armagh, told Evans-Wentz that 'my mother died in England, and she came to me in the spirit. I saw her plainly. I ran to catch her, but my hands ran through her form as if it were mere mist . . . The fairies', she added, 'once passed down this lane here on a Christmas morning; and I took them to be suffering souls out of Purgatory, going to mass.'

As we have seen, the fairies in Ireland were often credited with an ambiguous care of the dead, especially those who had died young. Thus, when the folklorist Jeremiah Curtin gathered from his Irish informants that fairies left corpses as substitutes 'when the persons borne away are marriageable young women' we hear again that poignant inability to believe that the young, full of life and the power of life, can really die. The corpse is not them, anymore than the disabled child is your child. Again, Lang heard from an Irishman that 'about half the people supposed dead are really with the fairies,' and after the Cleary case went so far as to infer that, for fairy believers, 'the fairies ... are in one respect only ancestral ghosts, living in a Hades which is neither heaven, hell, nor purgatory.' In a surprising number of cases, moreover, the dead were believed by their relatives to have *come back* from fairyland. While most of these instances were the result of elaborate frauds, a significant number of 'fairy sightings' (in and beyond Ireland) sound very much like encounters with real ghosts. Let us begin with the fraud.

Around mid-February 1834 a Tipperary widow, Mrs Kearns, received a visit from one Mary Mac, 'pretending to be "'a fairy woman", one who ... knew the haunts of "the good people", and was able even to raise the dead'. Mac told Kearns's daughter Mary ('a very handsome young woman') that her father was not in fact dead, but 'with the fairies'. A concealed accomplice stated 'I am your father,' and when the girl asked if he would stay, replied, 'No ... I cannot leave the fairies yet; but I shall be home with you in four days.' Mary was thereby induced to leave with Mac and her two accomplices, her mother presently returning to find her daughter and all their valuables gone. The trio of career fraudsters – who may in fact have been a family – were heard of in Monasterevin, County Kildare, but not caught, despite a £50 reward. Blackly comic as the story might now look, it must in reality have been horribly poignant for the bereaved Mary, and soon grew still more so for her mother. There is no record of the girl ever being found, and if she was not murdered, the fact of her being 'very handsome' may not have been to her advantage in such company.

Re-enter, next, the queen of the fairies, making her appearance in December 1843 at Kilkenny, where Catherine Muldowney has allowed her to come in for a drink of water. Looking initially like the thirty-year-old woman Mary Neill, Her Elfin Majesty presently reveals not only her true status, but the no less startling fact that she is also Muldowney's 'father-in-law, who had been dead for many years'. Adding to this the role of guardian angel, Neill explains that she has 'made it a constant practice to watch over the witness's family and shield them from all impending dangers'. There was, for example, a '"passage of the fairies" through the house', and if it were not for Neill, Muldowney's 'little girl would have been spirited away by the "good people", and her husband would have received a fairy dart in the right hip, which would have rendered him totally useless to her'. As well as leaving a fairy nectar for Muldowney to drink, Neill at one point burst into tears, explaining that 'her [that is, the father-in-law's] soul was suffering dreadfully for the good acts which she was doing for the witness's family', and that Muldowney should therefore give the priest gold to say Masses for him/her.

When Muldowney's husband heard of this he called her a fool, and a few days later Neill was arrested. At the subsequent trial she was acquitted for lack of evidence. Because Muldowney had no money when Neill called, the latter could steal only a gown and shawl by way of 'payment'. But if this was much less than the loss of a fortune or a daughter, we further learn that as a result of the affair Muldowney was turned out of her house, and apparently also her job, by Sir Wheeler Cuffe, in whose lodge she had originally offered hospitality to Neill. A further edge of upper-middle-class cruelty was seen in the trial. At one point in her evidence Muldowney 'burst into tears, and the Barrister told her not to be frightened, for she was now surrounded by anything but *good people* (laughter)'.

Elsewhere in the Emerald Isle, matters got stranger still. Some time before May 1848 a soldier, Matthew Lally, called on an elderly farming couple (also named Lally) in the Callows, County Longford. He was, he told them, their son – seemingly dead for sixteen years, yet now returned from fairyland. He showed them on his body a birthmark such as their son had had, outlined details of the events after his death and finally persuaded them to open the coffin. This had in it only a log of wood. Matthew further explained that 'though married to a high-up lady' among the fairies, he had been 'sent on earth for a season, with directions to go into the army and learn the new light infantry exercise'. With the Lallys' astonished neighbours crowded about him, he detailed 'the fate of many of their friends and relatives, whom he had met "in the hours of fairy revel"'. Once again, this account plainly implies a general though utterly heretical belief. The dead go not to heaven, but to fairyland.

Showered with gifts and affection like one very prodigal son, Lally for a time happily assisted his parents with their work until one day he suddenly vanished, seemingly for good. Months later he returned again, explaining that he had been taken overseas by the fairies, where he had taught the light infantry exercise to the Mexicans. Presently Lally attempted to buy his way out of the army. Although this was not permitted, the ensuing court martial was dropped when Lally's fairy story was heard and he was declared insane. Accordingly, he 'returned to the Callows, assuming the fairy man, foretelling events, and promising cures, thereby extracting money from the credulous infatuated poor'.

Lally's disappearance, after his first miraculous return, was clearly due to his army leave having ended. Young argues that Lally had managed to research the matter of the real Matthew's death and birthmark when his regiment had been stationed in the Callows, and that he had singled out the Lallys because he himself happened already to have a similar birthmark. The original corpse may, Young thinks, have been removed by the imposter, or stolen for sale by resurrection men. Young further establishes that, by May 1848, Lally's reputation as 'a fairy man' had led to his advising a girl called Killian about her dead father. With Mrs Killian now remarried to one Corrigan, Lally explained to the daughter that Mr Killian could be regained from the fairies if the stepfather was sent in his place. (Readers may imagine the intricate family dynamics of this at their leisure.) Discussing this – perhaps heatedly – with Lally in the pub one night, Corrigan got so drunk that on his way home he fell from a wagon and presently died. Local opinion held that his death greatly strengthened 'Lally's power with the fairies'.

Like many of the buried gems turned up in our excavations of the fairy past, this one flashes gleams of comedy at one moment, of poignant loss at another, and of exultant joy the next. Looking to us a little like some Talented Mr Ripley of fairyland, Lally succeeded because he was clever, daring, perhaps charming. And, most of all, because he knew that virtually everyone around him believed in fairies. Indeed, his stratagems seem only to have reinforced these beliefs among Callows residents. What happened to him? Despite Young's efforts, no more is known. Yet we must seriously consider this possibility: that the elderly Lallys had their remaining years gladdened by the miracle of their resurrected son's return; and that everyone around them persisted in this belief for decades to come.

Readers may still be wondering if Matthew Lally actually looked like the dead man of the Callows. Although we do not know, there is good reason to think that he did not have to. Young cites the broadly similar case of Bryan MacDonough, posing in May 1847 as a revived James Lyons, despite looking nothing like him. His true form, he assured Lyons's family, would be restored on New Year's Day by the elfin king. Meanwhile, in a case with family dynamics yet more richly delicious than those of the Killians, a widowed farmer, Paddy, presently remarried, living happily with his new wife on Island Bawn, Tipperary, until, one winter's night almost twenty years later, who should return from fairyland ... but, his first wife. After some initial reluctance, she was accepted as such by Paddy and by their son, and after this the lucky husband seems to have enjoyed an embarrassment of conjugal riches, living with both wives together. Again, it is hard to imagine that the returned woman looked identical to the dead one. Tellingly, after her return in 1820, our fairy escapee explained that her release from fairyland had been secured by 'the Virgin Mary'.

Stepping sideways for a moment into vampire country, we find these joyful Irish returns from the dead contrasting sharply with the revenants of Greece, Russia or Bulgaria. In at least four cases where the prematurely buried sat up in their coffins or escaped their graves, joy was conspicuously lacking. Despite looking almost exactly like the living people they had very recently been, these revenants were greeted with abject terror, and staked or stoned to death.

Back in fairyland, another case unearthed by Young surpasses even that of Matthew Lally. Around June 1863, a woman called Mary Doheny appeared in Carrick-on-Suir (again, in County Tipperary). She seems initially to have made her living by curing cattle, and at one point received a single payment of £5, this later being credited with bringing badly needed rain to the previously dry summer. But things got really interesting when Doheny attempted to cure the sick daughter of police constable Joseph Reeves. Although the child did presently die, a temporary recovery (writes Andrew Sneddon) impressed the parents so much that they, along with at least five others, fell under the potent spell of Doheny's black art. It was claimed at her trial in autumn 1864 that she had drugged them to achieve this 'infatuation', and this indeed seems possible, given her reputation as a herbalist and cow doctor. If so, one would certainly like to know what these drugs were. For, come summer 1864, Doheny had persuaded the Reeves family, and Sub-Constable James Hayes, that three dead people were alive. She had showed the Reeves child, Mrs Reeves's father-in-law, William Mullins, and another dead relative, Tom Sheehan, to the Reeves couple, their niece and Hayes. Not only that, but for weeks she oversaw the delivery of food, clothes, letters and tobacco to the dead, returning with letters from them to the Reeves family. One reason the case came to trial was that Joseph Reeves's colleague, Sub-Inspector W. H. Heard, noticed how badly in debt Reeves was getting as a result. Hayes, meanwhile, actually resigned his post after Doheny convinced him that he was soon to receive an extensive estate in Carrick.

Here are Mrs Reeves and magistrate Mr Hanna in court on 2 September 1864:

'Is your father dead?'

'He died about three years ago . . . but he is now living in Carrick-on-Suir.'

'Living! How can you say that?'
'Because I saw him!'

Doheny, she insisted, 'showed him to me, also Tom Sheehan ... and my own child. They were all alive (sensation in court).' These sightings all seem to have occurred at night, with no speech between the parties. Yet all these people, most of whom intimately knew the deceased, *swore in court* to having seen them. This included Anastatia Power (Mrs Reeves's niece), who stated that she had repeatedly given food to Sheehan, as recently as the night of 1 September. When Doheny was taken out of the court back to prison, Joseph Reeves took her by the hand and insisted that he still believed all he had seen. The 9 September newspaper report added that several others were under Doheny's spell; that remarks in court implied shared belief from some in the gallery; and that all of the statements by the Reeves couple and Hayes and Power were given in a very calm and collected manner.

As was so often the case in vampire or witch country, here in fairy territory official opinions, beliefs and powers were defiantly ignored by ordinary people. Doheny was certainly jailed for a year that October, but most of those giving evidence never believed in her guilt, and it was said that the food deliveries still persisted into late September, with general opinion holding that Doheny left her cell at night whenever she chose. Similarly, official theology here meant nothing if it stood in the way of personal beliefs about the resurrection of these dead relations.

Most of the papers reporting this case bandied about the terms 'witch' and 'witchery'. But Doheny was also described as a 'fairy woman', and this must have been the status accorded to her by those who paid her for services. Nobody ever seems to have explicitly stated that the dead of Carrick-on-Suir had returned from fairyland. Yet, given what else we have heard from Ireland (and Tipperary in particular), it seems hard not to believe that fairyland played an important role. I use this slightly cautious phrasing because it seems that those who saw 'the dead' may not have distinguished very clearly between Heaven, Purgatory and Fairyland. Joseph Reeves, for example, said in court that the letters he received had come 'from the other world' (they had in fact been written for the illiterate Doheny by a paid letter-writer).

From one angle, we might grudgingly admire Doheny for making such an impressive living in this way (she did, after all, have a blind husband to support). From another, we might ask about the Catholic priests who made an even better living from a theology that habitually and minutely insisted on the porous divide between living and dead. For, while this case was extraordinary, it was not unique. In autumn 1898, reports from Bavaria detailed the trial of the Wohlfahrt family, whose daughter Agnes had been taking payments and goods from the Kottrich family for five years. Why? Well, because Agnes was in touch with the Kottriches' dead daughter, Crescence. Agnes transferred letters to and from Heaven, and on learning that Crescence had married an angel and had a child by him, sent the happy couple at least 3,000 marks from the Kottriches, adding that, when the money arrived, 'all the angels in heaven blew their trumpets.' Among various gems of this trial was 'a receipt "from the Mother of Christ" for 150 marks' and the news that 'Frau Kottrich herself baked a fine tart for the Virgin Mary.' One of the earliest payments was 300 marks to secure Crescence's removal from Purgatory, and readers will not be surprised to learn that Kempten, scene of these 'letters from heaven', had an almost entirely Roman Catholic population.

Fairy Scapegoats

Before we move on to explore some of the peculiarly entangled relations between fairies, ghosts and poltergeists, we might briefly take stock of what fairies could do. They caused not only death but sickness, both mental and physical. One Irish girl who was ill for seven years was 'commonly believed to have been with the fairies' all this time. An elderly Donegal man, Neil Colton, recalled to Evans-Wentz how 'in olden times', the fairies 'used to take young folks and keep them and draw all the life out of their bodies'. As we have seen, this notion of an attack on life was one of the most basic beliefs of popular culture, whether the scapegoat was the witch, the vampire, the fairy or the fat-stealing pishtaco of the Andes.

If these attacks were the most serious of all, those on cattle or crops were not far behind – especially for people who had known severe hunger or even starvation as a result. In the first case, more-over, both sick livestock and sick humans were habitually understood to have been 'elf shot'. Alaric Hall has in fact argued that the first known use of the word 'elf' occurred as part of this phrase, in the ninth-century Anglo-Saxon medical text *Bald's Leechbook*. Our oldest surviving reference to British fairies, then, is clearly marked 'Danger'.

Writing from Scotland in 1699, the Welsh antiquary Edward Lhwyd explained: 'as to this elf-stricking, their opinion is that the fairies . . . do sometimes carry men away in the air, and furnishing them with bows and arrows, employ them to shoot men, cattle etc.' This seemingly oblique form of attack (by human proxy) was reported by many others – with some of the reluctant human archers claiming to have deliberately fired wide. One grain of concrete reality nestled in this belief was the actual flint arrowheads of Stone Age ancestors which people sometimes found when digging. Although Lhwyd dismissively writes these off as purely human artefacts ('just the same chipped flints the natives of New England head their arrows with at this day'), Robert Kirk had viewed them very differently, suspecting that these yellow flint arrowheads were 'cut by art and tools . . . beyond [the] human'. Not only that, but the wounds they inflicted on cattle were also, to him, clearly supernatural, being apparent under the skin, yet never having broken it.

If these explanations seem hopelessly uneconomical (ordinary cattle disease; no skin broken because no arrows used) one can only say, first, welcome to fairyland, and add that Kirk had seen these wounds and 'felt them with my hands'. Kirk also outlined at length how elf-shooting was especially dangerous during the quarterly migrations of fairy tribes, when they sailed invisibly through the air 'with bag and baggage'. The pious Kirk complained that, being aware of these dangerous times, Scots countryfolk would then feel forced to attend church for protection, where they were not seen 'again til the next quarter', as if 'all the use of worship and sermons were to save them from those arrows that fly in the dark'. Westropp found Irish fairy doctors still carrying elf-bags in Mayo and Sligo in 1918. Among other things these contained up to eight flint arrowheads, one of which was dipped in a curative liquid and used (with some hint of sympathetic magic) to cure cattle. In parts of Ireland farmers tied red rags on the horns of cattle to keep off the Gentry.

In the sphere of crops and weather, we have just heard of Mary Doheny being given the impressive sum of £5 to end what may have been a fairy drought. An unnamed 'scholarly priest' from the west of Ireland explained to Evans-Wentz that fairies were still, in 1908, 'believed to control crops and their ripening. A field of turnips may promise well, and its owner will count on so many tons to the acre, but if when the crop is gathered it is found to be far short of the estimate, the explanation is that the fairies have extracted so much substance from it.' Most devastatingly of all, according to most of the inhabitants of Tuam, in western Ireland, the fairies had also caused the Great Famine of 1846–7. This catastrophe, ultimately claiming over a million lives nationwide, was (explained elderly local Thady Steed) linked to the fact that he and hundreds of others had seen fairies 'fighting in the sky over Knock Ma and on towards Galway'.

One can well imagine that fairies were also held responsible for the unusually severe Irish winter of 1846–7 which so badly aggravated the Famine. On the island of Arranmore fairies were believed to cause storms at sea, and elsewhere could achieve yet more spectacular feats when angered. Walking by the ruined Pennard Castle on the Welsh Gower coast years ago, I had not known that, ages before,

The Luck of Edenhall, a
14th-century vase from
Syria or Egypt; one of
many fairy artefacts known
to popular culture.

Joseph Noel Paton, *The Quarrel of Oberon and Titania*, 1849, oil on canvas: one of
the most creative 19th-century versions of Shakespeare's play.

Natural harmony or fairy tyranny? John Anster Fitzgerald, *The Captive Robin*, c. 1864, oil on canvas.

Fairy imps and goblins. John Anster Fitzgerald, *The Fairies' Barque*, 1860, oil on canvas.

Fairy madness: Richard Dadd, *The Fairy Feller's Master-stroke*, 1855–64, oil on canvas.

One of several opium-inspired paintings by John Anster Fitzgerald, *The Stuff that Dreams are Made Of*, c. 1858, oil on wood.

Fairy voyeurism: Robert Huskisson, *Midsummer Night's Dream*, 1847, oil on canvas.

A Midsummer's icon: Robert Hughes, *Midsummer Eve*, c. 1908, oil on canvas.

Inner light or outer lust?
John Simmons, *Titania*,
1866, watercolour.

Fatal attraction: John William Waterhouse, *Hylas and the Nymphs*, 1896,
oil on canvas.

Otherness regained: Herbert James Draper, *Lamia*, 1909, oil on canvas.

Lamia tamed: John William Waterhouse, *Lamia*, 1909, oil on canvas.

Splendid isolation: Herbert James Draper, *The Kelpie*, 1913, oil on canvas.

Fairy energy: the Lost Boys from Walt Disney's *Peter Pan*, dir. Clyde Geronimi, Wilfred Jackson and Hamilton Luske (1953).

Fairy darkness on film: *Jonathan Strange and Mr Norrell*, dir. Toby Haynes (2015), BBC.

Loch na Beiste (Loch of the Beast), northwest Scotland: site of the Great Kelpie Hunt of Gairloch.

a violent sandstorm around it had been a work of fairy revenge. Furious at having their banquet disturbed one night, the fairies carried masses of sand from Ireland, dumping it on the Gower coast and allegedly burying an entire village in the process.

In some ways, the widespread and enduring belief that virtually any inexplicable misfortune was fairy work can be harder to credit than alleged sightings of the fairies themselves. We must remind ourselves, however, that in fairyland, the fairies were always in your head. Putting it another way, we might ask why, when you had such a useful and flexible scapegoat, you should put it to work on only a part-time basis. Given how many of the above examples are Irish, we should also remind ourselves that in England, Scotland and North America, such problems were habitually blamed on witches just over a hundred years ago. In those cases, the scapegoats were real people, who could suffer serious injury or death as a result.

Dangerous Landscapes

If I should offer to take you to a special fairy place in the country-side, you would probably expect somewhere extremely remote and tranquil, perhaps featuring a sheltered stream or woodland cave. Yet in Ireland, only a hundred years ago, someone might fulfil such a promise by flinging open the front and back doors of their house and warning: 'Out of the way – they're coming through!' Here espe-cially it was not so much a case of making an arduous pilgrimage to some lonely fairy place, as it was of finding a place which was *not* fairy territory, where you could safely live in peace. Rather like that invisible fairy kingdom of Rhys the Deep in Wales, fairy territory potently superimposed itself across your world.

There were three central areas of the fairy landscape which posed special danger. These were fairy trees, fairy forts and fairy paths. The first two at least had the advantage of being clearly obvious. In the last case, you might well find out too late – only when you had built your house on one, and the fairies began to express their anger in typically boisterous fashion. To some extent fairy paths parallel routes that were once useful and later forgotten. Readers of Robert Macfarlane's remarkable book *The Old Ways* might recall the sunken holloways of Britain, while Paul Devereux links Irish fairy paths with both the 'churchways' by which people walked to services in England and the old 'Mass paths' of Ireland. These latter were first used to reach places of outdoor worship during the English sup-pression of Catholicism, and later as routes to chapel or for carrying a corpse to its funeral.

In some cases Irish fairy paths seem to have been identifiable either because they were held to be direct routes between fairy forts, or because fairy thorns acted as waymarkers along them. Fairy men or women might also be consulted as to their location. In general, any sensible person took Standard Fairy Precautions before build-ing a house in the Irish countryside. You might mark the intended four corners of the house site with stakes or small heaps of stones.

If overnight the fairies knocked down any stones, or your stakes, you had been warned, and chose another spot. The fairies might also move the stakes to another area which did not encroach on their territory. Timothy Corrigan Correll cites a case where a practical joker one night moved them into a swamp, so that the resultant house was regularly flooded at the back. Once a house was completed, a last precaution was to 'place a bed, some other furniture, and plenty of food' in the new dwelling 'the night before the time fixed for moving into it; and if the food is not consumed, and the crumbs swept up by the door in the morning, the house cannot safely be occupied'. The Dublin University graduate who explained this to Evans-Wentz stated that the practice was still in use, and that he knew of 'two houses . . . that have never been occupied, because the fairies did not show their willingness and goodwill by taking food so offered to them'.

All across Ireland fear of the fairies dictated where people lived, how they farmed and where or how roads could be built. For a long time, a typical house-building for a family saw them hire a fiddler, gather all their friends and alternately dance and build throughout the day and night until their new cabin was complete. Yet, ironically, despite the often complete absence of legal building restrictions, people habitually feared the secret laws and penalties of the Middle Kingdom.

In Athlone, Westmeath, just before the First World War, the District Council seems to have had 'Fairy Building Objection' as a standing item on its agenda. Faced with a letter from labourer John Seery, in May 1911, surrendering tenancy of a cottage which 'he said was erected on a "fort" . . . the plot [being] haunted by fairies', so that 'he could not till it', Councillor Gilleran admitted that 'it was no place to select as a cottage site', adding, 'I suppose we cannot evict the fairies.' Councillor Molloy, similarly, conceded: 'No luck ever came out of interfering with such places.' Yet if Gilleran grew weary of such planning problems, he himself was rational enough to benefit from them a few months later. In February 1912 a labourer named

Kilduff gave up an acre of land, on which the Council had actually proposed to build a cottage for him (under the Labourer's Acts of 1883), because the site, at Lacken, had 'on it an old fort or rath which would have to be removed. On no account would he interfere with "the fairies' home". Despite his present house being on a site 'so windy that it would give rheumatism to a wild duck', Kilduff thus passed up a new cottage and farming plot, at which point Gilleran, now retired (possibly owing to fairy fatigue), stepped in and applied for the site himself. Perhaps despairing of finding another taker, the Council granted it to him.

Just what dangers did Seery and Kilduff fear? Much further north, in County Antrim, folklorist H. T. Browne heard of a man who recklessly cut down a fairy tree when drunk, and who was found the next morning alive, but with his head turned around backwards. Elsewhere you might suffer a problem and then identify the fairy source accordingly. Westropp heard of a Mullet family afflicted by sickness, who were told by the fairy doctor that this 'arose from the resentment of the fairy folk, owing to the defilement of their playground, by keeping a manure heap on the south side of one of the houses. It was removed, and soon afterwards the sickness, for very obvious reasons, disappeared.' In Kilmore, Armagh, a girl called Mary, aged around thirteen, suffered mental disorders and ultimately paralysis and death after falling asleep under bushes in her garden one hot summer's day. As her surviving sister explained many years later in 1859, Mary 'had intruded that day on "the Quality's" ground to sleep; the bushes was gentle bushes . . . [and] that's what come of doing what she did'.

Other problems were equally drastic. John Boylin told of how, during his Kilmessan childhood in the 1850s, he and his peers were subject to a fairy curfew each evening, always being brought indoors before a fairy procession came from Rath Ringlestown on a route which circled fairy bushes. On one occasion a man living in a house built close to this path came out at the wrong time, and was later found dead: 'the fairies had *taken* him because he interfered with their procession.' Writing to a London paper in April 1895, one Robert Day recalled a farmer's family from near Mitchelstown, County Cork, who moved from a house on a fairy track after two of the family died.

These are just a handful of several fatalities attributed to abuse of fairy territory. If we take all this only at the level of what people believed about fairy paths, forts and trees, it is already striking. Victims believed the fairies killed over such offences, and were ready to abandon their homes (or indeed never move in) because of this. Yet matters are about to get much stranger. For in a number of such cases, something bad really *was* happening, and its origin really was paranormal. A gulp of brandy and a relacing of boots are probably in order at this point. Over the next hill, our journey is about to take us into realms far stranger than any fairy island.

Fairy Poltergeists

An implicit link between fairies and poltergeists dates back to the Romans. Roman spirits of the dead (*manes*) were divided into two classes: those beneficial household spirits, the *lares*, and those problematic ones which made mysterious noises, the *lemures*. While fairies would later be bribed with bread and milk, the Romans had a whole festival, *lemuralia*, every May, to placate the *lemures*. Here activities which later would both be attributed to fairies are credited to two different types of household spirit. In 1518 the Scottish theologian John Major spoke of brownies as 'jocular spirits who do odd jobs about a house, throw stones and other objects, and are apt to provoke curiosity rather than alarm'. Citing this in 1963, Roger Lancelyn Green notes that this brownie 'owes something to the poltergeist'. In 1575 the influential French surgeon Ambroise Paré wrote of spirits which 'howl in the night ... move benches, tables ... children in the cradles ... walk up and down rooms' and much more – adding that these entities were 'called by divers names, as devils ... hobgoblins, fairies, Robin-good-fellows' and so forth.

As Paré already implies, poltergeists resemble fairies in that both are capable of very controlled activity, as well as chaotic and destructive outbursts. When children are moved in their cradles, for example, they are usually put down carefully, often unwoken. I know this, because that happened to Mike, my old sociology teacher, when he was a young parent in the 1960s. And, yes – this is the point where I state my belief that poltergeists are real. As a lifelong atheist and rationalist, I had almost no interest in them until they ambushed me in 2013, during research on vampires. It took me a long time to get my head around this subject, and if what follows gives you a headache, I sympathize. I have studied some very difficult things. But nothing ever made my head hurt like poltergeists. When I did begin to take them seriously, I found that people I had known for many years suddenly told me their own poltergeist stories. Mike had told his to our class in 1989, but back then it was too strange and isolated for me to begin to get to grips with it.

The barest guide to the poltergeist will assist us through what follows. The phenomena – including unsourced noises, inexplicable movements of objects, fires, invisible pinchings or beatings, and stones hurled from nowhere – typically involve not a haunted house but a haunted person. This is usually a child aged between about eight and fifteen. If the family flees the 'haunted house', the events therefore often follow them. The person on whom the events centre (hereafter 'agent') is almost always suffering emotional trauma of some kind. In modern cultures this can be sexual, interpersonal or the result of bereavement. In vampire and witch societies it is usually sheer supernatural terror. In each case, a ritual which calms the agent, whether psychoanalysis or the staking of a vampire, can stop the poltergeist activity. Readers may still be wondering: 'Are poltergeists ghosts?' We will come to this shortly.

In general, fairy believers often spoke of fairy assaults which sound like poltergeist episodes. The 'fairies' pinch', a proverbial phrase for the punishment of careless maids or householders, took on a sharply precise sting when a Cornish woman responded to an educated Victorian's fairy scepticism with, 'What! not believe in 'em, when my poor mother had been pinched black and blue by 'em?' Investigating a poltergeist incident at a remote farm in Derrygonnelly, County Fermanagh, in 1877, the physicist Sir William Barrett was told by the farmer: 'I would have thought, sir, it do be fairies, but them ... knowledgeable men will not allow such a thing.' Staying on the Hebridean island of Tiree in 1883, a Mr J. Sands heard of a house haunted so badly by fairies that the tenant abandoned it and built a new one. Unfortunately, having taken one stone from the old home to incorporate into the new, he found the problems as bad as ever in this next dwelling. Though details of the activity here are vague, the likelihood that poltergeist events simply followed one of the family is very strong. From Bospowes, Cornwall, the antiquary Henry Jenner told of how poltergeist knockings 'in a cottage not a hundred yards from where I am writing' caused the inhabitants to set out milk to placate the angry piskies during the winter of 1909–10.

On Man, Mrs Samuel Leece of Kirk Patrick recalled to Evans-Wentz how, around 1830, her mother had been 'in bed with her baby, but wide awake, when she felt the baby pulled off her arm and heard the rush of them. Then she mentioned the Almighty's name, and, as they were hurrying away, a little table alongside the bed went round about the floor twenty times.' While here the interference with a baby was naturally put down to fairies, the controlled movement of the table is classic poltergeist behaviour. Also well known are poltergeist missiles – sometimes oddly harmless, and sometimes with highly destructive effect. At Cae Drain in Holyhead, Anglesey, in February 1858 scores of windows were broken by stones, but no vandal was ever seen by the vigilant police and locals. Some thought the assaults demonic, 'while others affirm that the fairies have once more visited this haunted spot'.

Fairy poltergeists could also be found beyond the more typical Celtic fairy heartlands. Daniel Rabuzzi notes that in Norfolk 'the hyter sprite could ... be blamed if things went wrong in the house, à la poltergeists', and in Staffordshire sometime before 1896, the itinerant preacher and poet Elijah Cope jumped out of his chair one night when a poltergeist started rapping on the table of the farmhouse where he was staying. Notably calm about this apparently routine visitor, Cope's hostess told him that this was 'just a poor old fairy ... Old Nancy ... Been here ever so long; lost her husband and her children. It's bad to be left like that, all alone. I leave a bit o' cake on the table for her, and sometimes she fetches it, and sometimes she don't.'

But it was in Ireland that such problems were most often held to be precisely territorial. Silver cites Lang on the poltergeist events of 1907, in a Northern Ireland farmhouse, where the neighbours believed that 'fairies caused the problem, as the farmer had swept his chimney with a bough of holly, and the holly is "a gentle tree".' The Scottish Freemason William Harvey wrote of a case from Portarlington, Queen's County. Having saved £500 for a new house, a man

> erected the structure on what was reputed to be a fairy path ... all went well until the first night of his occupancy. About midnight strange noises were made; chairs, beds, and dishes began to move, at first gently, then with more violence, until at the end of an hour everything was smashed and the man himself was very seriously hurt.

Having sunk all his savings into the building, the man attempted after his recovery to reoccupy it. He was again forced out, and the house was still empty when Harvey wrote of it in December 1915.

In 1959, Diarmuid McManus told of how Paddy Baine, a man he knew, rashly built his new house without full fairy consultation. And, 'shortly after he and his bride, Biddy Callan, took up residence in the new house' near the Ox Mountains in County Sligo, 'they began to experience very frequent disturbances at one end of it which abutted on the little village road. Some nights it appeared as if the whole house was about to tumble down.' Local wise woman

Mairead ni Heine was called in, and she explained that one 'corner of the house . . . was interfering with the progress of the "good people"'. Paddy had a stonemason cut off the offending corner, and the problems apparently ceased. When McManus wrote of this, Baine's descendants were living there quite happily. While the photograph shown in McManus's book *The Middle Kingdom* gives a slightly hazy view of the sliced corner, Paul Devereux confirms that many houses in the west of Ireland were modified for this kind of reason.

Among many cases resulting from Devereux's impressive detective work on this subject, two are particularly interesting. At Knocknagashel in County Kerry, Eddie Lenihan was told by a local man about the building of a new public house three miles northeast of the village. During construction a passing stranger warned the builder: 'You're building the house on a path. Don't build it there.' The builder 'took little notice' and presently moved his family in, after which 'blankets would be pulled off beds by unseen hands, and strange, shadowy figures were seen around the house at night.' 'The fairies were all the time at the same house,' Lenihan's source told him.' In this case the solution was to call in a priest for a blessing. Notice, here, how the shorthand phrase 'a path' is assumed to be generally recognizable – echoing those Clare and Galway people who, when questioned by Lady Gregory, referred to such dwellings as simply 'in the way'.

An undated incident written down in the 1930s concerned the house of Billy Brennan at Cloonagh, County Mayo. Here the adjacent fairy path was blamed for the deaths of Brennan's cattle 'until a disembodied voice told him to stop throwing out dry ashes and to shift the position of his . . . roof end'. Impressively, Devereux's sleuthing led him not only to locate the house, but to find a local man, Sean Haran, who still knew the tradition of this fairy path in 2002, even though it had now disappeared.

At one level, all this offers us more concrete physical evidence of the weight of supernatural belief. Some of us may go to the trouble

A traditional corpse-door from Darum, West Jutland, drawn in the late 19th century by H. F. Feilberg.

not to walk under a ladder nowadays, but superstition does not usually make us move house or initiate substantial building work. Elsewhere one Michael Barrett pulled down half of his chimney-place to get rid of fairies, while in County Laoise a family suffering elfin disturbances were told by the wise woman Moll Anthony to block up two doors and break open a new one in another wall. Interestingly, these alterations seem often to exceed the trouble to which people went elsewhere to protect their houses from vampires or ghosts. In countries as diverse as Italy, Romania, Russia and Denmark the bereaved would make a special opening in their home to either release a dead person's soul, or to carry the corpse through it to its funeral. This was then blocked or bricked up to prevent the homesick soul returning through that same exit. The most substantial of these would be a whole rebricked 'corpse-door', as pictured here, from nineteenth-century Denmark; the simplest an open or broken window.

I have so far used the term 'superstition' as a kind of shorthand for a mixture of different beliefs and problems. But matters look different if we assume, hypothetically, that what some of these people complained of was *really happening*. The kind of violence inflicted in Portarlington is rare in poltergeist cases but not unknown, and the only other plausible explanation would be that the man was mad and did it all himself. The Baine case was probably also genuine, insofar as it involved real poltergeist activity. The agent could have been Paddy or his young wife, but once they had persuaded themselves that they had restored the fairy right of way, their nerves calmed and the problem stopped accordingly. In this sense, ironically, to believe in fairies was surprisingly useful: compare a completely 'rational' family who can find no way to stop a poltergeist episode because they have no sense of what is causing it. In the new pub, the mischief with the bedclothes is classic poltergeist stuff, reported time and again by just about every kind of witness. 'Shadowy figures' have been reported in ghost and poltergeist episodes, with one seen by two men at Peterhouse College, Cambridge, in April 1997, a few months before the college bursar saw a full-blown ghost in the same room. While Brennan's cattle no doubt had some ordinary disease, the 'disembodied voice' (assuming it was heard by more than one person) is interesting. These are rare, but the few on record have been heard by police, religious ministers, journalists and many others. Also notable is 'the rush' heard in Kirk Patrick: in many poltergeist incidents there are ambient sounds or sudden disturbances of the air. In Portarlington, the gradual build-up from gentle to violent matches numerous poltergeist outbreaks, including ones where ornaments are actually seen to vibrate before they explode or fly about a room.

Fairy Housework

Across centuries and countries poltergeist activity has been blamed on ghosts, vampires, witches and demons – as well as on human pranksters who in many cases were actually innocent. What is interesting about fairies as culprits is that they, like no other scapegoat, fit the dualistic chaos/control quality seen in so many poltergeist episodes. Appease the fairies, and they will help you. Upset them, and they will terrorize you.

We have to consider, then, the possibility that some of the 'fairy housework' reported in times past did *actually happen*. In some cases it was pure folklore; in others the work of homeless wanderers who knew the local customs and gained some minimal food and shelter in this way. But poltergeists could do housework. There are innumerable reliable reports of objects, such as glasses or vases of flowers, moved without spillage or breakage from place to place, sometimes around one or more corners. In a case privately described to me, a retired naval officer inspecting new building work in his house in 1998 found animal ornaments perfectly arranged across the doorway of one room, seconds after he had seen them on a shelf. In another, a man alone in his house found that towels he had hung over banisters had all been beautifully folded moments later. In fairy territory itself, we have the Monmouthshire farm of Molly Rosser. Here, some time before 1913, householders who put out milk for the resident *pwka* (or good spirit) came down in the morning to find 'the hearth ... cleaned up, kettles polished, dishes washed, and sometimes the cows washed and the horses harnessed'.

If this stretches credulity, I sympathize. But poltergeist interference with animals has been reported several times. As for the housework? Well – suspend your disbelief a moment and detour with me out of our Celtic fringes to Denton Hall near Newcastle. Katharine Briggs, our great fairy pioneer, had a friend who as a child often visited the old ladies of the Hall in the 1890s. The ladies had, they told her, 'a silkie' (glossed by Briggs as 'the Northumbrian brownie'), which on the one hand 'made it rather difficult to keep servants' but, on the other, often helped with housework, 'cleaning grates and laying fires'. She 'dressed in grey silk, and they often met her . . . on the stairs'. During the Second World War the friend returned to the Hall to find that the new occupants, although they never saw the silkie, certainly heard her. For 'the son of the house was so persecuted by intolerable bangings in his room that they did not stay long.' In this second phase the silkie behaved like a classic poltergeist, with the youthful son evidently being the agent for the hammerings.

Leaving Denton Hall for a few moments, we can compare it to a house occupied, sometime before 1989, by Jenny and Peter Bolton. This childless couple were told by the departing residents of their new home that the place had '"brownies" at the bottom of the garden' who did 'little jobs for them'. Having moved in, the Boltons would return from work to find dishes washed, or clothes put through the washing machine and transferred to the tumble dryer. The garden shed was tidied and clothes hung up in the wardrobes. Presently Jenny lost her temper on finding a box of fruit moved under the sink. Poltergeist mischief followed. Taps ran themselves; jam was rubbed into a carpet. That night a storm of smashed windows and hurtling crockery brought in the police and sent the Boltons off to a hotel. Like all those fairy-haunted families of Ireland, the Boltons themselves soon moved house. Recounting this story, Colin Parsons added circa 1989 that the current tenants, though happy enough, reported 'odd nice things' such as windows being opened for them if the house grew stuffy.

Phenomena experienced by three different sets of occupants would seem to rule out either hoaxing or any possibility of the acts being committed by residents while in some sort of trance state. Intriguingly, this case implies a paranormal force which interacts variously with different people and different emotions. Readers may further be wondering if both of these examples do not sound like haunted houses rather than haunted people. The thought had occurred to me also, and this is probably a good point at which to consider the question of fairies and ghosts.

Fairies, Ghosts and Poltergeists

At least a handful of readers will have seen a ghost. Others will know someone who has, and a few more will know such a person without realizing it – because that person has been too embarrassed to talk about their experience. Personally, I spent most of my life not believing in ghosts, and not really listening to people who told me they had seen them. Once I stumbled on poltergeists, I spent some months trying to explain them away as purely human outbursts of repressed energy, pursuing an unhappy agent from room to room and house to house. It is possible that some cases are just this. The Tina Resch affair, for example, contains almost nothing obviously ghostly. But others feature apparitions of the dead and sometimes even voices.

If we leave aside poltergeists for a moment, we can already see one basic similarity between fairies and ghosts. Simply, both often look like ordinary people, yet are able to magically vanish on the spot. Almost two millennia ago the Roman encyclopaedist Pliny the Elder had described how, 'in the deserts of Afric, you shall meet oftentimes with fairies appearing in the shape of men and women: but they vanish quite away like phantastical delusions.'

In traditional fairyland, we find the elderly Cornishman John Wilmet admitting to Evans-Wentz: 'Whether or not piskies are the same as ghosts I cannot tell, but I fancy the old folks thought they were.' At Pentraeth in Anglesey Evans-Wentz heard from an old woman, Catherine Jones, of how, aged about 24, she had been walking home on the island one night, when there appeared just before me a very pretty young lady of ordinary size. I had no fear, and when I came up to her, put out my hand to touch her, but my hand and arm went right through her form. I could not understand this, and so tried to touch her repeatedly with the same result; there was no solid substance in the body, yet it remained beside me, and was as beautiful a young lady as I ever saw.

This apparition, which followed Jones to her destination before disappearing, she 'always put . . . down as one of the Tylwyth Teg'.

Most strikingly of all, 86-year-old Biddy Grant of Upper Toughal habitually saw fairies which she held to be 'the spirits of our dead friends' and stated: 'I once touched a boy of theirs, and he was just like feathers in my hand; there was no substance in him'. This intriguingly nuanced description, of just perceptible materiality, matches the claim of two girls, when touching a female apparition in 1845, that it felt like 'gauze or muslin'. Grant also noted that these beings were 'as big as we are'.

We can add that fairy forts, whether old burial mounds or long-abandoned settlements, would be likely places for ghosts to appear. Westropp tells of the ghost of a headless young man seen sitting on a fence near a little mound in the Mullet, County Mayo, where certain peasants were buried after being massacred by yeomanry in 1798. 'It glides from the fence to the mound, into which it vanishes'. Westropp also knew of two adjacent farmers' houses between Kilkee and Liscrona where both families 'began to "see things"', including 'a little old man sitting on a sod of turf' in the early 1890s. Although unsure himself whether these beings 'were ghosts or elves', Westropp knew that the families had both fled in terror: 'one [man] fitted up a cow-house as his dwelling-place, and the other actually built a new house'. The old homes were never reoccupied, and lay in ruins when Westropp told of them in 1910.

Before we now undertake to grapple with our poltergeists, any dog-owning readers may want to fetch their pet along. Dogs in particular have often reacted very strongly to ghosts or poltergeists. This is interesting for two reasons. One is that dogs also show awareness of real things otherwise imperceptible to humans, anticipating both epileptic fits and electrical storms by some hours. Two: dogs do not have ideas about ghosts, poltergeists or fairies, and so are unlikely to merely imagine them. In 1961 a man walking his dog in daylight near St Asaph in Denbighshire tapped his muddy walking stick several times on a metal roadsign. Suddenly, a little man three feet tall 'appeared beside it, almost as if the tapping had summoned him'. The figure had 'a very malevolent air . . . a very ugly brown face, and was dressed all in green. The dog also felt ill-at-ease, for he growled and raised his hackles. The little man suddenly disappeared after only a short while.'

If we now return to Denton Hall, we find a fairy-poltergeist which is at once bizarre and yet very difficult to easily write off as pure folklore. After all, if it was pure folklore, would not different residents describe roughly the *same* signs of its presence? They do not, because one set of occupants somehow appease it and others anger it. Moreover, Denton Hall clearly did have a ghost. Throughout the nineteenth century occupants and visitors reported the apparition of an elderly woman dressed in either satin or silk (so that 'silkie' here may have a slightly ambiguous origin). One young woman allegedly held an extended conversation with her; a servant one day fled when 'silkie' blocked her entry to a room; and around 1847 two guests, sisters of the actor William Charles Macready, came down for breakfast and demanded to be taken from the house immediately, too traumatized even to describe their ghostly experiences of the previous night. Most interestingly of all, in 1884, a very few years before Briggs's friend visited, 'silkie took a sudden freak to move the furniture'. Occupants heard sounds of it being dragged through rooms and downstairs, though later finding nothing disturbed. This habit of imitating noises – often very exact, sometimes colossally violent – is again classic poltergeist behaviour, and was reported by the actor Bob Monkhouse, who heard it at Moor Hall in Berkshire in May 1946.

As argued, the incidents in the Bolton house offer even stronger evidence of some objective presence, which took differing forms as it interacted with the varying temperaments of successive residents. As also suggested, both cases seem like haunted houses, not haunted people. Yet the people themselves do make a difference, and there is probably a good chance that certain occupants might notice nothing at all. Again, I quite understand if some readers find this very hard to swallow. I can only say that, if you take the subject seriously enough to read and talk about it, you will probably be surprised at what you find. We can add that, whatever it was, something forced both the Denton residents and the Boltons to flee their homes, just as so many 'superstitious' fairy believers had done in their turn. It is also worth considering how mild some fairy poltergeist habits are. If these involved merely moving things around occasionally without damage, would people in a multiple-occupancy house actually *notice*? If you ever have suspicions here, then do *ask* your fellow tenants . . .

In one sense at least, then, fairies were real. People gave the name 'fairies' (or 'brownies') to mysterious forces which did real and otherwise inexplicable things in their homes. You really could appease or anger these forces. This in itself is remarkable. These apparently irrational and superstitious people were in a number of cases telling the truth. Or, put it another way. With something as bizarre, as anti-rational, as mysterious as poltergeist activity, to call it the work of fairies is about as good an explanation as anything else, and actually *more* rational than simply pretending it never happens. We come now to someone whose remarkable powers were frequently linked to the fairies, but who in reality evidently had psychic abilities – ones which would in fact have made her famous in any age or culture.

Biddy Early

'Biddy Early beat all women. No one could touch her.' Although Biddy died in 1874, the aura of power and danger surrounding her survived not only into the early twentieth century (when a Clare man spoke those words to Lady Gregory), but into the 1970s, when locals were awed by the bravery of Meda Ryan, a woman who dared research this perilous figure for a 1978 biography. Biddy was certainly one of the most extraordinary working-class women ever to have lived in Ireland. Born around 1798 in Faha, County Clare, Biddy was left to fend for herself by the age of sixteen, with both her impoverished parents dead before 1815. For much of her adult life, when she was famed as a healer for miles around her Feakle cottage, Biddy was denounced from the pulpit by indignant priests, with one allegedly whipping visitors away as they tried to pass him for medical visits to her home. Yet when she died, 27 priests attended her funeral. One of them reportedly said: 'we thought we had a demon amongst us in poor Biddy Early, but we had a saint, and we did not know it.'

Like other fairy doctors, Biddy was evidently an accomplished herbalist. Similarly, it was often stated to Lady Gregory that Biddy's powers involved her meeting or talking to the fairies, having gone 'away with them' at one point for seven years. In local belief, her powers were closely linked to a mysterious blue bottle which she had acquired at some point. In reality, there is good reason to believe that Biddy was not so much a magical as a psychic healer, gifted with mysterious but genuine powers. If all of her cures involved only herbs, then she must have been the most accomplished uneducated herbalist who ever lived. One man who came to Biddy's cottage for his sick boy found around fifty people waiting ahead of him. These people may well have been superstitious. But, like so many others in magical cultures, they valued Biddy because she was useful. Moreover, Biddy almost always only took presents (of meat and whiskey) for her services, very rarely accepting money. And she was also well known for refusing even these presents in the many cases where, after initial consultation, she would insist that the problem was beyond her powers.

Clearly, then, Biddy was not a charlatan, and the 'thousands of cures' attributed to her by one of Gregory's informants sounds like a realistic estimate. Wealthy and educated people also drove long distances for cures, and it was rumoured that one of these was a member of the English royal family. Moreover, scores of tales survive which credit her with detailed knowledge of people and events occurring miles from her, as well as with knowledge of future events. In one she knew that visitors who arrived at her door by car had substituted a cheap bottle of whiskey for a better one, and demanded the latter accordingly. She 'converted' one hostile priest by telling him intimate details about his personal life, and another by paralysing him and his horse on a bridge until he begged a passer-by for Biddy to release him.

It seems likely that Biddy's status as a folk heroine, able to defeat rich and powerful men, caused some tales to be embroidered. Yet the stories about her clairvoyance are interesting precisely because they do *not* appear recurrently in fairy folklore. Clairvoyance, now often termed 'remote viewing', has been taken seriously by the CIA for some time, as Jonathan Margolis's recent book on Uri Geller shows. It seems to me that Biddy, like our fairy poltergeists, offers an example of extraordinary things which did actually happen.

In many ways the best parallel with her career is that of modern psychic healer Matthew Manning. Now in his early sixties, Manning was beset by poltergeist phenomena in his teens, and had some of the most extraordinary experiences of ghosts recorded in the last century. His decades of work as a psychic healer have seen him treat Brian Clough, Pope John Paul VI and Prince Philip, and his work with cancer patients has received the support of 'Professor Karol Sikora, medical director of Cancer Partners UK … and former head of the World Health Organisation's Cancer Programme'. Robert Chalmers, reporting on this and much else in a GQ article of May 2014, added that when Manning held his hands a foot away from him, Chalmers felt something like the heat of a two-kilowatt electric fire. The most straightforward explanation of Manning and Biddy is that – as with poltergeist agents – there is and was something remarkable about them biologically. Whatever spiritual implications such powerful bodies have, they certainly deserve thorough scientific investigation.

Danger: Fairy Animals

The final pages of this chapter take us into territory where the nature of 'what actually happened' is doubtful, or local interpretations somewhat fantastical. But these incidents certainly did not lack their share of fairy terror. If some fairy animals – such as that Manx lamb – had an aura of the uncanny about them, others were outrightly terrifying or monstrous. In that Manx fairy stronghold where fairies could be heard and smelled, a fairy bull (or water bull) terrorized one farm so badly that the farmer finally imported a ferocious Spanish bull to deter it. This too was easily worsted on one memorable bellowing night. Again, folkloric as this seems (it has a Scottish version too), Gill gives some curiously precise details, including not just the Spanish bull, but the claim that after this the farm was never tenanted again.

Flying north into far wilder regions, we find the lakes of the isles of Uist haunted with fairy monsters of mythic horror. On the north of this island near the saltwater Loch Evort there still stand today a chambered Neolithic cairn, the Barpa Langass, and one of the most complete druidical stone circles in Scotland, Sòrnach Coir' Fhinn, associated with Fingal's kettle, cauldron and fireplace. Given what we have learned of the power of fairy hills and other unusual formations, it is no surprise to find that the hill of Langash was 'held in a kind of superstitious awe' beyond anywhere else in Scotland.

It was here, early one autumn morning in 1856, that Donald Ferguson rowed out to a small lake where he had left a trout net the night before. Hearing a splash, he peered over at what seemed at first to be a seal, around forty yards across the water. But, as it now reared up, there 'appeared the head and neck of a horse of prodigious size, without mane or any hair whatever, but a slimy black skin like that of a porpoise'. Fixing 'glaring eyes on the boat, [it] made a tremendous rush towards it' before sinking again below the surface. Frantically rowing for the shore, Ferguson saw, a few seconds later, just off his stern, the gigantic 'figure of a man, standing up to the navel in the water, staring him full in the face. His head was quite naked, and his skin was of the same description as that of the former horrible shape.' Finally gaining the shore after one more vanishing and reappearance of the monster, Ferguson flung himself down, vomiting copiously in shock. Having staggered home, he took to his bed for the next five days.

Not unlike Ferguson (a tall, strong Highlander toppled into a minor nervous breakdown), we here find ourselves stranded between the fathomless waters of myth and the mundane crackle of the pages of *The Times* – in which, that November, numerous genteel readers beheld this story in drawing rooms from Aberdeen to Bath. Certainly the Highlands and much of Scotland were, at this time, darkly peopled with such aqueous and protean monsters. E. C. Watson tells of the *uraisg*, a creature frequenting 'glens, corries, reedy lakes, and streams' that was 'half man, half goat, with abnormally long hair, teeth and claws'.

Our final words are reserved for a case no less memorable. On Lewis, northeast of Uist, Kate MacCaskill of Holm village was brought up before the Stornoway magistrate in summer 1899, charged with a breach of the peace. Her alleged victim, Mrs Mackay, explained in Gaelic that MacCaskill had threatened her with a fairy dog's tooth. Although not actually in possession of this formidable dental agent, MacCaskill remarked that, if she did have it, she would use it 'to cause witness's immediate destruction', and would also 'have put it down witness's chimney', in order to set the Mackay house on fire. For all the hilarity which this provoked in court, the tooth was clearly a very real and potent entity to certain of the islanders. A local crofter, Alexander Stewart, told the magistrate that he had seen it thirty years since. It was 'larger than a man's tooth, one end . . . red, and commencing to decay. It went by the name of "Fairy

Dog's Tooth". A Mrs Stewart, meanwhile, had seen and used it 34 years back. It was then in the possession of an 'old wife', who charged Stewart a shilling to borrow it. The tooth was carried from Melbost to Bayble to cure sick cattle, which were made to drink water in which it had been dipped. It was also believed able to heal people, and generally 'supposed to work cures better and cheaper than a doctor'. Still further back than this, the uncanny fang gleamed from the shadows of family history, for late one night, when Mackay's great-grandfather was coming home from Stornoway, 'something met him and gave him this tooth.'

Given how precisely territorial Lewis could still be when a friend of mine grew up there in the 1980s, it is no surprise to learn that much of the antipathy between MacCaskill and Mackay derived from the latter's outsider status – she having only 'migrated to Holm from the other side of the island some thirteen years ago'. Like so many magical agents, and like the fairies themselves, the fairy dog's tooth was neither purely good nor bad, but, more basically, powerful. Impressively, fairy power here threw its greater and denser shadow onto this one humble relic: something comically insignificant to the educated, yet reattached with imaginative awe by those four speakers to the animal which once bit with it, and the dark spirits which owned that fairy dog. In the relatively brief and spare report of this case, perhaps nothing sounds with so eerie a knell as that one opaque phrase associated with Mackay's great-grandfather: 'something met him' . . .

We now emerge – perhaps with some relief – from the rougher, wilder crags and vales of the real fairies, prising off mudcaked boots and pulling on slippers, brogues or court shoes to tread softly through our fairy library, and the muted polish of Victorian galleries and drawing rooms. We should not, though, too easily imagine that beyond those real and fearful beliefs, all ahead will be airily unreal. At its best, fairy literature, art and drama remake the fairies into new realities, writing or painting their way with exploratory force into the depths of the human psyche. Chapter Four takes us from the classics section of our fairy reading rooms, on through the Middle Ages and early modern period, and into the nineteenth century. Chapter Five deals largely with the twentieth – dipping back briefly to consider the links between fairies, femininity and childhood across the past two hundred years.

Four
Literature and Art

STAND A MOMENT, IN the surf. We are about to climb the beach to the oldest surviving fairy cave in the world. Before we do, we might want to relish this space upon the shoreline. Greek blues. A sky the colour of babies' dreams; a sunlight open, wide with three thousand years of untrodden possibilities. Nestled in pine sap, ideas sleep, waiting for later heat to breathe them free. This world is cleaner, younger; a world where gods and men touch hands. Here is Hermes, now, striding up the beach.

> up from the deep-blue sea he climbed to dry land
> and strode on till he reached the spacious cave
> where the nymph with lovely braids had made her home
> . . .
> A great fire
> blazed on the hearth and the smell of cedar
> cleanly split and sweetwood burning bright
> wafted a cloud of fragrance down the island.
> Deep inside she sang, the goddess Calypso, lifting
> her breathtaking voice as she glided back and forth
> before her loom, her golden shuttle weaving.
> Thick, luxuriant woods grew round the cave,
> alders and black poplars, pungent cypress too,
> and there birds roosted, folding their long wings,
> owls and hawks and the spread-beaked ravens of the sea,
> black skimmers who make their living off the waves.
> And round the mouth of the cavern trailed a vine

laden with clusters, bursting with ripe grapes.
Four springs in a row, bubbling clear and cold,
running side-by-side, took channels left and right.
Soft meadows spreading round were starred with violets,
lush with beds of parsley. Why, even a deathless god
who came upon that place would gaze in wonder,
heart entranced with pleasure.

In a perfect world, we would do nothing but gaze and breathe
and listen, spellbound as Hermes himself by Robert Fagles's mar-
vellous translation of the *Odyssey*. But, like Hermes, we must attack
this space with words, breaking and labelling it. What to say, then,
of this primal scene of fairy magic and captivity? The place where
Odysseus has been held prisoner is intensely feminine: song weaves
through the cloth; smoke drifts back into the woods that it was
split from. Life is sheltered here. Feathered warmth broods on eggs.
Juice swells grapeskins. Flowers, herbs, colour, scent and taste coil
through our nerves in heady synaesthesia. If this is a Greek Eden,
then it is one without the restless impulse that drives Adam and
Eve out into the shameful world of knowledge and toil.

Or rather, Calypso lacks that impulse. Odysseus, of course,
suffers a version of it. Troubled in this paradise, he sits at its margin.
It is here that Calypso finds him, when Hermes has persuaded her
to send him home:

... there on the headland, sitting, still,
weeping, his eyes never dry, his sweet life flowing away
with the tears he wept for his foiled journey home,
since the nymph no longer pleased. In the nights, true,
he'd sleep with her in the arching cave – he had no choice –
unwilling lover alongside lover all too willing ...
But all his days he'd sit on the rocks and beaches,
wrenching his heart with sobs and groans and anguish,
gazing out over the barren sea through blinding tears.

Buried in these lines is an older way of looking at the world – indeed, of being in it. Fagles's phrase 'sweet life', for example, translates the distinctive Greek word *aion*. For Homer, *aion* was a material, liquid form of life, saturating the flesh and linked especially with human seed and the cerebrospinal fluid. Odysseus' ebbing life, then, is not purely metaphorical. In Homer's world, what we now think of as metaphor did not have that modern sense of being faintly unnecessary, fanciful, unscientific. Feelings were always feelings of the body, and the tremor and flux of them through heart, lungs, brain and weeping eyes were a primal knowledge that fused together the concrete and the abstract, spiritual and physical. Here people had not forgotten that Ceres, Greek goddess of fertility, had left her mark not only on cereals, but on 'cerebral', too. The brain, ripe with earthy life, clasped a wisdom that was no less fecund: sap and sapient were one. Knowledge was organic, not mechanistic.

Perhaps, too, the feminine and masculine had not suffered the schism and the hierarchy which they would do under centuries of Christian misogyny. Odysseus, the great hero, warrior, adventurer, weeps openly. And even his impulse to voyage away from Calypso's sensuous abundance is in itself generated by another woman, his long-missed wife, Penelope.

Here at the edge of literature, at the threshold of history, is a world of fairy magic seemingly very different from the bruised skies and twilit underworlds of the Celtic fringe. But they have certain things in common. In both regions magic and wonder are potent forces. And in both there is a reverence for things beyond human control. As we now begin a journey which will take us into the rationalizing, industrializing, ultimately scientific and clinical realms of the Victorians, the Space Age and the World Wide Web, we might ask: where did magic go? At a glance we might see it, like the shyly nervous fairies, skittering away from the pounding rush of steam trains, poisoned by the caking filth of mines and chimneys, corroded by the acids of secular reason. Superstition was to be banished, sterilized by the forces of Enlightenment and progress – now only the stuff of poetry, childish whimsy or dubiously thrilling novels.

But it is not quite as simple, as linear as all that. We are all of us born into magic. Magic and wonder are, for over two precious years, the air we breathe and the food which makes us. In the womb the music of two bodies sings to us before we have even dreamed of language. Knowledge is pure sensation, untainted by words or concepts. Even once language moves in, slowly dividing us from ourselves and from reality, the world retains the magic of novelty. Watch an adult trying to move a small child through a park. The boy or girl is tangled up in nature, continually arrested by the everyday wonder of a leaf, a flower. Science itself tells us that a child's sense of time is vastly different from an adult's, and that their colour vision is far more intense. Where did magic go? It is right here, still, inside us. True, for adults it does not have the timeless brilliance known to a four-year-old on a summer's day, watching a ladybird on a grass-stalk, or a dragonfly twitching light along its wings.

But if it has gone to ground in us, it is still far from extinct. The hardest, driest columns of publishing profit and sales figures tell us as much. Harry Potter; Philip Pullman; behind these the durable appeal of *Alice's Adventures in Wonderland*, Narnia, and the elf-haunted world of the twentieth century's favourite book, *The Lord of the Rings*. Is there also a buried link between literature in general, and the early wonder of childhood? Why – to put it bluntly – does literature survive? What does it have that cinema, the Internet and computer games do not? Why, when a towering tsunami of post-war technology seems poised to smash the fragile word out of existence, will thousands of people queue up, before midnight, to buy a book in the first hour of its release? Let us whisper the answer, in hope that this secret will fly beneath the radar of government agencies, accountants and spin doctors. When you read a book, someone is *speaking to you inside your head*. Nothing else can do this. But once, someone did, at a just slightly greater distance, night after night.

We all grew up with stories. These stories were spoken to us. Those voices, those transporting words, which, like true magic, can take you somewhere else, are always with us. We are made of stories, given to us in the intimacy of human speech.

Certain kinds of literature also have the power not merely to recall to us this voice, but to build fleeting bridges between the world of the adult and the child. Shakespeare was brilliantly adept at shooting us right inside the skin of another person. Keats wanted poetry to tease us out of thought, back into wonder. Proust devoted his life to a book which, from one angle, simply said: what you were then, though entirely forgotten by your adult self, was *real*. They were just as real, just as important as you are now. Or, to quote the iconic storyteller of Neverland: 'On these magic shores children at play are forever beaching their coracles. We too have been there; we can still hear the sound of the surf, though we shall land no more.'

Like those precious springs on Calypso's island, the waters of magic and wonder at times run underground. They always burst free again. But in certain eras the hard weight of adult reality is the more dominant force. We might, then, imagine a kind of war between childlike wonder and adult reason, fought out on various literary battlefields across the centuries. Yet we must also grasp a more subtle and curious negotiation between these two poles. Children, we know, can wonder and marvel at stories. And that kind of early response, once lost, can never be fully recovered. Yet these very stories are themselves chosen by adults, and written by them. In producing these tales, what selections, what fantasies, misrememberings or pressures of loss and disappointment are involved? Even in reading them aloud, in drinking up the rapt absorption of the fairy-minded child, adults are often gaining a certain special pleasure, attempting somehow to *be* children themselves. To put this, again, a little bluntly: how far do adults exploit children as carriers of that precious, fragile, ever threatened commodity, wonder? This question will return with force in the context of the Victorians (sometimes credited with the invention of the child), and in the years of *Peter Pan* and *The Wind in the Willows*. Let us now move on, then, through the kaleidoscopic reinventions of fairyland, as it is forced through the prisms of literature and art.

Medieval Fairies

In the Anglo-Saxon and medieval periods, literature often had a kind of mythic force which – as with Homer – makes it difficult to cleanly split literary fictions from historical fact. Nowhere is this truer than in the case of King Arthur. Did he really exist? While scholars will probably never settle this question, we might well say that, if he had not, the British would have felt compelled to invent him. Enter this potent Celtic otherworld from almost any angle, and you have a good chance of meeting either fairies or someone very closely allied with them. Their demonic side glimmers darkly around Merlin, our archetypal British magus, through the legend that he was conceived on a sleeping nun by a horned devil. Most centrally of all, Morgan le Fay encodes in her very name a double sense of fairy magic. Not only does 'fay' mean 'fairy', but – as Stephen Knight reminds us – this ambiguous consort of Arthur was a shape-shifter who could fly, while among various possible origins of her first name, a strong candidate is the Irish water spirit, 'Muirgein'.

Avalon, the Isle of Apples where Morgan cares for the wounded Arthur, might well be seen as the prototype of later fairy islands. For, while Arthur's grave was supposedly discovered at Glastonbury in 1191 (this site having allegedly been once marsh-bound and filled with apple trees), the legend presently grew up that he was not dead, but had been taken by the fairies to Annwn, the Welsh otherworld, and would ultimately return. Annwn itself, a kind of pagan under-world Paradise, was clearly very different from the full-blown dualism of Christian afterlife. In this, it already resembles those popular figurings of fairyland as the sole form of afterlife for certain

Irish Christians. And, if the glamorous yet twilit courts visited by that truant schoolboy Elidyr had something of Hades about them, we seem to find a similar atmosphere in the fourteenth-century *Mabinogion*, where Annwn's courtiers wear robes of shining gold and brocaded silk. It was in this mythic Welsh collection that we met our fairy hunt, and it was here, later, that Prince Pwyll encountered the mysterious Rhiannon, a fairy woman speeding away on an impossibly swift white horse. Just as the human Pwyll can cross from the ordinary world into Annwn and back again, one early Welsh poem has Arthur and his warriors making a military raid on this ambiguous Land of the Dead. We find much of this darkly pagan world captured in the figure of Taliesin, the sixth-century bard who wrote about Merlin. Legend had it that a shepherd boy named Einon had descended into fairyland by a flight of steps, under a standing stone near Pentre Ifan; he had subsequently married a fairy called Olwen, and their offspring was Taliesin.

Around the end of the nineteenth century there would arise the theory that the fairies were, in a sense, real people. A separate, defeated race – smaller, more primitive, and keeping largely out of sight beneath 'fairy forts' – these marginalized Britons were in some versions Celtic and in others specifically the Druids, after their suppression by the Romans in the first century AD. Purely mythic as all this may now sound to us, the idea had credibility after it was first suggested by the folklorist David MacRitchie in 1890.

The Anglo-Saxon poem *Beowulf*, composed between the eighth and tenth centuries, falls in between Arthur and the later records of him (deriving largely from the twelfth century). The genealogy of the monster Grendel stretches back to the outcast Cain, held somehow responsible for all the 'ogres and elves and evil shades' of later times. Here we find a curious rival branch of that better-known heresy which traced fairies back directly to the fallen angels.

Reaching Chaucer – whose *Canterbury Tales* were probably written between 1388 and 1400 – we find fairies, elves, fauns and dryads all mentioned in passing. While fairy types are far from integral to any of these tales, elves in particular can certainly be sinister, if not quite demonic. In *The Miller's Tale* the sign of the cross is made against elves and evil men, and in *The Man of Law's Tale* a Turkish attempt to libel Constance, the Roman emperor's daughter, involves the claim that she was an elf and had given birth to a monstrous child as a result. Perhaps most interesting, though, is the Wife of Bath. Opening her tale with the claim that 'In th'olde dayes of the Kyng Arthour,/ ... Al was this land fulfild of fayerye', she presently explains that the vigorous piety of Catholic friars has banished fairies from her own time: 'This maketh that ther ben no fayeryes.' This passage has often been cited as a very early example of a recurrent fairy oddity: the tendency for each age to claim that there were many more fairies in the past, sometimes one or two generations back, sometimes centuries before. Nominally, Chaucer's example seems broadly founded on the opposition between lingering paganism and established Christianity. Yet, given how many times the claim has recurred, in such varying contexts, it is hard not to suspect a more basic origin for the belief. Was it, in fact, founded not on historic change, but on the subconscious memory of childhood wonder, openness and magic? The imagined fairy past was in reality not behind, but within us.

Shakespeare

Let us imagine something strange. Imagine a play in which a queen has sex with a monster, a man with the head of an ass. Imagine this, too, in a world where the real queen, Elizabeth, could order a man's right hand chopped off at Westminster for the offence of writing a pamphlet about her rumoured marriage plans. In one sense, then, *A Midsummer Night's Dream* is a very early example of one of the long-running uses of the supernatural in literature. Simply: once you inject the heady drug of fairyland, ghosts, demons or vampirism into your story, you can get away with things that you would – as it were – never dream of in a work of cold realism. Two girls can have breathy sapphic relations in 1872, and an upright Victorian man can enjoy a steamy *ménage à quatre* with three female vampires in 1897 (*Carmilla* and *Dracula*, for anyone still wondering and keen to purchase these lurid gems for scholarly research).

Some might respond that well, *A Midsummer Night's Dream* is 'just a play'. One answer to this is that playwrights and writers in general in Shakespeare's time got into a surprising deal of trouble for certain works: burning of books being a minor punishment, and prison a greater one. Puck's seemingly whimsical closure of the play, then ('If we shadows have offended,/ Think but this, and all is mended,/ That you have but slumbered here . . .') may be a little more significant and pragmatic than it first appears. Beyond these sociopolitical factors, we must also remind ourselves that we tend to look back at the play through a particoloured mist, formed of the spectacularly magical stagings of the last two centuries and the ravishing oils of Victorian painters.

So, let us suppose that alien beings, landed here by mistake, are about to flee in terror from the world we have created. Before they go, they have me by the scruff of the neck, desperate to know the truth about this play whose evergreen quotations have beamed on radio waves across the galaxy these past four hundred years: 'The course of true love never did run smooth'; 'So quick bright things come to confusion' . . . What can I tell them? They are clearly never coming back, and they deserve to leave with something good. I would tell them this. It is about fertility.

Peering down at the wildflower tangle of the play, certain more obvious blossoms strike us at once. It is shot through with jewel-like fragments of a natural world, minutely observed through elfin eyes:

And I serve the fairy queen,
To dew her orbs upon the green.
The cowslips tall her pensioners be:
In their gold coats spots you see;
Those be rubies, fairy favours,

In those freckles live their savours:
I must go seek some dewdrops here
And hang a pearl in every cowslip's ear.

So the play's first fairy tells the audience when he and Puck appear at the start of Act II, Scene i, perhaps slyly echoing off Lysander's earlier reference to the night when the moon will behold 'Her silver visage in the watery glass,/ Decking with liquid pearl the bladed grass'. Glanced at again when Puck, moments later, tells of how the warring Oberon and Titania on every meeting 'do square, that all their elves for fear/ Creep into acorn-cups and hide them there', this minutely delicate fairy world reaches its most artful distillation as Titania commands fairy service for her beloved Bottom:

Be kind and courteous to this gentleman;
Hop in his walks and gambol in his eyes;
Feed him with apricocks and dewberries,
With purple grapes, green figs, and mulberries;
The honey-bags steal from the humble-bees,
And for night-tapers crop their waxen thighs
And light them at the fiery glow-worm's eyes,
To have my love to bed and to arise;
And pluck the wings from painted butterflies
To fan the moonbeams from his sleeping eyes:
Nod to him, elves, and do him courtesies.

How did a writer manage to dream of this lyrically miniatur-ized nature, decades before the invention of efficient microscopes? Perhaps, indeed, by recalling the sharply detailed world of his own Arden childhood, or the more recent interests of his children, Susanna and the twins Hamnet and Judith, born in 1583 and 1585 respectively. At any rate, here we have fairies embedded in an intri-cate ecology, attentive to natural details in the way they still would be in 1849, in the poetry of William Allingham.

We also find, conversely, that the quarrel of Titania and Oberon is responsible for the temporary destruction of fertility:

> Therefore the winds, piping to us in vain,
> As in revenge, have suck'd up from the sea
> Contagious fogs; which falling in the land
> Have every pelting river made so proud
> That they have overborne their continents:
> The ox hath therefore stretch'd his yoke in vain,
> The ploughman lost his sweat, and the green corn
> Hath rotted ere his youth attain'd a beard;
> The fold stands empty in the drowned field,
> And crows are fatted with the murrion flock.

These and Titania's following lines remind us of the long-running scapegoating of fairies for natural disaster, including the Irish Famine. While Shakespeare may well have picked up such beliefs in his Stratford childhood, Annabel Patterson has also persuasively argued that the name 'Starveling' alludes to the bad weather and bad harvests suffered across 1595–6, citing summer riots in the former year in and around London. One of these involved a thousand people, and resulted in five executions on 24 July. Perhaps the darkest aspect of *Dream's* fairyworld, then, refers to the very real deprivation suffered by those for whom fertility was, in every sense, primal.

No less memorable than those fairy miniatures of dew, acorn cups and butterfly wings are two extraordinary speeches of Titania and Oberon. The former, defying her husband's egotistical demands for the Indian changeling, explains:

> His mother was a votaress of my order:
> And, in the spiced Indian air, by night,
> Full often hath she gossip'd by my side,
> And sat with me on Neptune's yellow sands,
> Marking the embarked traders on the flood,

When we have laugh'd to see the sails conceive
And grow big-bellied with the wanton wind;
Which she, with pretty and with swimming gait
Following – her womb then rich with my young squire –
Would imitate, and sail upon the land . . .

Gawping up at the players of the theatre in 1596, the most hardened and wearied apprentice might briefly drown in honey as this fluidly exoticized maternal world showered over him. The fabulous unreality of India, the melting cadences, the mysterious potency of the female body . . . Even the seemingly mundane 'gossip' of the two women signals what was then the tightly closed feminine circle of childbirth, overseen by female midwives and attended by the 'gossips' or 'god-sibs' of the expecting mother.

Yet, if this is one of the most impressive examples of Shakespeare burrowing into the skin of another, Oberon's following speech also nudges us into a further, more darkly buried level of fertility, closer to the roots of our tangled thicket. First vowing revenge on his defiant wife, Oberon then recalls to Puck how

Since once I sat upon a promontory,
And heard a mermaid on a dolphin's back
Uttering such dulcet and harmonious breath
That the rude sea grew civil at her song
And certain stars shot madly from their spheres,
To hear the sea-maid's music.

In this spellbound night, only Oberon saw

Flying between the cold moon and the earth,
Cupid all arm'd: a certain aim he took
At a fair vestal throned by the west,
And loosed his love-shaft smartly from his bow,
As it should pierce a hundred thousand hearts;

But I might see young Cupid's fiery shaft
Quench'd in the chaste beams of the watery moon,
And the imperial votaress passed on,
In maiden meditation, fancy-free.
Yet mark'd I where the bolt of Cupid fell:
It fell upon a little western flower,
Before milk-white, now purple with love's wound,
And maidens call it love-in-idleness.

Here, things get interesting. For this juice is, first, the catalytic sap of all the play's fertile chaos, the agent which makes Titania madly dote on Bottom, and triggers the abrupt comic reversals of the lovers' warring quartet. And look, secondly, at its exact origin. It arises from a defiance of chastity. (Daringly enough, the 'fair vestal' was almost certainly Queen Elizabeth herself.) Though Cupid's shaft is 'quench'd in the chaste beams of the watery moon', Oberon traces its ultimate descent, and with typical fairy attention to nature, ensures that *it is not wasted*. If we now link this to the threatened chastity of Hermia at the play's opening – obliged either to forsake her beloved Lysander or

be in shady cloister mew'd,
To live a barren sister all your life,
Chanting faint hymns to the cold fruitless moon

– we can begin to see how a covert war between sterility and fertility runs like a faultline through the entire play.

To appreciate this fully we need to bear in mind that Shakespeare's age also experienced a war over the validity and morality of theatre itself. Theatre and theatres (the first built only in 1576) were new and threatening. To most Puritans, indeed, theatre was a lie. Shakespeare most clearly attacks this position in *Measure for Measure*. But in a sense he was always at war with this naive Puritan literalism. If reality genuinely was a fixed, absolute, single and unchangeable thing, then drama was impossible. The greatest drama sends people in raging debate out of the theatre or cinema, defying the easy categories of good and evil, clear cause and effect. It is, indeed, a fertile chaos. In *Dream*, one role of the rude mechanicals is to obliquely mock Puritan literalism, via a theatre which insists on telling everyone clearly that 'this is not a real lion' and so forth.

Yet, if their failed theatre nicely satirizes such intellectual failings, the most powerful enemies of Puritan stasis and absolutism are Puck, the fairies and the lovers. Great drama is about conflict and about change. It is about the fertile chaos of these forces, let loose with impish mischief by someone who is continually saying: 'now, what if we tried *this?*', or 'what if the world, for a few hours, looked like *this?*' Here in 1596, the Shakespeare who would later be paired with the arch-magician Prospero is already paired with the riotously magical Puck, the amoral fairy id of the play: 'And those things do best please me/ That befall preposterously.'

The final defiance of Puritan myopia, however, comes not from the fairies or their exploits, but from Hippolyta:

> 'Tis strange my Theseus, that these
> lovers speak of.

Theseus, the voice of cool male reason, responds:

> More strange than true: I never may believe
> These antique fables, nor these fairy toys.
> Lovers and madmen have such seething brains,
> Such shaping fantasies, that apprehend
> More than cool reason ever comprehends.
> The lunatic, the lover and the poet
> Are of imagination all compact,

going on to dismiss their illusory visions as merely subjective and insubstantial things.

Yet Hippolyta, far more pithy and assured in her brevity, has the last word:

> But all the story of the night told over,
> And all their minds transfigured so together,
> More witnesseth than fancy's images
> And grows to something of great constancy;
> But, howsoever, strange and admirable.

What does this say? It says, at one level, that human feelings are real. And it also says, more indirectly, that poetry and drama are real. Literature, it defiantly whispers, is more real than reality. It dreams of the future with prescient clarity. It dreams of alternate universes. It will live, long after the powers of the city of London, their buildings and jewels, have been purged by fire. Shakespeare dared to dream of this four hundred years ago. Four hundred years later, it is inarguably true. And this graceful defiance is voiced by a woman, herself originally part of the wholly matriarchal society of the Amazons. If ever fairies and the feminine united in power, rather than prettiness, they did so here.

The Seventeenth Century

Like the bright vanishing which caught my eye that hot October day, fairies across these decades shoot from shade to light and back again, drinking with chameleon skill the various colours of the age or an author's temperament. In brighter times they are woven into myths of British national origins or unity; in darker ones, used to lead writer and readers into escapist pastorals.

Shakespeare's Warwickshire peer Michael Drayton roots them firmly in the medieval soils of Britain's mythic past in his ambitious national epic, *Poly-Olbion* (1612). Meaning both 'Many Blessings' and 'Multiple Albion', *Poly-Olbion* fantasized about a united island under the Scottish James I. Retelling how 'Merlin by his skill, and magique's wondrous might', brought Stonehenge over from Ireland in a single night, Drayton goes on to explain how the magician's plan to wall the monument around with brass was thwarted by his fairy lover, who first trapped his metal-workers underground by blocking up their cave mouth, before leading Merlin 'captive . . . unto the Fairie Land'. Picturing these noisy 'labouring spirits' as seeking to wake Merlin ('suppos'd by them to sleep'), Drayton might on another level be reminding his readers of the magic fairy powers rumbling beneath the very soil of the imagined nation.

Far from this Vulcan cacophony and its associated feats of strength, Drayton could also lean down in hushed wonder over fairy miniatures rivalling Shakespeare's. In his 1627 *Nimphidia* we behold a fairy palace magically suspended in air, whose 'walls of spiders' legs are made', its 'windows of the eyes of cats' and roof 'cover'd with the skins of bats'. Meanwhile, Queen Mab's chariot, made 'of a snail's fine shell', has 'four nimble gnats' for horses, and 'wheels compos'd of crickets' bones', wrapped in thistledown lest these should rattle their mistress all over the stones. Behind the surface whimsy, these lines offer us one more version of the distinctive power of literature. For even the most intricate Victorian painter, surely, could not translate this to the level of pure image: how would we ever recognize, for example, the spiders' legs or the thistledown?

Around the same time the poet William Browne echoed this nationalizing impulse, peopling his 1613 *Britannia's Pastorals* with rose-cheeked nymphs, piping shepherds, wild goats and deer. Yet, even as early as 1616, the second book of this project had grown – notes Michelle O'Callaghan – far more darkly satirical. Whether or not Browne yet dreamt of the Civil War chaos to be unleashed by James's son, Charles I, there was no hiding from it by the time that the Cavalier fairy poet Robert Herrick published his *Hesperides* in 1648. Or – was there? With the possible exception of the 'times trans-shifting', there is no whiff of blood or powder in the famous opening chords of this work:

I sing of brooks, of blossoms, birds, and bowers:
Of April, May, of June, and July-flowers.
I sing of may-poles, hock-carts, wassails, wakes,
Of bride-grooms, brides, and of their bridal-cakes.
. . .
I sing of times trans-shifting; and I write
How roses first came red, and lillies white.
I write of groves, of twilights, and I sing
The court of Mab, and of the fairie-king.

In following lines Oberon – as Diane Purkiss has noted – is revealed as Catholic, possessed of a 'Temple of Idolatry' where holy water is cradled in half a nutshell. Around this time, that uniquely elusive poet of English nature, Andrew Marvell, offered among other things the plaintive tones of a nymph speaking her own poem:

The wanton troopers riding by
Have shot my fawn, and it will die.

Smoothly defying any easy critical paraphrase, 'The Nymph Complaining for the Death of her Fawn' has the nervous shyness of the nymph herself. In it grief, death, solitude and unrequited love are varnished into a glassy beauty which – perhaps thanks to the authentically childlike tones of the nymphal voice – never quite ossifies or cloys.

Kensington Gardens

Come the eighteenth century Britain was busy trying to forget and indeed deny the traumas of Civil War, with these aims gradually hardening into a conservative injustice from which it has still not recovered over two centuries later. What place for the fairies here? In 1728 the government official and dilettante author Thomas Tickell found one – namely, Kensington Gardens – which would later be revisited by the more inspired hand of J. M. Barrie. While Tickell's poem has largely been shrunk down to a kind of fairy footnote to *Peter Pan*, it has its own distinctive qualities. Long after Browne and Drayton it attempts another curious myth of national origins.

Beginning with the fashionable promenading ground of its own time, *Kensington Gardens* quickly zooms back to the spot's 'ancient days', when 'its peopled ground/ With fairy domes and dazzling towers was crown'd'. Albion, Tickell reminds his readers, was a mythic British ruler born from yet one more coupling between Neptune and a mortal woman, Cleito. During Albion's rule the fairies – then seemingly more numerous, though already secluded in valleys or caves – stole one of his infant children. Also called Albion, this changeling was somehow kept down to fairy size. Grown to beautiful miniature adulthood, Albion falls for a fairy girl, Kenna, and through this star-crossed match catalyses open war with Oberon. During this epic conflict Neptune rushes in to Albion's aid, jamming his trident into the fairy city. In an apocalyptic moment, he hurls the whole uprooted metropolis into the fray:

> Aghast the legions, in th'approaching shade,
> Th'inverted spires and rocking domes survey'd,
> That, downward tumbling on the host below,
> Crush'd the whole nation at one dreadful blow.

Lying breathless and dazed beneath this titanic missile, the fairies and Oberon presently recover sufficiently to flee away. Surviving but vanquished, they seem more or less literally to be 'driven underground' – perhaps, indeed, to become that 'separate race' which late nineteenth-century thinkers would argue them to embody. Kenna, meanwhile, is unable to save the mortally wounded Albion, but with a Circean herb transforms him into a flower, ever after known as the snowdrop. She also now plants a kind of memorial garden in Kensington, leaving the place to fashionable society until it is later enlivened by Peter's impish irreverence.

What readers of *Peter Pan* would never guess is that Tickell imagines the eighteenth-century gardens' neat yew walks and topiared symmetries as the deliberate natural imitations of the lost fairy city. Bizarrely, his *Kensington Gardens* is a kind of inverted story of Eden: rather than humanity forced from the garden, fairies are forced from their metropolis. What does this say about the Enlightenment's attitude to ordered nature? And what about Tickell's own lingering sense of the traumas of civil war, as recalled by his parents and grandparents? Are we here offered a classicized version of the fairies as fallen angels? While we can now only guess at the answers, it is beguiling to think of all this richly mythic turbulence condensed into one pale flower, so easily crushed beneath Peter's scampering feet.

Romantic Fairies

Poised, now, on the threshold of the nineteenth century, we must be prepared to move with force and decision through the fairy riots that crowd us in from all sides – lest, exhausted with the onslaught of gorgeous sound, colour and spectacle, we fall benighted in some elfin glade, never reaching the Edwardian era at all. Once again, the fairies' greatest literary successes of this age occurred in poetry. Easy as it would be to see fairy worlds opening yet one more secret doorway of escape from the noise, poverty and pollution of the industrial age, the most potent kinds of fairy poetry produce something beyond mere escapism. For the Romantics, the fairies offered not some diaphanous retreat, but new forms of psychic power.

Faced with the grinding utilitarianism of industry, the pigheaded righteousness of Empire building, and the passionate love of misery that fired the hearts of British Protestants, the Romantics had one irresistibly defiant answer. Come with us, inside. If literature, at its best, is more real than reality, then the poetry of the Romantics wrote the map of a new reality with exploratory fearlessness greater than any Raleigh or Livingstone. Although fairies were only one region of this brave inner world, at best their capricious

energies fused with those of Blake, Coleridge, Shelley and Keats
to surge, crackle and smoulder through this expansive new inscape.

On the very cusp of this revolution, its most radical pioneer
was of course William Blake. Just dipping into his extraordinary
alternative cosmos, aided by the scholar John Adlard, we find Blake
stating that 'Shakespeare's fairies . . . are the rulers of the vegetable
world', opposing the fairies to the materialistic 'tyranny of experi-
mental science', and tellingly having his mythical city of Golgonooza
guarded not by angels, but by gnomes, nymphs and fairies. Perhaps
most memorably of all, we hear Blake asking a lady, 'Did you ever
see a fairy's funeral, madam?' and going on to describe the one he
had witnessed the previous night, featuring creatures 'the size and
colour of grey and green grasshoppers, bearing a body laid out on
a rose leaf'.

If Blake's fairies are often winged and miniature, they lack neither
energy nor power. A little later Wordsworth hints at the new spaces
which this fairy poetry would break open across the following decade.
His 1807 poem 'Though narrow be that old Man's cares' opposes the
seeming constriction of aged, uneducated poverty to a 'waking
empire, wide as dreams':

Rich are his walks with supernatural cheer;
The region of his inner spirit teems
With vital sounds and monitory gleams
Of high astonishment and pleasing fear.

. . .

For overhead are sweeping Gabriel's Hounds,
Doomed, with their impious Lord, the flying Hart
To chase for ever, on aerial grounds!

Did it matter that perhaps this old man mistook the distant sound
of geese for the yelping of the legendary fairy hunt above? Did
it matter that the well-fed and Cambridge-educated poet was
using his aged protagonist as a vehicle of a supernatural wonder

which he himself lacked? In some senses, no. As we have seen, the most powerful educated Christians could do nothing to talk their social inferiors out of their stubborn fairy heresies. And so here, as elsewhere, the fairies do indeed offer a certain freedom.

Ten years before Wordsworth wrote this poem, the fairies had already led Coleridge, his friend and sometime collaborator, into a much stranger and darker world. Or, some would argue, the fairies had allowed Coleridge a chance to explore some of the stranger and more troubling spaces of his inner self. His long unfinished poem *Christabel* has, as Jonas Spatz points out, been used by critics to argue for just about every psychosexual complex with which Coleridge could possibly be credited. Partly inspired by the success of 'Kubla Khan', yet rejected by Wordsworth for *Lyrical Ballads*, *Christabel* looks in some ways like a dress rehearsal for Keats's more successful ventures into Britain's elfin past. Its setting is medieval, northern, emphatically Catholic, and with a hint at the Britain of the druids. Praying one April night under an oak clad in mistletoe, Christabel is startled by a fine lady in white silk. Geraldine (rhyming with 'wine') claims to have been left here after an abduction. Who or what is she?

Silver notes various ominous signs given as Geraldine is taken into the castle of Christabel's father, including her inability to pass an iron threshold until carried over by Christabel. And she certainly has magical powers, enchanting the young girl into helpless complicity despite a horrific though implicit deformity, seen when Geraldine undresses (Coleridge having cancelled here an earlier stanza, Silver points out, which spoke of a breast and side 'lean and old and foul of hue'). Later, the castle's resident bard tells Christabel's father of a seemingly prophetic dream he has had, featuring a snake nestled down in the forest beside a dove; just after this Christabel sees Geraldine's eyes flicker into those of a serpent before they turn (with almost comic reversal) a melting feminine charm upon the widowed father. Despite the poem's opacity, a fairy demon seems more likely to lie within Geraldine than a witch.

In 1813, two years after being expelled from Oxford for atheism, Percy Bysshe Shelley published his philosophical poem *Queen Mab*. 'Easily the most widely read' of Shelley's poems for many years (notes Michael O'Neill), this fiercely revolutionary work drew charges of blasphemy down on publishers long after Shelley's early death. In it, the once daintily miniaturized Mab whirls the bewildered reader with visionary force to the limits of the universe, and of human revolutionary potential. The violent response to this early work amply bears out Shelley's claim that 'poets are the unacknowledged legislators of the world.' It also shows us how, in the right hands, literary fairies could regain a danger far exceeding that associated with sex or the demonic. Given how little interest Shelley seems to have had in folklore, it is intriguing to find here a type of fairy heresy separate from, yet rivalling, all those privately held about the ambiguous fallen angels of the Middle Kingdom.

Do fairies live forever? Thanks to Keats, at least a few of them will. His most explicit fairy poem, 'La Belle Dame sans Merci', has an unnamed narrator (probably a knight) meeting in the meadow a lady

> Full beautiful – a fairy's child;
> Her hair was long, her foot was light,
> And her eyes were wild.

After feeding him on 'roots of relish sweet,/ And honey wild, and manna-dew', she takes him 'to her elfin grot', where they sleep, and he dreams of all the past, seemingly damned lovers of this Celtic siren, 'their starved lips in the gloom,/ With horrid warning gapèd wide'.

> And this is why I sojourn here,
> Alone and palely loitering:
> Though the sedge is withered from the lake,
> And no birds sing.

Thus the poem ends as it began, its bleakly repeated chants folding in around the lost heat of fairy glamour. Was the belle dame a fairy, or 'a fairy's child' in the sense of one born from the union of fairy and mortal? Did the implied coupling ('She looked at me as she did love,/ And made sweet moan') produce *another* such hybrid, nine months on? Like so much of Keats, this briefly mesmerizing poem leaves us wondering, its words cut short but echoing on with the charged potency of those frozen figures around the Grecian urn. The most certain thing about this cold pastoral seems to be that fairy glamour has a danger beyond that of the headiest drug: for, against its memory, all present and future joys shrivel to ashes and dust.

'La Belle Dame' was inspired in part by a poem of that name written by Chaucer, and seems in itself to be medieval in setting (although the only strong clue to this atmosphere is the word 'wight'). It was written in April 1819, in a year which saw Keats produce seven of the greatest English poems ever written. One of these was *The Eve of St Agnes*.

> St Agnes' Eve – Ah, bitter chill it was!
> The owl, for all its feathers, was a-cold;
> The hare limped trembling through the frozen grass,
> And silent was the flock in woolly fold:

If you have never read this poem, then throw down my book and do so at once. You can take my copy. In this astonishing work, words fall with the ease of rain onto the page, and there seem as fixed and inevitable as the laws of nature. On St Agnes's Eve, 21 January,

> Young virgins might have visions of delight,
> And soft adorings from their loves receive
> Upon the honeyed middle of the night,
> If ceremonies due they did aright.
>
> . . .

Full of this whim was thoughtful Madeline:
The music, yearning like a God in pain,
She scarcely heard . . .

And so this gem of moon-chilled medievalism passes from the argent revelry of the baronial hall to the intimacy of Madeline's chamber, where her would-be lover, Porphyro, has connived with an elderly servant to hide himself in a closet:

Out went the taper as she hurried in;
Its little smoke, in pallid moonshine, died:
She closed the door, she panted, all akin
To spirits of the air, and visions wide

Espied as she kneels in prayer under a stained-glass window, 'which threw warm gules on Madeline's fair breast', Madeline is watched, with perhaps greater attention, as she undresses:

. . . by degrees
Her rich attire creeps rustling to her knees:
Half-hidden, like a mermaid in seaweed,
Pensive awhile she dreams awake . . .

Breathlessly, the voyeuristic tension builds, as richly gorgeous as the 'lucent syrops' and 'creamy curd' which Porphyro brings out from the closet as Madeline lies 'trembling in her soft and chilly nest . . . Until the poppied warmth of sleep' overtakes her. The freezing moonlight dreams the approaching lovers out of time. Even Porphyro's lute-playing (tellingly, 'an ancient ditty . . . called "La belle dame sans mercy"') cannot wholly break the spell. And now, the moment comes. Madeline opens her eyes; sees Porphyro; and is somehow both 'wide awake' and yet stranded between her dream of Porphyro and the living man before her. She begs him to sing again, begs him not to leave her. And,

Beyond a mortal man impassioned far
At these voluptuous accents, he rose,
Ethereal, flushed, and like a throbbing star
Seen 'mid the sapphire heaven's deep repose;
Into her dream he melted, as the rose
Blendeth its odour with the violet, –
Solution sweet . . .

When I say that, sometimes, literature is more real than reality, this is what I mean. Just what happens here? Those lines defy anyone to tell you, because they have said it all with a ravishing perfection beyond any cold paraphrase. We can say if we wish that Keats was Porphyro, having perhaps first consummated his relationship with Fanny Brawne just weeks before. Yet to then bluntly claim that we have somehow 'explained' the secret, panting heart of this poem as something merely sexual is to misunderstand its quiet triumph.

Enter, now, the fairies. They are woven artfully through the rich tapestry of the poem, framing it, perhaps spying in on Madeline like the moon, her lover, and the reader. In the fifth stanza the revellers are 'Numerous as shadows haunting fairily/ The brain', and in one of the last Porphryo hails the snow flying at the panes with 'Hark! 'tis an elfin-storm from fairy land.' Rapt in her visions of St Agnes and her imagined love, Madeline is 'hoodwinked with fairy fancy', and Porphyro himself dreams of presently watching her abed,

While legioned fairies pace the coverlet,
And pale enchantment held her sleepy-eyed.

The most densely evocative fairy lines, however, are also the most opaque. Immediately following the above, they close stanza XIX thus:

Never on such a night have lovers met,
Since Merlin paid his Demon all the monstrous debt.

This couplet has divided scholars, with some arguing that it refers precisely to Merlin's father, held, as we saw, to be an incubus, and others believing the 'demon' to be Merlin's fairy-sorceress lover, Vivien. Yet its exact meaning is far less important than those extraordinary fairy-struck stanzas in which Keats chips out a space where, just for one night, star-crossed lovers can actually touch:

> Into her dream he melted, as the rose
> Blendeth its odour with the violet, –

Airily defying all the sexual taboo and social snobbery which crippled human love in his age, Keats has two hearts melt across barriers which could have resisted bullets. If ever fairy glamour was successfully conjured out of those green hills where the Good People jealously guarded it, then it was here. And if ever we needed proof that the stern repressions of the nineteenth century could generate an eroticism far more powerful than the most explicit pornography, then here it lies. Could this space have existed without the fairies, or without their arch-magician, Merlin?

Without delving extensively into possible inspirations for such poems, we can add that Keats was heavily influenced by C. M. Wieland's German Romantic epic *Oberon*, published in 1780. And we can remind ourselves that the form of *St Agnes*, much as it might seem so well moulded to Keats's needs, was actually a direct imitation of the famous Spenserian stanzas of *The Faerie Queene*. Before we leave Keats, we must also glance at one other dazzling vision of fairy glamour – this, too, produced in his *annus mirabilis*, 1819.

> Upon a time, before the faery broods
> Drove nymph and satyr from the prosperous woods,

and before Oberon 'Frighted away the dryads and the fauns', the Greek god Hermes chanced upon a curious palpitating snake as he roamed the Cretan woods in search of a fair nymph. Mesmerized, he gazed down at

> . . . a gordian shape of dazzling hue,
> Vermilion-spotted, golden, green, and blue;
> Striped like a zebra, freckled like a pard,
> Eyed like a peacock, and all crimson barr'd;
> And full of silver moons, that, as she breathed,
> Dissolv'd, or brighter shone, or interwreathed
> Their lustres with the gloomier tapestries –
> So rainbow-sided, touch'd with miseries,
> She seem'd, at once, some penanced lady elf,
> Some demon's mistress, or the demon's self.

Just where are we, and what, exactly, are we looking at? Intriguingly, those very opening words ('before the faery broods') imply a whole separate genealogy of successive fairy types or races, pitching us back into a peculiarly ancient world of the shyest, most organically earthy nature spirits. Forcing our bewitched eyes, next, through the 'brilliance feminine' and particoloured labyrinth of the snake's body, we are reminded again of those synaesthetic raptures belonging to literature alone. Who could paint this? Who could film it? Knotted through its slithering coils are impossible intensities of colour, form, wildness and exoticism, which pitch us down into yet one further dimension when Lamia breathes her perilous life through all these gorgeous involutions, melting and heightening the original vision. Steadying ourselves under this sensory onslaught we are then left wondering about that closing trio of possible identities – one which in part recalls the uncertain demon persona overshadowing *St Agnes*.

On request from the eerily human mouth of this creature, Hermes uses his power to give her back her full woman's shape. This proves surpassingly beautiful. Lamia flees now to Corinth, where one Lycius falls in love with her, and for their nuptials a magical fairy hall is thrown up within moments:

There was a noise of wings, till in short space
The glowing banquet-room shone with wide-arched grace.
A haunting music, sole perhaps and lone
Supportress of the faery-roof, made moan
Throughout, as fearful the whole charm might fade.

There is, however, a spectre at the feast. This is the elderly sage Apollonius, whose withering gaze appears to pierce through Lamia to her doubtful origins or interior. Yet, where in *Christabel* this kind of figure (in the form of the castle bard) would seem a just and necessary warning against evil, for Keats, Apollonius represents something very different.

... Do not all charms fly
At the mere touch of cold philosophy?
...
Philosophy will clip an angel's wings,
Conquer all mysteries by rule and line,
Empty the haunted air, and gnomed mine –

Recalling those brave new inscapes of the Romantic poets, we here find the opaquely demonic Lamia as their champion, against the cold utilitarian rationalism of Apollonius. In this instance, Apollonius triumphs:

... the sophist's eye,
Like a sharp spear, went through her utterly,
Keen, cruel, perceant, stinging ...

Lamia vanishes at the sage's cry of 'serpent!' and Lycius dies, seemingly of grief, that same night.

We cannot now trace in detail the fairy wings which darted through Keats's letters, or dwell on 'the winged daemon king' which he so often used to symbolize the poetical imagination. But it is hard not to feel that there was something peculiarly elfin about the man himself. Standing just five feet tall, otherworldly, and irrepressibly energetic, if ever there was a sheer force of nature in poetry, it was Keats. Wracked through with sickness, harrassed by poverty, attacked with savage and vile mean-spiritedness by rich mediocrities whose words are now ashes, John Keats sat tight, kept his nerve, and wrote himself into eternity. To do that takes guts. But it also takes grace. Like some irrepressible fairy spirit, Keats darted with exuberant delight around the lumbering sloths who sought to drag him down, snatching beauty from the air as he went.

Victorian Fairies: Light and Dark

The Irish poet William Allingham (1824–1889) is now largely remembered for his fairy poems, along with his more political verse novel *Laurence Bloomfield in Ireland*, and his associations with Victorian luminaries such as Tennyson and Carlyle. His 1849 'The Fairies' has traces of whimsy (fairies living on 'crispy pancakes / Of yellow tide-foam … With frogs for their watch-dogs') and yet opens with a clear sense of the popular fears Allingham must have met in his native Donegal:

Up the airy mountain,
Down the rushy glen,
We daren't go a-hunting
For fear of little men

In addition to a warning against damaging fairy thorns, the sharpest edge of danger comes when we hear of how

They stole little Bridget
For seven years long;
When she came down again
Her friends were all gone.

They took her lightly back,
Between the night and morrow,
They thought that she was fast asleep,
But she was dead with sorrow.
They have kept her ever since
Deep within the lake,
On a bed of flag-leaves,
Watching till she wake.

Here Allingham seems to capture not just true fairy danger, but the mingled irresponsibility and incomprehension which sees the 'good folk' snatching pretty things, and failing to realize how easily they may be broken.

By contrast, a later and longer piece, 'Two Fairies in a Garden', looks like a poem intended to please children, rather than warn them of fairy perils. While the fairies of the airy mountain and rushy glen are little but not obviously miniature, those of the garden ride on bats, moths and dragonflies. This delicate scale is used to draw readers into just the kind of spaces that tamed fairies and privileged children might be assumed to appreciate: one fairy is off to 'warm myself/ In a thick red tulip's core' and the other to creep into 'the dim and deep snow-palace/ Of the closest lily-chalice'. The direct speech of the two elves in dialogue further aids such intimacy, and the simple AA rhyme scheme feels more childlike than the looser rhymes of 'The Fairies'. Leading an enclosed and limited existence, these two sprites' most active work involves warning a thrush against a hunter, or a robin of a hawk, as well as painstakingly strewing dew upon every leaf of the sycamore. One of the pair even laments the wicked sports of Puck, wishing he could have aided the housewife tormented by such mischief. Perhaps most tellingly of all, the male imp delights for purely innocent reasons in 'human children playing nigh', and wishes that 'we might/ Show ourselves to mortal sight/ Far more often!', while his female counterpart breaks out later:

Oh, brother, hush! I faint with fear!
A mortal footstep threatens near.

At one level, these fairies, mingling affection towards humans
with terror of them, would be unrecognizable to the peasants of
Donegal – and indeed the Isle of Man, where Allingham worked
briefly as a customs' officer. At another, the poem now reads like an
attempt to re-enchant a small, domesticated natural space with
more artificial versions of the rougher, earthier sprites which must
have influenced Allingham's Irish childhood. Flitting through the
piece is a whispered promise of magic at the bottom of the garden
if you – the child – are quiet enough and patient enough to catch
its murmurous gleams.

Goblin Market

If that begins to cloy, then come with me, beyond the garden,
and taste some rougher, darker fruits of fairyland . . .

> Plump unpecked cherries,
> Melons and raspberries,
> Bloom-down-cheeked peaches,
> Swart-headed mulberries,
> Wild free-born cranberries,
> Crab-apples, dewberries,
> Pine-apples, blackberries,
> Apricots, strawberries; –
> All ripe together
> In summer weather, –

Thus cry, in a sensuous nursery rhyme abundance, the goblin men of
Christina Rossetti's extraordinary poem *Goblin Market* (1862). The
barest outline of this richly ambiguous work is as follows: two sisters,
Lizzie and Laura, live alone in pastoral calm, disturbed only by these

uncanny vendors of forbidden fruits. Lizzie stands firm against the temptation of this succulent ripeness. Laura does not. Despite Lizzie's warnings as to the fate of Jeanie, who had previously succumbed, Laura eats. After this, she pines. At last, in an act of bold sisterly sacrifice, Lizzie herself goes among the goblin men to seek a cure. She achieves it, and Laura is restored, with both girls later becoming mothers who warn their own children against such goblin perils.

Before we venture bravely amid the furry claws of the goblin men, a word or two about our author. Sister of Dante Gabriel Rossetti, the poet and painter so central to the Pre-Raphaelite Brotherhood, Christina (1830–1894) was raised in a manner relatively enlightened for such sexist times, in a household continually enlivened by distinguished and inspiring company. Unfortunately, while Dante shook off the evangelical Anglicanism of their mother, this stern force kept its grip upon Christina throughout her life. It is not wholly clear how far her persistent ill-health was mental as well as physical. But, by the time she suffered a 'major religious crisis' in 1857 she had rejected two suitors, and seems to have rebuffed a third shortly after. She died a spinster, and – we can reasonably guess – a virgin.

If all this sounds rather overly biographical, well . . . follow me, and judge for yourself. Coiled together in the brookside rushes, the sisters hear the goblin cries, with Lizzie warning:

'We must not look at goblin men,
We must not buy their fruits:
Who knows upon what soil they fed
Their hungry thirsty roots?'

Can we perhaps read that first line as an oblique feeling that Christina herself must not look with desire on *any* men, goblin or human? The following question hints both at a sense of unknown, 'deep-rooted' contamination, which might seem founded on class prejudice, and also at a possible feeling that all sex, all male contact, has something intrinsically, darkly dirty about it. When Lizzie further battles off their sensuous lure with 'Their offers should not charm us,/ Their evil gifts would harm us,' it is hard not to think again of those charming yet rejected suitors of the years before the poem.

But what is so remarkable about *Goblin Market* is the way that it allows these evil gifts such a genuinely real and vibrant presence. When Laura clips off a lock of hair to buy the fruits, we hear of how she then

> . . . sucked their fruit globes fair or red:
> Sweeter than honey from the rock,
> Stronger than man-rejoicing wine,
>
> . . .
>
> She sucked and sucked and sucked the more
> Fruits which that unknown orchard bore;
> She sucked until her lips were sore . . .

And when Lizzie ventures among the goblins for her sister's sake, she

> Would not open lip from lip
> Lest they should cram a mouthful in:
> But laughed in heart to feel the drip
> Of juice that syrupped all her face,
> And lodged in dimples of her chin,
> And streaked her neck which quaked like curd,

before racing back to Laura, exclaiming,

> 'Did you miss me?
> Come and kiss me.
> Never mind my bruises,
> Hug me, kiss me, suck my juices
> Squeezed from goblin fruits for you,
> Goblin pulp and goblin dew.

192

Eat me, drink me, love me;
Laura, make much of me:
For your sake I have braved the glen
And had to do with goblin merchant men.'

By this stage, even the most chaste and virtuous reader may begin to understand why this poem would be published not only in versions designed for children, but by *Playboy* (graced, moreover, with illustrations which left little to the imagination). As with *St Agnes*, it would again be rash to too crudely reduce this to a merely suppressed lesbianism. Yet the sexual undertones here are surely more blatant, more unstable, than they are in any of Keats's work. Even the final 'had to do with goblin . . . men' could potentially slide into the sexual euphemism which those first four words often comprised. Another angle of approach might view Lizzie and Laura as two warring sides of Rossetti. For, when the latter begs, 'Have done with sorrow;/ I'll bring you plums tomorrow,' it is hard not to hear one part of Christina imploring the other.

Having said all this, we can still see how the poem would appeal to children – in part through its simple fairytale form and morality, and in part for lines precisely describing the goblin men:

One had a cat's face,
One whisked a tail,
One tramped at a rat's pace,
One crawled like a snail,
One like a wombat prowled obtuse and furry,
One like a ratel tumbled hurry skurry.

And again, later, approaching the selfless Lizzie:

Flying, running, leaping,
Puffing and blowing,
Chuckling, clapping, crowing,

Clucking and gobbling,
Mopping and mowing,
Full of airs and graces,
Pulling wry faces,
Demure grimaces,
Cat-like and rat-like,
Ratel- and wombat-like,
Snail-paced in a hurry,
Parrot-voiced and whistler,
Helter skelter, hurry skurry . . .

Shot through with the happy absurdity so beloved by children, and rhyming in a way they might get by heart, the animal vividness of these lines must have derived in part from Rossetti's visits to London Zoo, where she had been viewing the wombats since the late 1850s.

Had we but words enough and time, we could say far more about the poem's inner sense that something as deliciously forbidden as sex must be paid for dearly – with the bitter, white-haired sickness Laura suffers after eating, and before Lizzie effects her cure. We could further wonder about Rossetti slyly having her fruit and eating it, insofar as the cure itself involves that extraordinary union of the two girls: 'Eat me, drink me, love me' . . . In leaving it, let us just remind ourselves of something a little more basic. For here, as in 'La Belle Dame sans Merci', we again have a tale in which fairy glamour is dangerous just because it is so intoxicating. After tasting it, ordinary joys lose all their colour and, indeed, juice.

Fairy Paintings

At times it seems as if the Victorians were never more themselves than when fleeing themselves. Their paintings fled back into Shakespearean and medieval pasts; outwards to the wide, wide open seas rolling away behind marbled Greek terraces; inwards to the lustrous contours of a naked female body habitually imprisoned in layers of whalebone, linen and silk; away to scenes of gorgeous Roman or Oriental decadence and exoticism. Another way of saying this is to see the potently self-believing Victorians as creatures of paradox. Intensely repressed and profoundly erotic; rigidly temperate, while drowning in seas of opium; filled with humble Christian pacifism, and with righteous militant arrogance. And perhaps nowhere could this rich whirlpool of contradictions be better alchemized into art than in Victorian painting. You could not talk about the naked female body, yet you could paint it; you could not so easily say that dead, trapped, passive, vulnerable women were curiously attractive, but you could certainly make them look that way, leaving viewers rapt, teased out of thought before these highly coloured, intricately traced visions of the forbidden.

Before we engage with the fairies of Victorian art, we can briefly dart through some earlier works by posing a key question of elfin aesthetics. Just how did the fairies get their wings? It is tempting to see this now stereotypical feature as a diminished memory of their most ancient ancestors, the fallen angels themselves. There is indeed one scrap of obscure seventeenth-century poetry that evokes 'winged fairies', and which in fact refers to angels. But on the whole, folklore and fairy aesthetics rarely join up that seamlessly. So far as we can tell, it was a very urban, highly educated male poet who first pinned wings onto fairies. For, in *The Rape of the Lock* in 1717, Alexander Pope gave 'insect wings' to the sylphs of his poem. Around 1790 the painter Henry Fuseli gave his Puck the wings of a bat, and come 1797, when planning the illustrations for an edition of *The Rape of the Lock*, the painter Thomas Stothard had a friend suggest that he should give the sylphs of the poem butterfly wings. (To give yet another literary twist to this story, one critic has argued this friend to have been William Blake.) Stothard not only embraced this idea, but captured a real butterfly to paint from life, allegedly having to get another the following day after an obsessive housemaid threw away the first.

For a few years, then, two paths seem to have been open in the realm of fairy aesthetics. Could the darker, coarser, faintly uncanny bat wings of Fuseli, more easily evoking our fallen angels, have triumphed? If they had, perhaps the childish and feminine fairies would have been very marginal, even stillborn creatures. As we now know, however, our leather-winged sprites were soon worsted in this evolutionary battle, their sonar confounded by the miniature gale of all those filmy whirring pinions gusting through post-Romantic art.

Beyond this early division, we find two other broad ones persisting through the nineteenth century. As a painter, do you opt for fairy darkness, or fairy wonder and prettiness? Do you plunder Shakespeare for your subjects, or do you invent your own? In truth, once we get our knees dirty and peer more closely down through the leaves and mushrooms, we find some of the most famed fairy painters mingling traits from either side in both cases.

Take, first, Sir Joseph Noel Paton. Both of his mid-century depictions of Oberon and Titania are now so universally familiar that it is hard to imagine them never having existed. Many modern viewers could probably name them instantly as Victorian, even if they did not know the artist's name. Yet even in the two years between the 1847 *Reconciliation of Oberon and Titania* and the 1849 *Quarrel of Oberon and Titania* we see some clear changes. The first painting is certainly highly erotic, creative, and densely enlivened by inventive detail. But compare its Titania with that of the *Quarrel*. The earlier figure, while beautiful and voluptuous, has perhaps just an edge of the pallor of death clinging to her. The later one is softer, more supple, the planes and curves of her skin heated by a light which might be taken as the inner mystery of the feminine, as much as an illumination cast down from the tumbling coronet of elfs above her head.

And then, we have the other fairies . . . Here indeed is a Middle Kingdom as densely and variously peopled as our own. Famously, Lewis Carroll counted 165 of them when he stood before this sizeable canvas in the Scottish National Gallery in 1857. They range in size from the sinister horned Pan down to the minute goblin glancing in fear at a spider bigger than his own head, with many gradations between. And, allowing for that hoary old Victorian bedroom line, 'you can keep your wings on,' many are naked. How did the Victorians get away with this? We are so used to that paradox that perhaps we hardly notice it any more. In this instance, what at one glance seems a hybrid between the classical nude, the pastoral and some woodland fairy orgy might have escaped censure just because the sheer bewildering multiplicity of the scene deflects lustful focus from any single pair of breasts or legs. Beyond that, the abundant, faintly grotesque scattering of goblins – bald, bug-eyed, and with at least one tail – also counters the perils of all those lustrous, inviting bodies.

If there is little fairy darkness here (aside from the night itself, sharply heightening all that naked pallor), the eroticism might yet be seen as a kind of transfigured danger. As for invention: despite the popular Shakespearean pretext, Paton has here made the subject his own – largely through sheer labour and inventiveness. Clearly there was no hint in *A Midsummer Night's Dream* itself of all this teeming multitude of extras, while even the Victorian stage could not boast such a cast, or such a range of aesthetics.

Paton's Scottish origins may have played some role in the success of these pictures. The Irish background of John Anster Fitzgerald was certainly relevant to both his persona and his many fairy paintings. Viewing works such as *The Fairies' Banquet* (1859), *The Fairies' Funeral* (1864) or *The Captive Robin* (c. 1865) from a distance, most would probably be struck above all by the gorgeous excess of artfully juxtaposed colours. For some, this could evoke the more cloying sides of Victorian art. Fitzgerald's paintings seem eminently Victorian in their ravishing chromatism as much as in their beguiling fusion of fairies and nature. Coming closer, this fusion is the next thing to strike us. Amid all the flowers, the fairies themselves are dressed or capped in petals; canopied by a leaf; riding on mice; or gathered around a mushroom table. And yet, leaning in a little closer still, we also find many shades of fairy darkness. Although chained with flowers, the robin is indeed a prisoner, thereby typifying the selfish irresponsibility of the fairy id and its innumerable thefts of human infants. In *The Chase of the White Mice* (1864) the bird (as Jeremy Maas notes) is being goaded with a briskly wielded thorn. With nice irony, other fairies attack a bat, as if still aware that its leathern wings might yet overshadow those of the butterfly. Perhaps most of all, once our eyes move away from those beguiling reds and blues and purples of the fairy dresses, we are struck by all the more ambiguous figures lurking around them.

Just what are they? Here beside our robin, something with green curving horns leans morosely on his stick; to its left another squats like some antennaed pixie; while just behind the gorgeous blue-petalled fairy, that bearded orange imp has shades of Fitzgerald himself. In *The Fairies' Barque* (1860) the one clutching an oar is undeniably (if whimsically) demonic, and below him the two puffing musicians look like nothing so much as their own inimitable crazy selves (having said which, do we now perhaps see something of the ageing hippy in the seated figure?). It has been rightly argued by Maas and others that these lively goblins were inspired by the similarly whimsical figures which crowd the paintings of Hieronymus Bosch (*c.* 1450–1516) and Jan Bruegel the Elder (1568–1625).

Yet these sources still raise another question. Why should Fitzgerald revive these rambunctious imps at just this time? And how was it that he, in the midst of Victorian fairy images derived from Shakespeare, should prove so inventive, and so unmistakably iconic? Maas gives two intriguing answers. The first is opium. Whether or not he himself took it, Fitzgerald certainly found this distinctive Victorian narcotic a potent source of subject-matter. Around 1870 he painted *The Pipe Dream*, in which a surreal assemblage of figures struggles to emerge from the smoke of an opium pipe. In *The Artist's Dream* (1857) it is he himself who fantasizes the grotesque figures around his own sleeping form; and in this and the following year he painted and repainted an opium dream in which a young woman's poppied slumbers sprout the same Boschian forms, along with fainter, human ones (*The Stuff that Dreams are Made Of*, c. 1858). Her troubled sleep is reflected in her twisting motion on the bed, and the Oriental decadence of the drug visually echoed by her colourful Turkish jacket.

Interestingly, while Fitzgerald carefully repainted the image, and the woman in particular, to produce pictures far more fit for respectable consumption, two opium-inspired qualities grew stronger in these later versions. One was the imps, whose merry drumming, fiddling, piping and clashing of cymbals injects another level of hallucinatory pandemonium. And the other, more basically, was colour. For, as Maas emphasizes, 'opium dreams tended to intensify colours: reds became redder, darkening to maroons and blood crimsons . . . yellows became yellower and more luminescent'. And when he further cites an American doctor of 1862 on how opium 'exaggerates . . . multiplies . . . colours' and 'gives fantastic shapes', we meet a pithy gloss of both Fitzgerald's opium images and his seemingly childlike fairy paintings.

Maas's second explanation leads in a more worldly direction. For, almost timeless as Fitzgerald's gorgeously coloured scenes may now appear, both their pigments and their light were in fact inspired by the dazzling new technical feats bursting from the stages of Victorian London. Central to so many fairytale vistas of plays and pantomimes were gaslight (developed in Britain from 1795 to 1820) and the slightly newer limelight. The latter was known to have been used as early as 1826, and come 1839 it underpinned the 'stupendous panorama al-fresco of Mount Hecla', erupting spectacularly and punctually every night at 8 p.m. in the Royal Surrey Zoological Gardens. In December 1859 an improved, more stable version of limelight was dazzling viewers at the Crystal Palace, precisely as Fitzgerald's fairy colours began to hit their prolific stride. By the early 1860s limelight was brightening the northern provinces, producing summer sun on a real stage waterfall in Newcastle, and a moonlit fairy ballet in Sheffield.

While Fitzgerald might therefore be seen to have alchemized fairy glories from both the drugs of the East and the modern innovations of industry, our third fairy artist threw onto his canvas inventions whose eerie shades and haunting ingenuities had essentially one basic source – namely, his own fevered brain. Seen here in reproduction, Richard Dadd's painting *The Fairy Feller's Masterstroke* (1855–64) is both unforgettable and troubling. You, like myself, may even find it slightly painful to look at. Leaves, grasses and fauna have something of the hard shine of metal; perspective is slippery, if not in places bewildering. And once we shift from paper to the original oils in London's Tate gallery, further layers of strangeness creep up. As Alice Huxley found when standing in front of the original picture during research for her brilliant dissertation on Victorian fairy types, only here can you appreciate the painstaking way in which the artist applied subtly graded layers of paint.

If we now compare this to one of Dadd's earlier fairy paintings, *Titania Sleeping* (c. 1841), it is difficult to believe them both the work of the same artist. The earlier creation certainly seems inventive at first glance. Yet the intricate frame of flowers and musical goblins around the bower was borrowed from the fairy painter Daniel Maclise, and the dancing bacchantes to the left from Poussin. Arguably the most original feature is the outer frame of darkly gleaming bat wings, perhaps hinting back to Fuseli, yet producing a Gothic tone which now evokes so many of the century's darker novels. Details and touches of danger aside, this definitely looks above all like a recognizably Victorian painting.

How, then, did Dadd travel from that respectable Shakespearean scene to the uncanny creations and obsessive focus of the *Masterstroke*? Simply, he went mad. While in Rome in April 1843 during a long European tour he became 'irrationally excited and quarrelsome' and allegedly considered an attack on the pope. Back in England that August, he murdered his own father with 'a knife bought specifically for the purpose', later explaining that 'he had killed the devil in disguise'. After a temporary escape to France and a second attempted murder, Dadd was confined in Bethlem asylum. Diagnosed as schizophrenic, he was allowed painting materials, and 'worked with the intensity of a man possessed' on both the *Master-stroke* and a strikingly different Shakespearean scene from that of 1841, titled *Contradiction: Oberon and Titania.*

Described by one recent critic as 'arguably now the two most famous 19th-century fairy subjects', Dadd's two asylum paintings were in fact unknown in his lifetime. The second of these intensely private imaginings, with its wingless humanoid fairies and the axe poised over the hazelnut, took Dadd perhaps nine years to complete, maybe longer. Since 1800, the fairy escapism that was already visible in Shakespeare and Drayton has multiplied endlessly across stage, page, canvas and screen. And yet . . . could there ever be a fairy escape more purely artistic and individual than those experienced by Richard Dadd? Painted without models, the *Master-stroke* in particular seems to have sprung from no one but himself, to have given meaning and purpose and beauty to a tormented life, lived amid 'the most brutal behaviour', and to have been executed initially for no one but himself, despite its apparent dedication to G. H. Haydon, Steward of Bethlem Hospital.

Certain very minor painters of this era would somehow absorb the prevailing colours and tones of Victorian fairyland with a success that they otherwise lacked in their brief or marginal careers. Robert Huskisson's 1847 scenes from *A Midsummer Night's Dream* and *The Tempest* memorably counter background darkness with enticing feminine pallor and sparing touches of potent, at times almost jewel-like colour; while the still more obscure John Simmons left a butterfly-winged *Titania* (1866), whose lustrous skin tones might be the fierce heat of a male voyeur as easily as the inner light of maidenly purity. Most notably of all, we find that Edward Robert Hughes (nephew of the more famous Pre-Raphaelite Arthur), though not meriting an entry in the *Dictionary of National Biography*, was nevertheless able to produce one of the most iconic fairy images of his day. Around 1908, his watercolour *Midsummer Eve* fuses intimacy and wonder around the rapt figure of an ambiguous girl (human? fairy?) as she gazes into the delicate lights of a fairy circle stripped of all danger.

Edging sideways to some less typical fairy types, we find striking renderings from John William Waterhouse and the more obscure Herbert James Draper. Confronted with the 1896 painting *Hylas and the Nymphs*, the art critic of *The Times* noted with mild condescension that while Waterhouse's theme had 'given him the opportunity to paint a number of very pretty faces', these unfortunately seemed 'as if they had all been painted from one model'. The *Daily Mail* – by no means averse, even in 1897, to semi-clad nymphs – felt their 'white arms and shoulders [to] . . . gleam invitingly', adding too that there was 'more variety [than usual] in the profiles and limbs' of the women. Viewing this work now, it is hard to find much power or threat in these slight figures – even if their large eyes and faintly inhuman attentiveness give them a certain tinge of otherness.

Waterhouse also painted two versions of the Lamia figure. In the 1905 image the seated knight dominates the composition, suggesting an ambiguous conflation of both Keats's *Lamia* and 'La Belle Dame sans Merci'. In 1909 the elusive gorgeousness of the snakeskin is well captured, offering a ravishing counterpart to Lamia's pale pink dress. Stunned by colour as the viewer may be, however, both eroticism and danger are largely absent. Without the aid of a title, most would probably at first glance see an attractive female subject rather than anything otherworldly.

Set beside Waterhouse's second attempt, Draper's painting of the same year achieves a faintly smouldering eroticism, the profiled figure marked by an independence shading into otherness. The aquiline nose, hints of unstable energy in the just-ruffled hair, and the snake creeping over the forearm all contribute to an impression which requires no explanatory title to urge its extra-human qualities upon the viewer. By contrast, his 1913 work *The Kelpie* arguably does need the label by way of guidance. Yet once this is absorbed, we notice similar attributes: even under the sun which gilds her, the kelpie has a certain defiant wildness. Comparing the finished oil to an earlier pencil sketch, it is clear that Draper was at pains to sharpen the facial features of his model to this end, by both loosening her hair and altering the original contours themselves.

By the time that certain of these Edwardian images had been realized, a new and more androgynous associate of the fairies was unleashing his peculiar energies upon the London stage.

Five

Fairy Magic:
1800 to the Present

IT IS 7.46 P.M. on Tuesday, 27 December 1904, in the Duke of York's Theatre, London. A man in a dog suit is shuffling about the stage, airing the children's pyjamas. Waiting in the wings to go on as Wendy, the actress Hilda Trevelyan suddenly hears from the audience 'a shout of joy which simply beggars description'. Why? They have just realized that the dog is *really* a nanny . . . Enter Peter Pan. What bliss it was in that theatre to be alive, that cold December eve; but . . . to be young . . .? was very heaven. Three acts later, heads spinning with the memory of all those pirates, Red Indians, flying children, ticking crocodiles, mermaids and that strange, elusive creature called Peter Pan, the children whose glittering eyes had beheld this must have been at least as ravished with delight as our gentle author, when at age eight he sat watching *Star Wars* on a rare cinematic outing with the Cub Scouts.

There seem to have been fewer children at the first night of *Peter Pan* than one might have expected. Yet the adult reactions left to us show that when Barrie supposedly wrote in the prompt-book, 'Always remember that every person in the audience is a child,' his gamble more than paid off. Citing his instruction, the *Daily Mail* considered that 'this, in a nutshell, is the secret of Mr Barrie's success as a dramatist.' *The Times* found the play 'from beginning to end a thing of pure delight', with Peter triumphant as 'a prose Puck, a 20th century Ariel'. A Scottish reviewer sounded a not uncommon note of ambivalence when he called Barrie 'a playwright despot who makes us obey him willy-nilly . . . compels us to laugh heartily . . . at what we do, say, and believe', giving in swiftly to this half-forced infantilization when he added that, in *Peter Pan*, 'Mr Barrie has given us a freedom to fancy which is as astonishing as it is delightful.'

The *Edinburgh Evening News* partly echoed this sense of happy confusion when its initial perplexity melted into admiration: 'it is described on the bill as a play, but it is really . . . a medley of farce, of fairy tale, of pantomine . . . it abounds in fun and revels in absurdity.' Another reviewer, similarly, found in the play an 'elusive unanalyzable quality that seems to touch magically the meanest and most trivial thing,' adding that 'Peter Pan himself is a puzzle; he has something of the spirit of a pierrot.' (Barrie evidently thought so too, given that he later suggested the role to Charlie Chaplin for a silent film version.) Years later Nina Boucicault, the play's first Peter on that opening night, was 'sure the play took them by surprise . . . [being] so utterly different from any other play'. Like so many other geniuses, Barrie had broken the rules and got away with it. Like so many other masterpieces, *Peter Pan* offered audiences something which was captivating precisely because it was so new; because it could not be fully understood or explained as it burst in a hurtling, impish rush of whimsy from the stage on that December night. Among other wonders, it seems that that most upright, repressed and self-conscious of animals, the Edwardian Briton, had just realized, for perhaps the first time in a communal setting, that it was very good fun to be a child again . . .

And this strange, perhaps almost indecent freedom focused its delights most sharply in one unforgettable moment. For, with the poisoned Tinker Bell dying, Peter hears her murmur that

> she thinks she could get well again if children believed in fairies! (*He rises and throws out his arms he knows not to whom, perhaps to the boys and girls of whom he is not one.*) Do you believe in fairies? Say quick that you believe! If you believe, clap your hands! (*Many clap, some don't, a few hiss . . .*). Oh, thank you, thank you, thank you! And now to rescue Wendy!

As the first night approached, Nina and others in the exhausted, over-rehearsed cast had much to be nervous about – not least because those flying over the stage had been required to take out life insurance. Nina was especially anxious, however, on one point. What should she do if, as the light used to conjure the illusion of Tinker Bell grew fainter, and her appeal rang out, *no one clapped?* In fact, with the orchestra primed to start the applause if need be, and despite the largely adult audience, Nina's plea was greeted with a response so wildly, thunderously spontaneous that she found herself reduced to tears.

Like other moments of genius, this one was clearly not entirely planned. Barrie, with his faintly cynical stage directions about abstainers and hissing, surely never guessed just what he would create. Like nothing else, these few extraordinary minutes played theatre for all it was worth. Let us not forget, in our age of exact mechanical duplication, when everything can be so easily seen again and again at such cool distance, what only live events can do for us. To myself – and perhaps for other lecturers of my generation – there is something strangely precious about the idea of speaking with passion for an hour to people who will be the sole carriers of what passed in that crowded, many-eyed room. Yet how much stronger was the special vulnerability, the unstable generosity of theatre in an age when theatre was still all that you had? And this, with its odd mixture of intimacy in community, was all the more defiantly non-repeatable in the case of a play which the author compulsively rewrote, week by week and year by year.

If that first night had the advantage of surprise, the life-saving applause seemed no less ardently spontaneous come 1909, when the Duke of York's stage was littered with thrown thimbles and violets, and the air wild with 'the cheering of the Peter Pan Club'. 'Either we are a nation of hypocrites,' wrote one reviewer, 'or we have a secret belief in the supernatural, for the torrent of hand-clapping which came to the rescue of the expiring Tinker Bell was so overwhelming that even Peter seemed surprised.' In 1925 the

Mail's theatre critic thought that some children clapped because 'they really believe in fairies' and others 'because their elders prompt them to do so', yet admitted that 'it is impossible to think of a parallel happening.' Come 1996, Paul Taylor of *The Independent* recalled that even as a child he had wondered, at this moment, 'how you were supposed to clap your hands when both your arms were being twisted behind your back', while the ferociously materialist philosopher A. J. Ayer, having vowed at the outset of his second childhood trip to the play that he would *not* clap, found himself doing precisely that in the general tidal rush of applause.

We can fairly assume that few of the clapping adults actually did believe in fairies. And yet, given that they had already half-consciously regressed into a childhood when they *had* believed . . . Meanwhile, at the child's level, matters were much more densely powerful. One of the special qualities of theatre or cinema is that we are caught up in the magic of artistic creation, yielding ourselves (childishly, again) to the whole unstoppable experience for two or three hours, in a way that we rarely would when reading a book. Part of the pleasure of this is to *lose control* – albeit in a safe, familiar sort of way. But what happens to this special theatrical quality when, for a five- or six-year-old child, it appears that the play is about to break down and throw you all off the magic ride? What happens in the case of *Peter Pan* is that you, the child, are then curiously *given* a sort of control. In other words, at this extraordinary breathless moment, you – the little individual whose Edwardian life was a continual labyrinth of rules, errors, cautions and subjugations – were given *power*. Magical power; the power of life or death . . .

What I had not guessed, however, until I stumbled on the following recollection, was that you might also be given a peculiar taste of something like love. In December 1914 Madge Titheradge was playing Peter. Noël Coward (on stage with her in the part of Slightly) recalled Titheradge as too fiercely commanding at this moment, so that 'little children whimpered and clung to their mothers instead of clapping their hands.' But this was not how Giles Playfair, a New England professor, remembered it in 1962:

> I was only four years old at the time, but I remember the agony of suspense she aroused while Tink was dying and then the wild relief and the overwhelming response – not simply polite, formal clapping but a standing ovation – and finally her 'thank you, thank you, thank you', which every child in the audience could take as being meant for him personally, and which was surely the sweetest caress he had ever received in his whole young life . . . I still find it difficult to believe how short the scene actually is; I still cannot imagine how she was able to create such an effect, and such a lasting impression on me in so few lines.

By 1944 the Tinker Bell moment had broken out of the theatre, with a *Daily Mail* columnist, 'the Colonel', telling of the apparently terminal winter sickness of his bull terrier – a beast named Tinker Bell precisely because it was nothing like a fairy. One day at tea the Colonel's small niece said, 'If you believe in fairies, clap your hands. Don't let Tinker Bell die,' after which the animal 'took a turn for the better' and was soon 'restored to her un-fairylike habits'. One suspects that this was not the only case in which Barrie's fertile invention became a curious form of illicit prayer.

We can imagine that children may not have answered Peter's plea with such urgency if they had not already been dazzled by the technical wizardry of the play: Peter makes his first entrance in flight; 'ordinary children' learn to fly; and the treetops scene and Wendy house evidently beguiled even hardened adults. Little wonder that the original first night should have been delayed by five days while mechanical fine tuning polished this box of tricks to perfection. For all that, Peter conjured magic over the dying Tinker Bell with nothing more artful than an electric light and strong acting. Moving away from the stage, we also find a great deal of wonder and magic in the text of *Peter and Wendy*, the longest published version of the story, which appeared in 1911.

What did Barrie make of fairies here? Without wishing to crudely explain away the whole tale in psychoanalytic terms, a few words on Barrie's own childhood are necessary before we make the flight to Neverland. Bruce Hanson, citing Lisa Chaney, reminds us that, when Jamie was just six, his thirteen-year-old brother, David, was killed in a skating accident. Barrie, 'already aware that he was not his mother's favourite . . . must have been deeply hurt by the rejection he experienced after his brother's death'. Perhaps most poignantly of all, he would later recall how, one night when his mother was sleeping, she heard him stir and twice called out 'Is that you?' Barrie, taking this to refer to the dead David, finally replied 'No, it's no' him, it's just me.' Urged by his sisters, 'Jamie tried to replace his brother by acting as much like David as he could' – the broad result evidently being that he never quite grew out of this distorted childhood.

Those who remember just one thing about the play almost certainly remember the power of children's belief in fairies. While the Tinker Bell scene is naturally weaker in the book, Peter himself is closely associated with fairies. Their otherworldly glamour sprinkles its dust over him by association, sparkling in Wendy's eyes when Peter mentions his acquaintance with the fairy world: 'She gave him a look of the most intense admiration,' to which Peter responds: 'when the first baby laughed for the first time, its laugh broke into a thousand pieces, and they all went skipping about, and that was the beginning of fairies.' Drawing us back again to the importance of childish belief, Peter has to admit, however, that 'children know such a lot now' so that 'they soon don't believe in fairies, and every time a child says "I don't believe in fairies" there is a fairy somewhere that falls down dead.'

Peter would probably not have been the beguiling, evergreen puzzle he is if he had been something quite as *definite* as a fairy. Something of his earthy otherness is of course that of the original

Pan, figuring nature's power and unpredictability rather than its goodness. Yet Peter clearly has fairy traits. Like the real fairies, he has prodigious energy. We are told that Neverland, rather lazy in his absence, can be heard 'seething with life' upon his return. His flying, if not authentic for true fairy believers, obviously fitted popular views well before 1904. Perhaps most central and most potent of Peter's fairy qualities is his sheer selfish independence and irresponsibility – that special 'fairy id' which we met at the outset of our quest. At one level, this might indeed be the selfishness of a child. At another, it has something of all those selfish maverick heroes who are somehow the more attractive because their occasional heroism is unexpected or wayward. Notoriously, Barrie had refused to offer Nina any more direction for her part beyond telling her that 'Peter is a bird; and he is one day old' (this being echoed in a stage direction where Peter's cockiness infuriates Hook in the manner of a sparrow darting about a lion). Little wonder, then, that when Peter answers the fighting pirate captain's 'who and what art thou?' with 'I'm youth, I'm joy . . . I'm a little bird that's broken out of the egg,' Barrie swiftly bats away this stable definition: 'this of course was nonsense.' On stage, Peter also has a certain fairy otherness, because, as he explains to Wendy, 'no one must ever touch me,' with Barrie adding in a stage direction, 'he is never touched by any one in the play.'

Next, we have the question of childhood. Children must believe in fairies. Babies create fairies every time they laugh. Peter's associates are the 'Lost Boys' – a gaggle of motherless children who are keen to kidnap Wendy as their ambiguous mother. Peter is the boy who will never grow up, and both play and novel are brilliantly adept at the whimsical absurdity of the best children's fiction, right down to the humbled Mr Darling in Nana's dog kennel. Here again, children often have the selfish thoughtlessness of fairies. When Wendy in the play is trying to impress on the Lost Boys how heartbroken are the parents of missing children ('Think, o think, of the empty beds'), 'the heartless ones think of them with glee'. Meanwhile, though all children can fly at first, they lose this talent as they grow, because 'it is only the gay and innocent and heartless who can fly.'

If the flight of the young child stands for freedom, possibility and a kind of faith in the joy of life, it also very basically stands for the sheer joy of movement. As we saw earlier, the single most important thing about life is that it moves. At the start of the novel Barrie explains:

> I don't know whether you have ever seen a map of a person's mind. Doctors sometimes draw maps of other parts of you ... but catch them trying to draw a map of a child's mind, which is not only confused, but keeps going round all the time.

Then, briskly unravelling any stable outline this chart may have had, Barrie whisks it through Neverland and numerous childish experiences, before admitting that 'it is all rather confusing, especially as nothing will stand still.' In reality, of course, nothing ever does stand still. Children are just rather more at ease with this than adults, who gain a certain dubious power by analysing or approaching the world as though it were a dead thing or a machine. Clearly very fairylike in its restless motion, it is also intriguing to note how the child's mind, in all its fluid instability, recalls to us those childhood 'daemons' of Philip Pullman's *Northern Lights*: creatures that become fixed and unchangeable only at a certain age.

At the furthest pole from this very fluid and very particular world of the young child, we have, of course, the adult male. Mr Darling, for all his comically childish behaviour at home, is initially the epitome of the colourless, abstract man. In the play we are told that 'in the city where he sits on a stool all day, as fixed as a postage stamp, he is so like all the others on stools that you recognise him not by his face but by his stool,' and he presently compounds this greyly anti-magical status with his belief that he can sell Peter's shadow: 'I shall take it to the British Museum to-morrow and have it priced.'

Given the sexism of an age when women could not vote, it is perhaps little surprise to find them in some ways more closely allied with children than with men. The central fairy of the tale is of course ultra-feminine. Tinker Bell is capricious, catty (hating Wendy with 'the fury of a very woman'), elusive, vain, and conspicuously miniaturized, with her boudoir the size of a birdcage and all its delicate furnishings. She is also (even before Disney gets hold of her) 'exquisitely gowned in a skeleton leaf, cut low and square, through which her figure could be seen to the best advantage', and 'slightly inclined to *embonpoint*' – this last delicious euphemism meaning, basically, breasts.

Yet, if Tinker Bell's persona and figure may now look sexist, she is a veritable suffragette by comparison with Mrs Darling or Wendy. In both cases their femininity has the secret, elusive interior particularity of traditional gender stereotypes. Mrs Darling's 'romantic mind was like the tiny boxes, one within the other, that come from the puzzling East, however many you discover there is always one more; and her sweet mocking mouth had one kiss on it that Wendy could never get'. This idealized otherness, easily evading the clumsy male grasp, prompts a startling moment in the play, when Peter is so tantalized by all the stories Wendy knows that 'he would like to rip those stories out of her; he is dangerous now'.

It is hard to say just what Wendy herself is, or what Barrie wanted her to be. There is the faintest whisper of Eve when her alluring 'I know such lots of stories' prompts from the narrator: 'there can be no denying that it was she who first tempted him'. But on the whole, despite some ambiguous flirtation with the asexual Peter, Wendy is a child, playing at motherhood in a way which is far from being 'only fun'. '"Wendy," says Peter slyly, as he seeks to lure her into Neverland, "you could tuck us in at night." "Oo!" . . . and her arms went out to him. "And you could darn our clothes, and make pockets for us. None of us has any pockets." How could she resist?'

How indeed? While there is already an abundance of similar sexism in the play, *Peter and Wendy* etches the line that bit deeper with its closing pages on Wendy the adult mother, trying to explain growing up to her own daughter. Almost comical as such stereotyping can now seem, it was perfectly natural for many late Victorian and Edwardian men and women. Leonard Woolf's wry memories of his ideal and naive Victorian mother in his memoir, *Sowing*, offer us one example among many. Another – albeit more ambiguous – came from Nina Boucicault, when she insisted in 1923 that *Peter Pan* was 'a wistful commentary on human nature, taking as its theme the supreme selfishness of man and the supreme unselfishness of woman'.

Yet Barrie's part in this undoubtedly sexist world was of course a very distinctive one. He was nervous with women – partly, it seems, because of his height, being only five feet tall. His unhappy marriage was childless, and he seems to have been impotent. But most of all, Barrie idealized women in an impossible way because of the rejection he had experienced from his own mother following David's tragic death. Was Peter really Barrie? He was, of course, much much more. Yet the two surely touch hands in that poignant moment when Wendy states that a mother 'would always leave the window open' for her wayward child to come back, and Peter responds:

Wendy, you are wrong about mothers. I thought like you about the window, so I stayed away for moons and moons, and then I flew back, but the window was barred, for my mother had forgotten all about me and there was another little boy sleeping in my bed.

A compilation of *Peter Pan* theatrical reviews alone would make a weighty book, running with almost unbroken continuity from 1904 to the present. Yet Peter of course broke out of the merely fictional, into the 'real world', in many different ways. He not only proved, once again, that sometimes literature is more real than reality; he showed with unusual force how literature can make new realities, and how it can give a class of people new ways to think about themselves.

Beyond the royalties bequeathed to Great Ormond Street Children's Hospital, Barrie left us with two other great gifts. The first was the myth of the boy who would not grow up. In this, Barrie became part of a special elite: that little club of authors whose creations are understood when they are evoked by name alone. Jekyll and Hyde, Sherlock Holmes, Peter Pan and James Bond are accordingly used in many languages by non-English speakers. For some reason which has never been fully explained, a very high number of these literary myths were born within a period of less than twenty years, from Hyde in 1886 to Peter in 1904 (or, strictly, 1902). In between we have Holmes, Dorian Gray, Dracula (now the most universal visual icon of the group) and, in different but powerful senses, H. G. Wells's Time Machine and Invisible Man. Peter was the last of these. In a certain curious sense, then, Peter and this clutch of privileged associates return us to the mythic force with which we began: neither Homer, Shakespeare, nor the creations of Stevenson, Doyle or Barrie can be brushed aside as 'merely literature'.

What does it mean to be 'a bit of a Peter Pan'? The epithet was bestowed on the deceased American poet Walt Whitman as early as 1910, and in October 1918, as the First World War ground to a close, one journalist felt that the average British Tommy was playful but good-hearted, 'just a big overgrown boy with a bit of Peter Pan in him'. When Julius Gordon, Dean of Pretoria, died suddenly in 1932 the Bishop of St Albans felt that this lovable eccentric had 'lived young and died young. Like Peter Pan he never grew up; the imp in him was always there.' Not long after the release of Hook (1984), its director, Steven Spielberg, admitted, 'I still feel like Peter Pan,' adding: 'the one thing I don't want to lose is the fairy dust. I don't think any film-maker can afford to lose that kind of magic.'

To be the most successful kind of Peter Pan, you probably have to be creative, if not quite a genius. These people have their childishness not only forgiven, but celebrated. For a long time it seems that these Peter Pans would almost always be men. Yet this early gendering is quickly complicated when we probe the persona. Peter

Pan the work was highly feminized, and Peter himself was notably androgynous, not least because all leads in the play were female until 1982. The subversive mockery of City gent Mr Darling is also interesting when we consider how sharply he contrasts with Barrie's own personality. We should further remind ourselves that that great English national treasure, Kate Bush, still retains something of Peter Pan, almost forty years after she plundered a children's toy chest and sang those haunting verses of youthful shyness and wonder, 'In Search of Peter Pan'.

Probing a little deeper, it is also hard not to suspect that for many people in past decades there was always something a little irresponsible, unworldly and in the end *feminine* about male 'airy-fairy' creative types. Although not obviously singling out writers or artists, as early as 1933 Dr Maurice Newfield, discussing 'the Peter Pan complex', warned readers that 'there are far too many grown-up children in the world ... an adult who refuses to adopt all the responsibilities that are demanded of a grown person is neither desirable personally nor socially useful.' If Newfield ever watched *A Midsummer Night's Dream*, he must surely have sided in Act Five with Theseus, not Hippolyta. Like the fairies, creativity is, for more analytic minds, irresponsible, insubstantial, and ultimately useless. Looking at this parallel another way, we can respond that, like the fairies, creativity is powerful. Whether or not creativity is 'feminine', or some special union of male and female principles, it is certainly magical – not least in the sense that it so airily produces something where there was nothing, or turns this into *that* ...

Theseus, Freud and Newfield would probably tell you that the Peter Pan types of the past century have all been neurotics; and one psychiatric line on schizophrenics is indeed that they are people who have failed to make the transition between childhood and adulthood. Yet fans of Spielberg alone make a weighty opposition to this analytic stance. One great gift from Barrie – a man himself ferociously psychoanalysed by many critics and biographers – has been to give these 'grown-up children' a new and powerful way to think about themselves: an identity at once as definite as that slight, impish figure, and as expansively mythic as the skies over Neverland.

His second gift can only be hinted at here. Across over a hundred years of war, atrocity and terrorism, adults living between 1914 and the present have enjoyed a strange relationship with childhood. For many years now, millions of adults have periodically counted the hours to the midnight release of the new Harry Potter book. In children's literature, as we saw, adult and child sometimes enact a curious dance of nostalgia, regression or selection, whether the adult is reader or writer of the bedtime story. And at the start of the twentieth century, J. M. Barrie got in first. Before *The Wind in the Willows*, before *Swallows and Amazons*, before Narnia or Middle earth or Pullman or Potter, there was *Peter Pan*. The anthropologist Joseph Campbell once described the scenes in *Star Wars'* Mos Eisley space-bar as 'the jumping off point' – the place where somehow the transition between the familiar and the magical becomes possible. From Lewis's wardrobe, through to Rowling's Platform Nine and Three-quarters, these liminal zones have been central to the great escapes of children's literature. Although anticipated to some extent by Alice's rabbit hole, the leap of imagination which viewers and readers took with Peter and co. through that nursery window must have helped many later authors defy adult gravity.

How far, then, do we owe our peculiar century of childhood to Barrie, the man whose own childhood was curiously arrested and distorted at age six? One thing we can say for certain is this. It is a great and magical art to take the bad things which happen to you and bewitch them into something good. J. M. Barrie magicked his neurosis into myth. And in the end, it is this he most deserves to be remembered for.

Pretty Fairies: Children and the Feminine

If fairies were everything ever said about them, they would be very confused creatures indeed. Even as their formidable power and danger persisted in the minds of thousands of British country-dwellers, they were being prettified, miniaturized and indeed more or less commodified for the pleasure of privileged children. In 1800 the phrase 'pretty fairies' seems to have been little used – a rare example from this year employs it to refer not just to children, but to little girls in particular. But across the following two-hundred-odd years, variants of this association abounded in art, literature, stage, screen and fashion.

In Part II of *Christabel* in 1800, Coleridge pictured

A little child, a limber elf,
Singing, dancing to itself,
A fairy thing with red round cheeks

and over a century later, in 1917, the children's author Rose Fyleman immortalized the idea of 'fairies at the bottom of the garden'. In between, children and fairies enjoyed an ambiguous relationship on the stage.

Famously, the eight-year-old Ellen Terry appeared as Puck atop a mechanical mushroom in 1856, while in the following year her elder sister, Kate, played Ariel atop a dolphin's back, and riding upon a bat. Yet around these now celebrated islands of fairy theatre, the ephemeral and dazzling froth of more obscure entertainments may well have been the first and strongest impression which many children had of fairyland. A 'fairy pantomime' called *Harlequin Puck* was gracing the Royal Surrey Theatre on Boxing Day 1842, and in following decades that term became an alluring form of re-branding for many children's plays, from *Cinderella* to *Puss in Boots*.

The ambiguity of these stage delights arose because, increasingly, many of them featured children. As Diane Purkiss has emphasized, what may have seemed magical for those in the stalls could feel like long, grinding, underpaid labour for the young children who performed. She estimates around 1,000 seasonal fairies working in London for Victorian Christmas theatre, and around 5,000 across the country as a whole. Nominally aged between seven and twelve, some of these paid imps may have been as young as five. In December 1878 one London *Cinderella* featured a hundred child actors, and come 1908 *Pinkie and the Fairies* was one among several plays for children and acted by them. (This example, with inspired opportunism, featured not only elves and fairies but Cinderella, Jack the Giant Killer and Sleeping Beauty.) While these pieces were indebted to *Peter Pan*, it had been the 1901 panto *Bluebell in Fairy Land* which gave ideas to one J. M. Barrie when he took the Llewelyn Davies children to see it that December. Tellingly, its star, Ellaline Terriss (previously known for playing Carroll's Alice), felt obliged in a *Daily Mail* interview to emphasize how well-fed and tutored child actors were, recalling the many 'ragged, half-starved children' who had applied for work in *Alice*, and the beneficial transformation they underwent in their new employment.

For those who could afford the luxury of a sheltered middle-class childhood, the magic was still alive from the First to the Second World War. Fyleman's poem of May 1917 caught the spirit of the times, prompting five publishers to write to her within a week, and three further volumes of fairy poems from her hand in the following eight years.

> There are fairies at the bottom of our garden!
> It's not so very, very far away . . .

Spoken by a small girl, this famous piece partly echoes Allingham with its sense of everyday fairy magic for those careful enough to see it. And yet, at the risk of sounding like the miserable tyke who would not lift a hand to save Tinker Bell, I have to say that the deftly evoked proximity of all this elfin magic is not quite what it seems.

For the speaker goes on to direct the reader past the gardener's shed, and on to a small wood with a stream running through it. To me, this sounds pretty far away from the house, and any neighbours, roads or modern industry. So, yes, there might be fairies at the bottom of your garden, if your garden is large enough to feature a private wood, a stream and a shed for your paid gardener ... Readers may not be surprised to learn that Fyleman was privately educated, nor that when she failed to make it to university she was given £200 to go and learn singing in Paris, Berlin and London.

Still, any such sceptics must, in summer 1923, have been silenced when 'twenty thousand fairies' gathered 'in the brightest valley of Robin Hood's country' to sing to the visiting Prince of Wales and 30,000 other spectators. Although the 20,000 were in fact children, there is no evidence that they were *dressed* as fairies – the above quotations from the *Mail* thereby implying that by this time children and fairies were increasingly synonymous. Just a few months later, the *Nottingham Evening Post* offered children the chance to become at least Associate Fairies, if they could afford the price of a stamp and do 'one kind action every day'. The Tinker Bell Club enrolment form appeared in the second issue of the paper's new children's column, 'The Wendy Hut'. Kicking off on 3 March 1924, this feature ran daily for years, and was still an intermittent regular until September 1941. Along with a very solidly built Wendy house, the opener seen here offers a Tinker Bell not remotely inclined to *embonpoint*, and looking indeed rather like a flapper practising the Charleston. So successful was 'The Wendy Hut' that it even spawned a brief run of parodic fairy newspapers in the *Post*: 'Fairyland News' had a bright green banner, cost 'one violet', and offered an ironic re-creation of the fairies' ability to mirror so much of human life. The recent visit of Tinker Bell to the court of King Oberon and Queen Titania, for example, had prompted the introduction of radio broadcasting in fairyland, while the News in Brief told of how 'Peter Pan's friends half hoped he might have had a birthday this year'. Meanwhile, back in 'The Wendy Hut' itself, Peter had been reimagined as 'half boy, half fairy', while the waspish Tinker Bell had somehow become 'the sweetest fairy . . . always trying to do kind things for Peter and the boys'.

Across this period, then, children might see, hear or read of fairies, or in some curious way *be* fairies, when looked down upon by rose-misted adults. Yet there was also one more possible relationship. As we saw, Newfield sternly reproached those adult 'Peter Pans' who refused to adopt 'the responsibilities . . . of a grown up person'. At the same time, many adults gave children the responsibility to continue believing in fairies, and to somehow preserve a more general spirit of wonder, long since battered from the grown-up world by industry, reason and war. In 1881 Robert Hunt, a scientist whose West Country childhood prompted him to collect and publish fairy folklore as *Popular Romances of the West of England*, told of how 'a scientific friend . . . deep in the cold thrall of positivism' had accused him of inventing most of the stories in the book. Being thus prompted to lament an age when 'our most sacred things are being sneered at, and the poetry of life is being repressed by the prose of a cold infidelity,' Hunt opposed that mentality to his own childhood. As a boy 'I drank deeply from the stream of legendary lore which was at that time flowing, as from a well of living waters,' imbibing this nourishment in part through a young woman who took him 'to seek for the fairies on Lelant Towans. The maiden and the boy frequently sat for hours, entranced by the stories of an old woman, who lived in a cottage on the edge of . . . that region.' Such things, Hunt adds, 'make a strong impression on the mind of the child' and 'are rarely obliterated by . . . education.'

Given his profession as a Victorian chemist, Hunt's sense of the undying power of childhood wonder is especially striking. At the other end of the scale, Edmund Gosse (1849–1928) registered the general right of children to imaginative fancy when he recalled how miserably lacking it had been in his own starkly Puritan childhood.

Not a single fiction was read or told to me during my infancy . . .
Never . . . did anyone address to me the affecting preamble, 'Once
upon a time!' I was told about missionaries, but never about pirates;
I was familiar with humming-birds, but I had never heard of fairies.

Yet, if 'the soft folds of supernatural fancy' were for Gosse's luckier
peers as natural and familiar as a favourite blanket, matters had
changed in some quarters by January 1930. 'The Teachers' College of
Columbia', the *Mail* had learned, 'is banishing "insidious fairy tales"
for ones with strictly practical value'. An imagined dialogue between
mother and child – "'Look, mummy, a fairy!'"; "'No dear, you are
deceived, take up your Encyclopedia and look up British entomol-
ogy'" – is followed by the indignant assertion that 'magic was before
science and will be after it. Fairies live longer than pedagogues.'

Come 1895 the *American Journal of Psychology* was referring to a
'secret organisation' of homosexuals in New York, calling itself 'The
Fairies'. As Noel Williams has noted, an association between fairies
and gay men may have existed as early as the sixteenth century.
Despite the often pejorative use of 'fairies' in this context in later
decades, the label seems to have been self-selected by this avant-
garde of gay men during the 1890s. Why? Fairy femininity is one
obvious reason. The peculiarly inbetween character of traditional
fairies may have been another; and the necessary secrecy of gay
culture might also have played some part. Perhaps, too, those who
selected and used this term were aware of the potent glamour which
had shimmered so darkly around the real fairies of the Celtic hills.

A strong degree of ambiguity certainly clung to the 'pretty fairies'
of the other sex. After all, a good way into the twentieth century
women were still treated like children in many ways. Married women
gained full rights over their own property only in 1893, and women
had no voting rights of any sort until 1918. Henrik Ibsen had created
outrage in 1879 when, in *A Doll's House*, he had the infantilized
Nora finally object to her status as a child handed down from father
to husband.

For a long time, some women actively embraced their fairy status. Offered the chance to be magically ethereal, elusive, mysterious and capricious, how could they resist? At Victorian society fancy dress balls both Titania and Ariel were popular characters, and by the twentieth century a loose alliance was being formed between fairyland and the more self-conscious modern fashion industry. The rounded 'Peter Pan' collar invented by the first Broadway Peter, Maude Adams, in 1905, was catching on in Britain by 1909, and still popular in dresses made by plumo in 2012; while in summer 1923 the *Daily Mirror*'s London Fashion Fair prompted the reflection that 'fashion is one of the greatest ruling fairies in the world, for with her magic touch she produced a real and perfect union of the women of all nations.'

And what, of course, could better fit the graceful superfluity, the whimsical extravagance, of feminine adornment than ... fairy wings? From the 1980s to Paris Fashion Week of 2004, when they sprouted from one of John Galliano's creations, these seemed well suited to the anorexic modern fancy dress of high fashion. The difference now, of course, was that it was all rather more self-conscious fun: one of those temporary feminine performances which a woman might adopt before reverting to jeans, DM boots or combat trousers. Or – was it? Viewed from certain angles, this picture gets surprisingly complicated. In 1999, for example, Jane Lovatt found her eleven-year-old daughter already looking with contempt on childish fairy-winged dresses, and when referring that same year to the newly opened outlet *Girl Heaven*, Daisy Waugh felt that little girls of her time 'grow out of fairy wings before they grow out of cots.'

Surely, then, they were now banished from everywhere but under-twelves fancy dress and the studied mannerism of the catwalk? But, 21 years after the UK's first female prime minister, and eighteen after the first male Peter Pan, fairy wings were still fluttering through Canterbury. Here in 2000, Miranda Seymour was surprised to have a young woman called Anoushka Hardy tell her, 'I'm a fairy. I wear wings.' She wore them, indeed, not only to go clubbing, but while doing housework (possibly with that iconic washing-up liquid in her hand), and owned 23 pairs, 'not counting my best midnight blue ones'. Anoushka was perfectly happy with people laughing at these appendages in public, explaining that 'wearing wings means you're going to be treated like a child . . . it's all about innocence'. At the time of writing, Anoushka was only one of many twenty-something women who could be seen out drinking in wings, glitter and tulip-petalled chiffon skirts. Such innocence came relatively cheap, with Topshop retailing a wings-and-wand fairy set for just £10.

Cottingley

In December 1920 the fairies came to London. For once, they were not rehearsing the latest Christmas panto. And, although they had travelled all the way from Yorkshire to the great capital of the Empire, they were not in the least shy or intimidated. From the pages of the *Strand* magazine their photographs stared out at gawping Londoners, and their champion was none other than Sir Arthur Conan Doyle himself. In July and September 1917 two Yorkshire cousins, Frances Griffiths and Elsie Wright, had taken two fairy photographs at the beck beneath their home in Cottingley. Because Elsie's mother, Polly, was interested in Theosophy, these presently caught the attention of Edward Gardner, a prominent member of the Theosophical Society, and next that of Doyle.

Thanks to the arduous labours of Joe Cooper (on whose work much of the following depends) we know that Doyle was initially sceptical of these first two photographs. He was not alone. Kenneth Styles, a 'fairy authority' of the day, expressed his suspicions to Doyle, as did physicist and paranormal researcher Sir Oliver Lodge, who was perhaps the first to note the sprites' oddly Parisienne hair. But matters changed when in summer 1920 Gardner travelled to Cottingley and the girls managed to take three further fairy photographs. In summer 1921 a medium, Geoffrey Hodson, spent much time in Cottingley with the girls. Though no new photographs resulted, we still have many minutely detailed descriptions of fairies allegedly seen by himself and the cousins.

Doyle's own attitude, though still fluid, now became at times almost messianic. In his tellingly titled 1922 book *The Coming of the Fairies*, he writes:

> the series of incidents set forth in this little volume represent either the most elaborate and ingenious hoax ever played upon the public, or else they constitute an event in human history which may in the future appear to have been epoch-making in its character.

Seen as a whole, this work seems to display a man still getting to grips with the whole affair. But at his most optimistic, Doyle is fervent indeed:

> I must confess that after months of thought I am unable to get the true bearings of this event. One or two consequences are obvious. The experiences of children will be taken more seriously. Cameras will be forthcoming. Other well-authenticated cases will come along. These little folk who appear to be our neighbours, with only some small difference of vibration to separate us, will become familiar. The thought of them, even when unseen, will add a charm to every brook and valley . . . The recognition of their existence will jolt the material twentieth-century mind out of its heavy ruts in the mud, and will make it admit that there is a glamour and a mystery to life.

He then goes on to compare the whole matter to the European discovery of the Americas, seeing the girls' spiritual world as a similarly life-changing new continent. The cruel irony of the third sentence above hardly needs emphasizing. Readers will also by now probably notice how the once perilous magical glamour of the true fairies has here taken on a very different shine. We might add that, for the spiritualist who had lost both a son and a brother to the First

The century's most famous fairies: Frances Griffiths and the fairies, taken by Elsie Wright, 1917.

World War, those 'heavy ruts' sound grimly like the tracks of wheeled cannon. Notice too, though, an internal contradiction: can these new, camera-friendly fairies really be both familiar *and* mysterious?

For decades the photographs, and Frances and Elsie, played an artful game of cat and mouse with sceptics and the media. Doubters were already vocal in the 1920s. Having referred to one fairy's 'up-to-date dress' and bobbed hair in March 1921, the *Daily Mail* found the pictures useful artillery two years later, during an outburst of indignation at new photographs exhibited by Doyle, claiming to show 'massed spirits of dead soldiers hovering over the crowds' at the Whitehall Cenotaph. That this memorial 'should become the centre now of sensational theories, absolutely unproved and probably as grossly faked as the famous photographs of Hampstead Heath fairies, with gauze wings and bobbed hair, is revolting to hundreds of thousands of men and women in this country'. Our learned reporter does not explain how they had managed to interview all these men and women, or why the fairies had fled Cottingley for north London. Nor is it clear why the emphatically Christian paper objects to the spirits of war heroes looking down from Heaven at their loved ones. Once again, fairies sit very low, here, in an implicit hierarchy of supernatural beliefs.

At a 1927 clairvoyant demonstration in Dover Town Hall, one Howard Bradley showed how closely the Cottingley photos were bound up with the validity of spiritualism per se when he asked: 'is it not a fact that Sir Arthur Conan Doyle's fairy photographs have proved to be taken from a well-known advertisement?' Doyle himself seems to have gone to his grave, in 1930, still persuaded of the genuineness of the images. But the story lived on – and grew. When a *Daily Express* reporter tracked Elsie down in May 1965, she already sounded rather ambiguous: 'as for the photographs, let's say they are pictures of figments of our imagination, Frances and mine, and leave it at that.' Cooper, who cites this, also gives an interesting moment from a Yorkshire Television interview of 1976. Referring to Hodson, presenter Austin Mitchell states:

'You told him you saw fairies – were you pulling his leg or not?' Frances: 'No. We saw them.'

Both women, however, now laugh, and admit that they had at times played mischievous games with Hodson, describing to him non-existent sprites in the belief that he 'was a phony'. In 1978 the American magician and arch-sceptic James Randi had the results of supposedly cutting-edge computer analysis published in *New Scientist*. The report emphasized, 'among other evidence of fakery, the strings holding up the fairies'. Although no such strings ever existed, they nonetheless set Randi's mind at rest, and helped him confirm what he already knew.

It was in fact the more open-minded Cooper who first heard the truth, in September 1981. A faintly ominous phone message from Frances ('there are things you should know') resulted in a drive to Canterbury, where Cooper was asked to wait in a coffee shop while Frances, interestingly, paid a brief (confessional?) visit to the cathedral, before rejoining him at their table.'Frances eyed me', writes Cooper,'with amusement."From where I was, I could see the hat-pins holding up the figures. I've always marvelled that anybody ever took it seriously."' Even now, however, Frances insisted that one of the five shots (the'fairy sunbath', with neither girl in frame) was genuine. "'Elsie didn't have anything ready, so we had to take one of them building up in the bushes.""So that's the first photo ever of real fairies?""Yes."'

When the two women confessed more publicly to the press in March 1983, Elsie's stance was notably ambiguous. With *The Times* announcing that'the reputations of the world's most famous fairies and Sir Arthur Conan Doyle . . . are in tatters', and pointing up how Doyle had taken one hatpin for a fairy's navel, Elsie, now 82, insisted that'she was proud of the one photograph which her cousin believes is genuine' – adding, rather pointedly,'I am sorry someone has stabbed all our fairies to death with a hatpin.' Those clinging to this last piece of hard fairy evidence were to be jolted that April when Geoffrey Crawley (now owner of the photographs) wrote to *The Times*, explaining that this picture was merely an unintended double exposure.

By now some readers may have hovering in their minds that refreshingly blunt question of our opening pages, 'Do fairies exist?' I will say more about this – and the question of whether fairies existed at Cottingley – in a moment. Before I do, it is hardly less intriguing to ask,'what did the Cottingley fairies *mean* to the world, across a century of war, terrorism, and unprecedented technological change?' And what, first of all, did they mean to Frances and Elsie? As we saw, Doyle was one of that small elite who created literary myths, instantly recognizable by name, from the 1880s on. And, thirty years after the birth of Sherlock Holmes, two very ordinary girls created their own unforgettable icons, aided by Holmes's cre-ator. These images are now so famous and so potent that it is hard to imagine them never having existed. Challenged only by the Disney version of Peter Pan or Tinker Bell, they are perhaps the most easily recognizable fairies of the past hundred years. Surely, then, for both Elsie and Frances in the decades down to 1983, the Cottingley fairies were a source of strange and amazing *power* . . .

And, neatly enough, this power had the secrecy and the play-fulness of the true fairies themselves. Nowhere was that impish defiance of cold positivism more obvious than in the unfinished play which Elsie began in 1978, just weeks after the slightly comical 'expo-sure' of the pictures by Randi and co. This drama opened with Puck gesturing to the unseen stage behind the theatre curtains, where a giant oyster shell was surrounded by reporters, still vainly trying to prise it open sixty years on. The pearl nestled inside, Puck explained, was either 'a pearl bursting joke' or 'a lustrous pearl of beauty . . . capable of whisking people's imaginations off to gorgeous . . . fairy land places'. When the curtains open, all but one of the weary jour-nalists wander off. Having climbed up to sit in baffled contemplation on the giant shell, he finds to his astonishment that 'two wings expand from each side of the shell' and float him away.

What else did the Cottingley fairies mean to the wider world? They seemed very quickly to become a kind of British national treasure. In its earliest years this pearl was closely bound up with the shattering horrors of war. After the traumas of the Somme and Verdun, these five extraordinary frames might appear to distil much of the beauty, peace, grace and innocence which British soldiers had fought to preserve. It is hard to imagine that this nostalgic treasure would have been prized so fiercely had it arisen from the cunning tricks of two boys, rather than girls. Fairies had been heavily fem-inized for decades by this time, and it was the perfect moment to oppose this new version of spiritualized femininity to the masculine suffering and the masculine lunacy of the war and its aftermath.

And youth, too, was vital to the mixture. We know this at one level because of the recurrent hint that children could see fairies when most adults could not. An article of 1921 quoted Elsie as saying, 'in their more recent appearances the fairies were more "transparent" than in 1916 and 1917, when they were "rather hard . . . You see, we were young then.'" Both Doyle and Gardner also felt that, with the girls growing up fast by 1920, there was little time to be lost if new evidence was to be secured. At another level, we know that youth was important precisely because of the way it was falsely imposed on so many versions of the affair. The 1997 film *Fairytale*, for example, has the nineteen-year-old Elsie played by a girl who looks no more than fourteen, and also oddly collapses the events of 1917 and 1920 together, as if keen to preserve the girls, Peter Pan style, in that one ageless Yorkshire summer of the first pictures. Any doubts as to the 'childishness' of Elsie are easily scotched by a glance at the assured and stylish young woman seated beside Hodson in a photograph of 1921.

Similarly, *Fairytale* manages to play up the idyllic rural side of Cottingley in a way that is less than faithful to its more urban qualities. Perhaps most strikingly, it invents a severely wounded soldier, missing almost half his face, who is first met by Frances on a train and who later rescues the innocent girls from a slimy reporter. When the soldier's notably tremulous query to the girls about the reality of the fairies is answered in the affirmative, the force of his relief ('I knew it; I just knew it') is almost metaphysical. This invention not only highlights the sense that, after a certain point, the cousins could not bear to disappoint all the believers they had created, but again underlines the impression that the whole potent fusion (fairies, girls, English nature) offered something free and pure, something worth fighting for and living for, once the smoke of war had faded.

It was still being fought for, a little more prosaically, in 1998, when Arthur Wright's original cameras and prints came up for sale. *Fairytale* had been produced by Mel Gibson's company, Icon Productions, and Gibson himself makes a fleeting uncredited cameo appearance in the film as Frances's just-returned soldier father. He now bid high for Wright's Cottingley artefacts, thus threatening to take part of the British national treasure abroad. Touchingly, Geoffrey Crawley, who owned the cameras and prints, agreed to let them stay in the UK provided £14,000 was raised, even though he could have sold to Gibson for much more. This sum was reached with public help, and donations from Canon, Jessops and Olympus. In June 1998 the Midg and Cameo cameras which had shot the fairy photographs were given to Bradford's National Museum of Photography 'in front of a 2,000 strong crowd chanting "Fairies coming home"' ('Fairytale Ending . . ', *The Times*, 8 October 1998).

Having said all this, a few further words are in order about photographs. The cousins were not in fact the first people to think of this possibility. Back in more traditional fairy territory, Cyril Allies of Inisbofin was once out rabbit-shooting when he was informed by 'an old man that a crowd of fairy girls were around him. He offered a large reward to be shown one or to be allowed to photograph one,' but down to Westropp's visit in 1911 the reward was unclaimed. For many, there seems to be something beguilingly paradoxical about the very idea of fairy photographs. These are two words which just should not go together, any more than you can put a leprechaun in a workhouse, or an angel in a zoo. As Cooper shows, two reporters of the early 1920s were deeply offended by the whole possibility, with the *South Wales Argus* warning that 'the day we kill Santa Claus with our statistics and our photographs we shall have plunged a glorious world into deepest darkness,' and the North American *Sun* feeling that Doyle 'does not bring the fairies nearer to us. The soul of the fairy is its evanescence. Its charm is the eternal doubt, rose-tinted with the shadow of a hope.' Keats, whose fairy Lamia was destroyed by the piercing (photographic?) eye of Apollonius, would surely agree.

On the other side of the coin, Doyle and Gardner clearly valued the pictures just because they seemed to be the ultimate in hard evidence. In this, they were part of a notable unofficial group who across the long twentieth century attempted to weigh the soul or have it photographed leaving the body at death, to autopsy aliens, or to X-ray the recently fabricated fairy posted on the Internet, nestled on (what else?) a police evidence bag.

At the heart of all this lie some powerful questions. Why have many of us come to value the permanently visible over what people tell us? In a court of law the latter is taken very seriously indeed; elsewhere, it is often degraded to the status of the 'merely anecdotal'. Let us assume that all five of the Cottingley photographs were fakes. And now listen to what Frances told Cooper about a childhood trip to the beck. Struck by the shaking of just one single willow leaf, though there was no wind, 'as I watched, a small man, all dressed in green, stood on the branch with the stem of the leaf in his hand, which he seemed to be shaking at something.' Presently 'he looked straight at me and disappeared.' Echoing what we have heard earlier, when Elsie was asked by Mitchell in 1976 why the cousins no longer saw fairies at the beck, she replied, 'I think it's really because we were only children – we were very young then.'

Let us assume for a second (and we had better whisper this) that fairies do exist . . . Are children for some reason more likely to see them? Two stories told directly to me by very hard-headed people indicate that children certainly can see ghosts, when these are felt by, though not visible to, adults. Why? I wish I knew; but something about the relative blankness of the child's mind, its less rigid sense of the impossible, is probably important. Much more on the seeing of fairies in a few moments. But let us close our visit to Cottingley with what Cooper heard, in the early 1980s, from local forester and ex-wrestler Ronnie Bennett, a man who for twenty years had worked in woods in and around Cottingley, often sleeping there through the night. Of his brief encounter with woodland fairies, he stated: 'I didn't see one, I saw three . . . and I didn't sleep for three nights after I'd seen what I'd seen.'

Fairy Magic?

The Cottingley affair shows that for some, mechanized warfare only made fairies the more magical by contrast. Yet, across the hundred years between 1917 and 2017, machinery and technology have often threatened to bludgeon the numinous otherness of the fairies out of existence.

How far has this process been the result of Disneyfication? This term, which began to appear in the 1950s, shortly after the first Disneyland site opened in California, is defined by the *Oxford English Dictionary* as 'the simplification, sanitization, or romanticization of a place or concept' in ways typical of Disney's films and theme parks. The earliest Disney films certainly thrived on the commercialization of magic and fairy tales. Not unlike Shakespeare, Disney took some simple elemental stories and made them his own. Also like Shakespeare, he had a knack for pleasing almost everyone, from the smallest children to the most sophisticated adults.

The 1940 *Pinocchio* indeed offers us a good deal of reductive and shallow moralizing, supervised by the Blue Fairy: a blonde, winged, middle-class American mother, with uncredited voiceover by the Columbia pictures actress Evelyn Venable. Perhaps the sugary glow suffusing this character helped obscure the basic fact that she had, like some female Prometheus, *given life* to a wooden puppet – a blasphemy or heresy ranking with those of traditional fairy believers. In that same year, *Fantasia's* sugar plum fairy has a more conventional life-giving role, as her miniaturized, rather more erotic figure jewels flowers and spiderwebs with fairy dust, visually echoing the elfin labours of *A Midsummer Night's Dream*, or Allingham's Victorian poetry. Underpinned by Tchaikovsky's famous score, this brief vignette is arguably Disney's most magical fairy moment, its strong colours gaining force from the violet darkness against which the fairies dive and swirl.

Come the 1953 *Peter Pan*, it is hard not to see shades of the Blue Fairy in Disney's Wendy – a portrayal arguably still more sexist than Barrie's original, and (largely owing to her voice) often positively soppy. Peter, too, is over-simplified, losing much of his extra-human quality during flirtations with Tinker Bell, Wendy or Tiger Lily. Tellingly, perhaps the best elements of this version are rather masculine ones. The tumultuous slapstick of the Lost Boys exploits high-speed animation for every kilojoule of tumbling mayhem. Yet, while one can well imagine any watching fairies fistling away in delight, this boyish exuberance contrasts sharply with the controlling domestic instincts of their honorary mother, Wendy.

Were we able to pitch some true Celtic fairy believer down one midnight under the Bavarian towers and pennants of Disneyland, they might well fancy themselves in an enchanted fairy castle. As for the modern Disneyland experience, this itself has changed radically across sixty years. The status of a child's one-off visit to this American otherworld must surely have diminished in the last two decades, when they can constantly pre-visit or revisit the site via Internet stills or personal films.

The Disneyland figures of Peter Pan or the Blue Fairy have of course been as crudely reduced as anything the studio ever created. Arguably, when in costume these actors would be swiftly recognizable as their given types in the densest city crowd in New York or Tokyo. Internet responses to them nevertheless suggest that they yet retain that peculiarly inbetween glamour we encountered in our opening pages. In this sense, they might indeed be seen as ironic celebrities: like Johnny Depp or Keira Knightley they spend a lot of time in public trying not to look like themselves, albeit for very different reasons.

Meanwhile, back on film, Disney's Tinker Bell franchise offers children as young as three some very brittle and worldly glamour. Promotional shots of Tinker Bell and her friends look at first glance like some kind of fairy girls' night out, and the ultra-stylized types are so easily transferable that they can, via a partial costume change, effortlessly become 'fairy musketeers', with their elfin status guaranteed by wings alone. Interestingly, this Disneyfied Tinker Bell may be recognized by many children via her exaggerated eyes rather than her wings, suggesting a link with the facial types of the massively successful *Frozen*.

Among the myriad ironic contrasts between these children's fairies and the terrifying child thieves of the past, perhaps two are more easily forgotten. Once, fairy glamour depended on that astonishing single encounter with a riot of colour and riches such as you would, literally, never see again. Simply, precious things and precious colours. For many Western children, versions of fairy glamour are now endlessly available, while its cacophonous pigments are a mundane norm, rather than a dazzling exception. Moreover, even within Disney's own commercial lifespan, the aggressive hues of the fairy wardrobe have recently hardened beneath a flat digital veneer which makes *Fantasia* seem richly, hazily numinous by comparison.

How far has this aesthetic reductionism tainted other recent fairy offerings? Whatever the cause, it seems generally agreed that *Peter Pan* defeated the remarkable directing talents of both Steven Spielberg and Joe Wright. For many critics the 1991 *Hook* was the weakest film of Spielberg's career to date, kept sadly earthbound by its prosaic new plot and the weight of its high-tech budget. Come 2015, the usually virtuosic Wright met the same fate, with another redrafted Pan story sapping the vital energies so conspicuous in films such as *Pride and Prejudice* or *Atonement*. Once again, the overload of CGI came under fire from many critics of *Pan*. At times, this clash between fairy magic and heavyweight machinery found its way onto the stage as well. In 1996 the parents of three-year-old Morris Mitchener attempted to sue the West Yorkshire Playhouse after the child fled under his seat, yelling 'Get me out!', in the opening minutes of the theatre's new *Peter Pan*. One element of the Playhouse's defence was to respond that the terrifying voiceover ('like Peter Cushing at 100 decibels', according to Amanda Mitchener) had been broadly signalled by a programme note declaring the performance unsuitable for under-sevens.

In the face of this we might at least hope that fairies, fled from the high-tech thunder of modern cinema, found refuge on the printed page. This is not entirely true, given the mechanized and vastly successful fairies of the Rainbow Magic book franchise. Where once the fairies might steal away children on 31 October, here Trixie the Halloween Fairy is their saviour, making 'sure that Halloween is fun-filled and exciting for everyone'. Stepping sideways slightly, we do find film, technology and fairy darkness united to magical effect in Jim Henson's 1986 *Labyrinth*, and Guillermo del Toro's more recent *Pan's Labyrinth* (2006). In both cases, children's forays into the underworld are powerful elements; a female friend of mine, recalling the former from her own childhood, remains bewildered by how sexual the experience was for her. In terms of edge, Disney itself does offer one striking counterpoint to its more typical fairy ventures. Robert Stromberg's 2014 film *Maleficent* is dominated by an iconic fairy figure whose Pan-like horns and majestic wings defy easy or familiar categories. Weaving a poetical chiaroscuro around this ambiguous heroine, the picture offers some closing scenes in which Angelina Jolie dramatically rediscovers those fallen angels with whom our story began.

Yet broadly the contrast does seem to hold good. The freedom of literature gives the fairies life, where the vampiric camera often drains it away. Probably the most powerful and popular example is Tolkien's elf-haunted epic, *The Lord of the Rings*. We might also glance at the revived Merlin figure, Merriman Lyon, in Susan Cooper's eerie novel *The Dark is Rising*. The bleakly luminous atmosphere of that snow-bound work reminds us that, in many cases, fairy magic cannot really shine without an edge of darkness to sharpen it. Undoubtedly the best literary example of this in the past twenty years has been Susanna Clarke's extraordinary creation, *Jonathan Strange and Mr Norrell* (2004). The potent Northern fairy twilight and threat of this book are somehow only intensified by the satire of the hopelessly academic and antiquarian York Society of Magicians, and all its attendant Regency trappings – rather as if M. R. James had been asked to produce a fairy version of his archetypal ghost stories. Interestingly, the darkling glamour of the novel's fairy gentleman does not lose its magic when seen through the camera's eye. The 2015 Canadian screen version brilliantly re-imagines the fantastic shadows of the fairy underworld and the Northern landscapes of the human realm.

No less recently, the fairies crept sideways into the work of one of Britain's most accomplished writers, David Mitchell. Towards the close of *Slade House* Doctor Iris Marinus-Fenby nervously drops a wild strawberry which would reduce her to being one more victim of the house's mysterious twins, explaining: 'In all the tales, the myths, the rule is, if you eat or drink anything – pomegranate seeds, faerie wine, whatever – the place has a hold on you.' In doing so she causes readers to reconceptualize the pivotal role of the 'banjax' which the novel's previous victims had to imbibe voluntarily to fall into the clutches of Norah and Jonah.

For me, however, the most haunting brush with fairy literature of the modern age occurred on the October evening when I sat spellbound in the lamplit hush of the British Library's rare books room, inhaling the scent of old paper that rose from Maurice Hewlett's 1913 work, *The Lore of Proserpine*. Just what was I reading? Beginning like a conventional autobiography, the book swiftly tumbled me down a rabbit hole, as Hewlett moved from a photographically precise evocation of a twilit Sunday walk to the moment when, lagging behind his family, he stood in damp greying woods before a fairy boy calmly throttling a rabbit. No less arrestingly realist was the story of a Wiltshire bank clerk, Stephen Beckwith, who around 10 p.m. on 30 November 1887 chances on an injured fairy girl while out with his dog. Months after Beckwith has taken the girl into his family home, she disappears with his young daughter, Flossie, who is never seen again. Frustrating as it is trying to convey the haunting voices of this extraordinary work, I would strongly recommend readers to try it for themselves: failing an appointment with those thickly textured pages in London, the online versions should be intoxicating enough, if imbibed in tranquil leisure. For now, the best summary of Hewlett's fairy world is to say that it is perhaps second only to *The Lord of the Rings* in the way that it so brilliantly remakes the *inbetween* quality of our traditional fairies. At times *The Lore of Proserpine* seems almost to be a unique genre in its own right. The driest, most measured tones recount the utterly impossible in a way that leaves one rapturously stranded between fact and fiction.

At that stage, however, I had no idea how sharply new fairy images might still surprise me. The following January, on a dark afternoon two days before I travelled to the funeral of my old friend Christopher, my teacher friend Emily dropped into my lap a riot of fairy colour and energy. Learning that there had indeed nearly been a riot among the impatient children of Wadhurst Primary School when a broken photocopier delayed their fairy artistry, I sat rapt and startled as the bewildering range of fairy types fistled past our eyes.

To say that only four of the 66 creations lacked wings is to say very little at all about their breezy defiance of the expected current stereotypes. Some were tribal; some insectile or reptilian; some spiky; at least two faintly New Age; one cannibalistic; a couple witch-like; and another strikingly extraterrestrial. Quite often, a closer look at what seemed to be a girl's picture showed it to be a boy's work, or vice versa. Smaller children (the age range being six to eleven) seemed just as likely to create dark and jagged images as prettily feminine ones.

The general range of size (which children were asked to give in writing) was usually small: typically 2–10 centimetres, or 'as small as a hazelnut . . . as big as a rubber'. Those who felt fairies to be straightforwardly good slightly outnumbered those who felt them to be 'naughty and evil'. On the whole, however, most descriptions broadly captured the capricious ambiguity of traditional fairy types, with 'mischievous,' 'naughty' and 'cheeky' appearing many times, and the line 'I think fairies are good and bad' (beneath a marvellously fat and ebullient horned imp) being echoed with variations on numerous images. The eleven-year-old girl who felt fairies to be 'similar to humans, but more magical and smaller . . . I don't think they all wear long dresses, and I think they live very similar lives to ours' very nicely captured the older diversity and the uncanny mirroring qualities of Celtic fairyland, and was not the only child to do so.

In a perfect world I should have printed all the drawings, or indeed ranged them in a gallery sponsored by Disney. Failing that,

I would recommend that anyone who finds themself in charge of four or more children sets them to draw fairies, giving them plenty of crayons and no directions. Narrowing matters down to the two which we have space for here, my own impressions are far less valuable than the pictures themselves. At risk of stating the obvious, David Gourd's Blakean fairy offers a striking fusion of energy, power and even joy, and his description ('as big as a squirrel and really fast') aptly distils much of the hurtling kinetic mischief which has bustled through our early chapters. A year younger than David at age ten, Mimi Weller depicts a 'Fairy of War' whose green pixie boots are less immediately obvious than its quasi-Viking headgear, devilishly scarlet wings and outflung bow and arrow. Five centimetres it may be, but then so is a hornet.

Overall, the bristling kaleidoscope of fairy life which tumbled out of Wadhurst Primary School warns us not to forget how resistant children can be to the potentially deadening forces of commercial stereotyping. As with any good performance of *Peter Pan*, they will bring much of the magic with them. We were all of us born into magic, and against considerable odds fairy magic keeps being reborn around us. What we are now about to encounter indeed suggests that at times this process may be surprisingly literal.

Sightings

'In the year 1900–1901, during the South African War, when I was about five years of age, I lived in Gillingham, Kent. Every night for some months, after my mother had kissed me goodnight and shut my bedroom door, there was a short interval, and then I would begin to hear distant, massed Liliputian bands playing.' This music grew louder, and by the light of a nightlight, our witness saw

> column after column of tiny soldiers marching up from the right of my bed over my eiderdown (I remember its pattern and colour

clearly) and across to the other side where they disappeared over the bedside. Each soldier was about nine inches high and wore a red coat. There was battalion after battalion of them, and each was headed by a brass band. As these passed, they played minute martial music, far more exciting than any music I had ever heard in the daytime. The march-past lasted for a few minutes, and then I fell asleep. The direction was always from right to left. I never tried to touch the soldiers, but they were completely real. I actually did see them, and I should be prepared to state this on oath, if necessary, in any Court of Law.

This account was written in 1951 by Victor Purcell. By this time Purcell had fought, been wounded and been taken prisoner in the First World War, acted as a major colonial administrator in Malaya, and become a history lecturer at Cambridge, where he remained until 1963. In short, he was hardly fanciful or unworldly. Like Sir John Randolph Leslie, writing after that leprechaun frenzy of 1938, Purcell thought his evidence good enough for a court of law. The comparison is important, because it reminds us that spoken statements, often derided as 'merely anecdotal', are taken very seriously in certain contexts.

And yet, late in 1951, after press reports that a Limerick housing project had been suspended because workmen, believing a fairy fort to be sited there, 'would not go within miles of it', a very different opinion was heard from Irish Labour MP Sean Dunne. This report, sent out by an Irish news agency, was for Dunne 'one of the most scandalous productions that ever went out of this country'. Was this, he demanded, conducive towards 'the building up of greater respect abroad for the Irish people?'

At a certain stage it became dangerous to believe in fairies, rather than dangerous to disbelieve in them. Nothing could be more ridiculous, childish or irrational than fairy belief. Implicitly, even belief in witches, with all its attendant violence, was less absurd than this. When starting this book, I never imagined that I would spend more

Full name: David Thomas Gourd   Class: Ocelots   [age:] 11

What do you think fairies are like? (good/bad/kind/naughty) Try to write a sentence of two below.

I think fairy's are cheeky and mistires and will show some trouble but wont solves it but doing some thing but they dont know what they have done.

How big do you think fairies are? (Make a comparison, e.g. as tall as a....... / or estimate in cm)

As big as a squirrel and really fast

Blakean fairy: David Gourd, age eleven, 2016.

Fairy of War

called Red

Full name: Mimi Weller age 10 Class: Ocelots

What do you think fairies are like? (good/bad/kind/naughty) Try to write a sentence of two below.

Some fairies are good and some are bad!

How big do you think fairies are? (Make a comparison, e.g. as tall as a......... / or estimate in cm)

5cm

'Fairy of War: called Red', Mimi Weller, age ten, 2016.

than a few lines handling the seemingly straightforward question, 'Do fairies exist?' By now, after reading dozens of accounts like Purcell's, I certainly would not write them off very easily. Selecting the tiniest handful of fairy sightings, I give them here in approximate date order.

In August 1920, though sceptical of the Cottingley fairy photographs, the physicist Sir Oliver Lodge was corresponding with a woman who recalled her childhood experiences of fairies.

> I can remember when I was five years of age . . . slipping out of bed at dawn and going into the garden to talk with the fairies . . . They were always beautiful, never old, not very young, just without age . . . Sometimes as a child I would at night suddenly awake feeling rigid with fright, and I used at once to send a call to the fairies to come to me, and first I would hear faint music growing louder and louder till my room was filled with music and from every side little fairies came and glided along the coverlet of my bed and all my fear was turned to joy, and they put me to sleep again. They have nearly always been accompanied by music.

Politely emphasizing that, with ferocious sceptics at his back, he must probe this account rigorously, Lodge further asks this woman (who is given the pseudonym of Celia Alleyne) if she was really awake during these experiences. Alleyne is quite clear on this point.

> I must tell you that I have been found in the garden in the early morning wet through with the dew, and severely scolded by my mother for slipping out. I can well remember standing on a hall chair to unfasten the bolt and the ugly squeak it made, which I hated so much, not for fear of waking up the household but because 'ugly noises frightened away the fairies' and I thought they would hear. It had to be still and quiet or I could not see them.

For all their compelling detail, these two accounts involve benign fairies, of the sort which children in this era might be expected to imagine. Both feature music, and the soldiers of Purcell's bedtime seem the kind of likely variant one would expect for a boy growing up during a famous war. Matters change, however, when we hear of a woman staying in an old Gloucestershire house, whose garden ended in the forest of Birdlip Beeches. She had washed her hair and was out in the forest, drying it in the sun, when

> suddenly, I felt something tugging at my hair and turned to look. A most extraordinary sight met my eyes. He was about nine inches high, and the most dreadfully ugly, dreadfully misshapen, most wrinkled and tiniest mannikin I have ever seen. He was the colour of dead aspen leaves, sort of yellow-brown – with a high, squeaky voice. He was caught in the strands of my hair . . . struggling to escape . . . telling me I had no right to be there, troubling honest folk, and that I might have strangled him with my hair.

Aside from being emphatically ugly and arrestingly detailed in the woman's memory, this creature is strikingly indignant at her very existence. In this he resembles not only certain other fairies, but some ghosts, possessed of a powerful sense that we, the living, are the marginal intruders. Such instances cannot help but suggest some sudden, illegitimate fracturing of dimensions which should ideally be separate and ignorant of one another. The woman adds that, when describing the experience to a professor at Bristol University, he knew the forest to be one of the last surviving fairy haunts in the country – so much so that 'no one could go there because of it'.

An undated twentieth-century account is equally compelling in its realism.

> It was about 11am on a summer morning, in a place where a river flowed below a large area of wild [Welsh] moorland. I was fly-fishing for trout on the left bank, casting to the opposite bank ... [Presently]

I hooked a half-pound trout, and while playing it clear of the weeds, I became aware of an excited chatter in a high-pitched voice on the far bank slightly upstream of me.

This intruder was speaking English with a Welsh accent, and

as far as I can remember the words were 'Catch him, Tommy, I like to eat trouts, Tommy man; give him to me, Tommy.' I glanced up ... and saw that my visitor, although not tiny enough to be in the Little People category, was small and looked like an oldish man of, say, 65, hatless, with wisps of grey hair and a short, grizzled beard. He was in his shirt-sleeves (colour forgotten) and had very bright green trousers, which came high up his waist. He was dancing about and waving his arms. I was naturally astonished and annoyed, as fishing is, for me, a solitary vice; but I said, 'All right, but I haven't got him yet,' or something of the sort. He paid no attention to this remark, but kept on with his gabble: 'I like trouts, Tommy!' I concentrated for a few seconds on extricating the fish from the weed. During that time I was delighted to notice that the gabble had ceased. As I drew the fish into the shallows, I looked up and my visitor had evaporated. This really did give me a shock, and my heart missed a beat. He had disappeared completely in open ground, as he could not have regained the stile at the end of the road-bridge some 150 yards away and uphill in the few seconds during which I had looked away. I made enquiries in the village, but nobody knew or had seen anyone in any way like the visitor I had described. *How did he know my name?*

Any readers who detected a certain no-nonsense precision in our narrator's tone will be interested to know that he was one Commander T. A. Powell – a man who, in giving his account, emphasized strongly that he was 'not the type ... to see visions'. Indeed, he sounds no more that type than does Purcell, and his memory of this elfin trout-fancier, with its ghostlike ability to dematerialize, comes not from childhood but from adulthood.

Quite recently, a childhood memory was recalled with no less clarity, and supplied in the 1990s by E.J.A. Reynolds to Janet Bord. Staying in Horsham, Sussex, in 1948 during the school holidays, the ten-year-old Reynolds was out one moonlit night setting rabbit traps.

> As I sat still and waited I suddenly realised that a small hairy man had stepped out from a blackberry bush. He was no more than 18" high and covered in hair. His face was bare but had a leathery look. The nose seemed sharp. I noticed it when it turned away in profile. It definitely had hands. Its arms seemed longer than a human being's. I did not notice his feet. It was definitely substantial, real. It did not notice me, or if it did it did not show it. It turned and disappeared back into the blackberry bush. When I told the couple I was staying with they laughed at me.

'A few days later', adds Bord, 'Mr Reynolds saw the creature again when travelling upstairs on a bus. This was during the daytime, and in a different location in Horsham. He saw the little man walking across the lawn in a large garden.'

Do fairies exist? This certainly now seems to me a far more important question than it did at the outset of this book. To put it another way: all those people sound to me as if they saw what they say they saw. Why, then, are their accounts still so hard to believe? Aside from fear of ridicule, the best answer is probably this: we do not know what fairies are, or where they might come from. They fail to make sense in a way much more radical way than do aliens or ghosts. Having said that, I would emphasize again that there is far more evidence for their existence than there is for the existence of the Christian God. Taken as a whole the above descriptions cannot simply be reduced to some kind of cultural archetype or stereotype. Some are beautiful or delightful, some angry or ugly. They vary in size between nine inches and (in Powell's account) at least three or four feet. Neither Powell nor the Birdlip woman sound as if they *wanted* to see fairies, and both those incidents also appear to be complete one-offs. The only one of the five reporters who saw fairies all their life was Alleyne. Though three cases occur in the countryside, two take place indoors.

Meanwhile, if Liverpool in 1964 might seem the epitome of swinging British modernity, the near-riot which occurred there that July had nothing to do with The Beatles.

> I certainly [remember leprechauns], and I actually saw a few of them on Kensington Fields, close to the library ... This would be one afternoon in early July 1964, around 4.30pm, and I remember it as if it were yesterday. I was 10 at the time and on my way to play football with my mates and saw these little (I'd say just a few inches tall) men dressed in red and black, standing in the grass, looking at me. I'm sure one of them had some type of hat on. I panicked and ran all the way home.

Liverpool radio presenter Tom Slemen not only collected this statement, but gave a sighting of a figure 'about two feet in height or less, with pale yellow-green skin' which had appeared in a garden on Edge Lane to two women, on the afternoon of 1 July. Back at the bowling green park, local constable James Nolan found himself obliged to call in police cars and motorcyclists to clear the hundreds of children swarming about for a glimpse of the leprechauns. In October 2009 a man who had been at Brae Street School in 1964 wrote to the *Liverpool Echo*, insisting that he and his schoolmates 'all saw them popping in and out of a window overlooking the school yard; there were about four of them, all tiny dressed like a school book idea of a typical gnome, and they sat swinging their legs on the window ledge getting in and out'.

Among other things, such accounts raise the question of why and how we believe in the strange or improbable. There seem to be various implicit levels of persuasion or mental clarity involved. If I had loosely paraphrased the above reports, they would probably form an easily dismissed blur for most readers. But add in names, dates, places and physical descriptions, and their focus sharpens considerably. And, if our best friend were to tell us a similar tale . . .? This point bears emphasizing, because a lot of people have looked me in the eye and told me of encounters with ghosts. With fairy reports, of course, there is always the possibility that what we take for realistic persuasion is something else. We grew up with wonder. We were made of stories, the early oxygen of our formative years. Do we then perhaps unknowingly relapse into that childish state when we read such accounts, happily giving up for a few moments the rigid, dry laws of adulthood?

In 1996 the Albert Hall's director of building development, Ian Blackburn, was interviewed by the *Daily Telegraph* about repeated ghost sightings in the famous venue. 'When people keep saying the same things to you, you have to take notice and try and get to the bottom of it,' Mr Blackburn said. This is a very good motto indeed for the question of ghost sightings, and a pretty good one for the problem of fairy encounters. But it raises another question. Sometimes, when a lot of people say the same thing, they get listened to. At other times, they sound like folklore. Why? It is partly for this reason that I have separated the encounters in traditional fairy territory, and those given here. I have also tended to privilege reports from educated people, or those with a certain kind of reputation to lose. (I am not sure this is fair, but if we do not know the reporter, many of us do look to their social status.)

A few final words about stories. I spent most of my life refusing to believe in ghosts, and tending not to listen properly to people who told me about them. Once I had heard enough of these stories, I had to change my mind. I may have a certain bias towards stories, as these are my job. I have been trained to spot their tone, credibility, consistency, and so on. Yet there seems to be no doubt, now, that if you want proof of something strange, you are better off trusting to stories than to pictures. As far back as Cottingley, a formidable photographic hoax could be achieved by two young girls, and in my lifetime digital and computer innovations have reduced the old phrase 'the camera never lies' to a ragged irony. In the realm of the paranormal, the best bet is of course to see it for yourself. If not, stick with a very old human method. Talk to people; listen to them; and keep listening.

Conclusion:
The Green Mist

I' th' spring tha want . . . to every field in to'n, and lifted a spud o' yarth fro' th' mools, and tha' said stra'ange and quare wo'ds, as tha' cudna scarce unnerstann thersels; but the same as ad bin said for hunnerds o' ye'ars. An' ivery mornin' at tha first dawn, tha stood a' the door-sil wi' salt an' bread i' ther hans, watchin' an' waitin' for the green mist's rose fro the fields n' could that tha yarth wor' wake agean; and the life wor comin' to th' trees an' the pla'ants, an the seeds wor' bustin' wi' thee beginnin' o' the spring.

ON THIS FATEFUL MORNING, all across the Lincolnshire valley where we earlier met Tiddy Mun and the Strangers, people would then crumble the bread and salt onto the earth as a kind of fertility offering. For most people across most of history, this kind of attitude to nature has been the norm. Patient, minutely attentive, reverent of mystery, and holistic in its sense of mutual reciprocity, this broadly animistic or pagan stance contrasts strikingly with the pseudo-rationalism and utilitarianism of a predatory, mechanistic attitude to nature. In this latter case the one-way plunder which drains land of its vitality prompts the intensive farmers or loggers or hunters to simply move on, denying any chance of the tightly localized, intimate relationship seen above. Richly detailed in Annie Proulx's novel *Barkskins*, this predatory stance has also been acknowledged by the scientific call, in August 2016, for the declaration of a new geological epoch. The Anthropocene, due to be dated from around 1950, would be the first such epoch in which Man, rather than Nature, is the dominant force, and would be marked by global traces of radiation and plastic pollution. Any Christians moved to criticize the pagan behaviour of those Lincolnshire farmers may like to bear in mind that the most severe damage to nature in recent centuries has been committed by avowed Christians, reaching its nadir in the United States, the most intensely Christian country in the developed world. Here in Britain, meanwhile, the current Archbishop of Canterbury, Justin Welby, trained for his vocation by working for eleven years as an oil executive.

In both broader and very precise ways fairy beliefs helped to counter the predatory behaviour of industrialism and capitalism. Long before the uncanny wandering trees of *The Lord of the Rings*, nature spirits rustled through woods and forests. Trees associated with Greek nymphs might be held to bleed when cut, and we find very real echoes of such caution or reverence lingering into Greek agricultural habits of the twentieth century. In eighteenth-century Wales the cutting of a female oak could entail dangerous retribution, and in the German Kammerforst – a forest near Trier – the nature guardian known as Pulch would take revenge on those who harmed trees or took wood without permission. In the Cotswolds the elder was believed to bleed when cut, while back in Lincolnshire anyone cutting this tree must not only ask permission, but promise some of their own wood in return, 'when I grows inter a tree'.

All across traditional fairy country, this bond with nature and fertility could at times appear still more starkly pagan. One story about the young Merlin held that he narrowly escaped being used as a blood sacrifice to build a Welsh castle, and on Iona, the sacred heart of Celtic Christendom was said to have drunk the blood of one of its most pious devotees. In a written history later suppressed by the Church, it was stated that Columba requested the burial of a living human sacrifice beneath the first Iona monastery, to protect it from evil spirits – this dubious privilege falling on a man named Odran.

Come the early twentieth century, people in Wexford and other parts of Ireland were still celebrating St Martin's Day (11 November) by sprinkling the blood of a cock around their houses and outhouses to bring St Martin's blessing on the household and livestock in the coming year. In the 1930s Canon Meehan of Roscommon recalled how, in his youth in Westmeath, 'no house would be built without putting some *live* animal under the foundation stone – a chicken, kitten, rabbit, etc.'; while the horse's skull found in Man was echoed by numerous other examples routinely buried beneath peasant houses across Ireland. Citing these archaeological finds, Barry O'Reilly reminds us that such dwellings were not only physically porous, but psychologically so: the self-built house was 'regarded as an interface between the human and supernatural worlds and . . . its portals – doors, windows and chimneys – were liminal zones or points of contact between these worlds'. Neatly underlining this pagan behaviour of nominal Christians, Garland Sunday (the first in August) once involved an annual pilgrimage by Welsh or Irish peasants to local fairy places.

The potent links between fairies and fertility which we saw in Chapter Three prompted the neighbours of Tiddy Mun to hold that, 'in the spring of the year' the Strangers 'fell to shaking and pinching the tree buds to make them come open . . . Folks thought that they helped the corn to ripen, and that they painted the pretty colours of the flowers, and the reds and browns of the fruit in autumn, and the yellowing leaves.' As late as 1997, Bord took seriously the view that the ubiquitous fairy habit of either leaping or dancing was in part designed to 'produce energy which helps the crops to grow.'

Anyone who has read Evans-Wentz's *Fairy Faith* has also felt this earthy energy, vibrating through the author's bootsoles as he stamped joyously across the hills and valleys of Celtic Britain. Back in his native America Evans-Wentz's animism had expressed itself in bouts of naked sun-worshipping on the banks of the Delaware river, and come 1911 he would insist that his physical 'immersion in the most striking natural and social environment of the Celtic race, gave me an insight into the mind, the religion, the mysticism, and the very heart of the Celt himself, such as no mere study in libraries ever could do'. As much as I sympathize with those sceptical of the Oxford-educated, privately funded Evans-Wentz's ability to genuinely 'participate in the innermost thoughts' of Celtic peasants, I also find powerfully evocative his view from a Barra mountainside, when 'the rocky backbone' of the Hebrides under the sunset 'seemed more like some magic vision, reflected from Faerie . . . than a thing of our own world'.

While Evans-Wentz's elfin animism propelled him into outright fairy belief, literary renderings of such emotions could be no less powerful. For 1911 saw not only the publication of *The Fairy Faith*, but that of the British nature classic *The Wind in the Willows*. Hunting downriver on Midsummer's Night for the missing otter baby, Portly, Rat and Mole are suddenly stunned out of thought by the sound of an unearthly music. A few moments later, with the bird-heavy trees all eerily silent, they see on an island before them 'the backward sweep of the curved horns . . . the stern, hooked nose . . . the bearded mouth [and] the long supple hand still holding the pan-pipes only just fallen from the parted lips', lastly spying Portly, sleeping beneath the shaggy limbs and satyr's hooves. For, yes, the piper at the gates of dawn is none other than Pan himself, his liquid music floating down the fertile stream, over three hundred years after Puck, Hippolyta and Shakespeare had celebrated the irrepressible spirit of growth on that very same night. Convulsed with some unspeakable fusion of love and terror, Rat and Mole, 'crouching to the earth, bowed their heads and did worship'. Moments later 'a capricious little breeze', blown 'caressingly in their faces', bestowed from Pan 'the gift of forgetfulness' – a happy oblivion which allowed them to forget this haunting beauty in a way that Keats's fairy-haunted lover never could.

Within this broadly pagan and animistic frame, fairies and fairy believers enacted a curious ecological dance. At first glance, we might imagine a simple parting of the ways opening there in 1911: Evans-Wentz's fairy literalism leads him ever further into the social and intellectual margins, while the mass appeal of *The Wind in the Willows* is gained by taking a route both fictional and childish. In fact, matters are not quite so simple. Fairy ecology does not merely dilute itself into something purely whimsical and unworldly, as the twentieth century gives way to our own. Probably the most central and recurrent oppositions of this story are utility versus reverence, and mechanism versus mystery. This is not to say that the older stance was by any means unselfish; but it was typically a selfishness which deferred to nature, and which knew, in its bones, cells and guts, that it was part of nature, bound into it, and not towering arrogantly over it.

Across Ireland smaller, localized examples of eco-reverence abounded among fairy believers. A priest who grew up in Connemara recalled how 'on November Eve the fairies passed over blackberries and sloes', making them unfit to eat and causing serious illness in anyone who did: 'I laugh now when I think how we used to gorge ourselves with berries on the last day of October, and then for weeks after pass by bushes full of the most luscious fruit, and with mouths watering for we couldn't eat it.' More seriously, Westropp heard of how

> in 1839 seal-hunting was stopped in County Mayo from Down-patrick Head to Kilcummin. Two boys had declared that, when killing seals in one of the caves of that reach of coast, a white seal sat up and cried, 'Spare your old grandfather, Daniel O'Dowd!' They were naturally astonished, for O'Dowd had long before died and been buried in Dunfeeny . . . so they argued with the seal, who, however, convinced them that he was their relative. He had for his sins done in the body been condemned for a certain time to walk the night as a seal. He bade them to give up murdering seals, 'who may be nearer to yourselves than you think'. The boys, especially his grandson, Tim O'Dowd, firmly believed all this and so convinced their neighbours that they . . . gave up their lucrative seal trade.

'People on Galway Bay, on Inishofen and Inishark', Westropp added, firmly believed in the Coneely family 'being of seal blood, and regard shooting a seal as murder, and eating its flesh as cannibalism'.

Back inland, in 1954 the elderly Walter Furlough, of the White Mountain, County Wexford, recalled a story from the days of his father's youth. 'A man from Ballybawn had a sick cow, and after every remedy he tried failed he sent his son over to a fairy man in Newtownbarry.' The fairy man told the son that 'his father was a very bad class of a man, that he killed all the pigeons that were around the place and also stopped that little window in the back of the house which he had no right to do' – quoting a direct complaint from the fairies, whose path this had blocked. Still quoting, the fairy man explained: 'if you promise on behalf of your father that you'll open that window and let back the pigeons, your cow will live. If not, she'll die.' Was this fairy man – like Biddy Early – genuinely psychic? Even if he was not, fairy ecology here triumphed once again. On a still smaller scale, Hunt found in Cornwall that the local peasantry, believing ants to be 'the Small People in their state of decay from off the earth', held it 'most unlucky to destroy a colony of ants'.

The fairy ecology of larger scale land-use, meanwhile, takes us right across the British Isles, first striking northeast from Cornwall to the marshy Lincolnshire fens where that watery fairy figure, Tiddy Mun, cried his eerie lapwing call of an evening. Here in the late eighteenth century the notoriously unhealthy fen country was systematically drained with the aid of Dutch engineers. Over a century later, in 1891, locals talking to M. C. Balfour still recalled how no one would give food, shelter or bedding to these Dutch meddlers. Why not? At a glance this seems like a good example of a case where rural inertia was misguided, and where scientific intervention could positively alter an environment which produced malaria in local inhabitants. But anthropologist Darwin Horn saw a different story here. First, he explained how Tiddy Mun had acted as a fertility spirit specifically linked to water levels. When floods threatened cottages, people went out and directly invoked him. And, following the mass drainage projects, his anger was all too visible: livestock and infants sickened, ponies were lamed, and cottage walls and roofs slipped or crumbled. Tiddy Mun aside, Horn argued that the locals were broadly right in linking this to the recent hydro-engineering: the drainage affected the acid balance of soil and pasture, causing Johne's disease in cattle; made the ground harder for wandering ponies; and caused the desiccated land levels to fall by almost as much as five feet in places, thereby prompting subsidence in local cottages. It may also have caused an increase in malaria, after the loss of marsh predators which had previously fed on mosquitoes.

Here science seems to have laid its well-meaning but clumsy hand upon a complex local ecology. In northwest Scotland's Gairloch, two incidents offer a far more aggressive human attempt to hunt fairy mystery out of the woods and waters. In the late eighteenth century, many locals claimed to have seen the Gille Dubh or black boy of the woods. Osgood Hanbury Mackenzie had often heard of him during his own early Victorian boyhood: 'his haunts were in the birch-woods that still cluster round the southern end' of Loch a Druing. He was named Gille Dubh after the black colour of his hair, and 'his dress, if dress it could be called, was merely leaves of trees and green moss. He was seen by very many people and on many occasions during a period of more than forty years in the latter half of the eighteenth century ... and was generally regarded as a beneficent fairy.' The only person he ever spoke to was a young girl named Jessie Macrae, whom he rescued when she was lost in the woods one night.

Despite this, some strange whim prompted Sir Hector Mackenzie of Gairloch (1758–1826) to invite four other Mackenzies on a shooting expedition, aimed solely at the fairy boy of the woods. Clad in Highland dress, they were well feasted by John Mackenzie, then tenant of the estate, before spending the night in his barn on couches of heather. Happily, a thorough scouring of the woods the following day yielded no sight of the Gille Dubh. Yet one cannot help suspect that he did actually exist. He may not have worn leaves and moss, but he could well have been one of those marginal figures, perhaps mentally disabled, whom we glimpsed in Chapter Three, surviving on the fringes of ordinary society by blending into its established fairy mythology. There is something very appealing about this wild boy of the woods, slipping with animal stealth out of sight or shotgun range, at once as present and absent, as familiar and mysterious, as the fairies themselves. Moreover, a further thread of romance winds through this tale, given that by this time Jessie Macrae was married to the tenant, John Mackenzie. Did she in fact slip out into the woods that night as the hunters lay on the heather, to warn the fairy boy of the imminent hunt?

Meanwhile, in the Gairloch waters there lurked something almost as elusive, but far more terrifying than the Black Boy. The Gairloch kelpie had allegedly been seen by many locals, including church elder Sandy Macleod, who one Sunday saw it, looking like 'a big boat with its keel turned up'. Its size is vividly indicated by the tale of one unusually dauntless man seen fishing for it with a whole sheep as bait. The loch in which it resided was known as Loch na Beiste, or Loch of the Beast, and so great was the terror it inspired that locals pestered Meyrick Bankes, the proprietor of the estate from 1835, to eradicate it. How could this be done? Being a nineteenth-century industrialist as well as landowner, the English Bankes was little daunted. His yacht the *Iris* sailed up from Liverpool bearing 'a huge pump and a large number of cast-iron pipes', after which 'a squad of men worked this pump with two horses, with the object of emptying the loch'. Now looking broadly like a low-tech version of the later attempts to sonar Loch Ness for uncanny bodies, this plan failed, as the burn feeding the loch amply replenished it.

Accordingly, it was now 'proposed to poison the Beast with lime, and the *Iris* was sent to Broadford in Skye to procure it'. With no local man daring to sit in the boat that carried fourteen barrels of hot anti-kelpie lime across the waters, Bankes's own sailors laboriously plumbed the loch with their oars until they discovered one suspiciously deep hole, and poured every barrel into it. Recounting this incident in 1921, Osgood assures us that, 'needless to say, the Beast was not discovered, nor has it been further disturbed up to the present time.' As Osgood himself (born 1842) often saw the imported pipes stored in a shed, the Great Kelpie Hunt of Gairloch probably occurred in the 1850s.

Given the role of the local Scots in catalysing it, this hunt is not a simple case of Industry versus Mystery, or Science versus Nature. But it is interesting to further note that Bankes, in his rage at this defeat of his godlike mechanical powers, then turned on his tenants, fining them all a pound a head. Overall, there is indeed a satisfying sense of basic oppositions here: fluid and watery mystery eludes hard utilitarian mechanics, and the ancient monster of the Scottish wilds triumphs over the brash wealth of the English Bankes – a man notorious in Scotland for clearances, and owner of a Wigan colliery where many were injured in an accident in 1870.

Readers may not be surprised to learn that, come the twentieth century, clashes between Progress and Fairy Ecology were largely fought out on Irish soil. In spring 1905 the *Daily Mail* reported: 'as soon as earth is dumped into a ravine near Ballintra to make a bed for the new Donegal and Ballyshannon railway, it disappears down the hillside. A "fairy thorn" has been removed to make way for the track, and local opinion lays the difficulty at the door of the angry fairies.' Was this in fact human eco-terrorism, prompted by local fear of the fairies? It would certainly be odd for railway engineers of this period to have been simply defeated by purely natural processes.

Come the 1950s, the indignation of MP Sean Dunne at press coverage of that fairy strike in Limerick might again suggest that now it was more dangerous to believe in fairies than to disbelieve in them. But a fuller look at this affair suggests otherwise. In November 1951 Limerick city mayor Matthew Macken declared: 'if I have to get a gun to defend the fort' from the bulldozers, 'I will certainly do it.' After 'workmen employed by Limerick Corporation to build 475 houses refused to clear the mound on the site because it was a fairy fort,' Macken concluded: 'we will have to give in to the fairies. We have decided to leave the fort standing.' Corporation overseer John McNamara claimed that 'several members of the bulldozer crew said they saw leprechauns making shoes there that night' – adding that when replacement labourers, from adjoining County Clare, came in and 'built a few house gables . . . next morning not one of the gables was standing.' The result was that thirty of the proposed houses went unbuilt. In April 1958 a strike by Mayo workmen due to build a fence was resolved only after P. J. Lindsay, a former cabinet minister, agreed with the men that the fence could go round rather than through a fairy fort at Toorglass near Belmullet.

Sitting back to celebrate one more victory, the fairies watched Beatlemania, the Space Race and the Berlin Wall, Thatcherism and CND come and go – only to find, in 1999, that one of their trees was under threat from a motorway bypass between Newmarket-on-Fergus and Ennis. Here Eddie Lenihan stepped in, getting the bypass to also bypass the tree, which can now be seen safely fenced in, just off the hard shoulder. Nor does the twenty-first century seem to have daunted the eco-fairies of the Emerald Isle. In 2007 they were blamed for the repeated toppling of new electricity poles installed close to a fairy fort in Sooey, County Sligo.

At first this set of incidents looks rather disparate. A railway or a motorway might well be seen as chemical and noise pollution, but the harmless necessary fence and houses are surely rather different. Looking at this from another angle, however, we can see a very clear opposition forming on these fairy landscapes. It is, simply, straight versus curved. Both railways and motorways are of course man-made triumphs of the former. By contrast, all the curves of those Irish forts, and the roads and fences which so frequently swerve around them or around fairy trees ally themselves to the feminine meanderings of rivers, streams, and indeed all those British country lanes which escaped the ruthless utilitarianism of Roman road-builders.

You do not have to be a fairy believer to at least feel ambivalent about a world of straight lines, as phrases such as 'like a motorway' and 'off the grid' still show. There again, the ambivalence of Dunne about Irish stereotypes hardened occasionally into violent hostility among some of his countrymen where fairies were concerned. In 1900 the anti-clerical lawyer Michael McCarthy stated of Irish forts that 'these accursed ... remains of barbarism should be levelled to the ground by every man who wishes to see Ireland prosper', and it may have been a similar antagonism to 'backward traditions' which prompted an unknown vandal to hack branches off the Ennis fairy tree in August 2002. What of the 'fairy doors' attached to trees in rural Ireland and America? The labour involved in constructing these certainly implies a serious desire to somehow respiritualize nature. In the longer view, of course, attempts to ease fairy passage into the human world would have horrified those country dwellers who spent far more energy seeking to keep nature spirits at bay.

Meanwhile, a rare English battle over a fairy tree in Berkshire in 1985 gained a similar colouring of the quaintly irrational when the *Daily Mail* presented the story from the viewpoint of two sisters, Eloise and Naomi Forsyth, aged nine and seven. Eloise, who was said to hear an owl talking to the fairies in the partly hollow old ash, wrote to Environment Minister Kenneth Baker explaining that the proposed new housing development in Bugs Bottom would see the tree cut down, and the fairies made homeless. The fairies, Eloise said, were 'tiny, tiny, and dressed in petals' – hugging the tree as she added that the wasps buzzing round it were guarding the fairies within. By the time that the housing project was finally approved in 1990, Eloise was no longer a child, and the phrase 'tree hugger' – more or less unknown in 1985 – was becoming common.

In the next few years, as Andy Letcher reminds us, the Tory government initiated a massive wave of new road-building projects, which in turn catalysed highly publicized eco-protests, including that centred on the Newbury bypass in Berkshire. Letcher, who was part of the Newbury protest camp, describes the attendant eco-paganism of this culture as a direct, intuitive form of religion which in many ways resembles the quiet heresies and the sensuous reverence of traditional fairy believers. Like the fairies themselves, protesters were at times living underground, in the tunnels built as part of various obstructive tactics. More explicitly, British eco-sabotage was termed 'pixieing', the first camp at Newbury was 'the pixie village', and at Fairmile in Devon one set of protesters referred to themselves as 'fairies' and another as 'trolls'. Matt Tweed, lead singer of a prominent protest band, the Space Goats, changed his name to Poc (as in Puck), and penned a song lyric which ran: 'Who are the pixie people, are you one of the fairy folk?/Do you like your planet, or do you want to see it go up in smoke?'

Letcher saw in such cases a broad parallel with Tolkien's 'scouring of the shire', in which the returning hobbits rose against the industrial desecration inflicted on their home by Saruman. Nor was he alone. He cites George Monbiot, who in 1998 claimed that 'the road protests have already taken their place in the folklore of these islands; the 1990s will be remembered as the time when the gargantuan monsters of corruption and repression were slain by the little folk.' Neither the courage of these protesters, nor the final outcome, which saw the government cut its road budget from £23 billion to £6 billion, were merely quaint or childish.

But perhaps it was no accident that, by 2015, after Tory privatization had produced one of the most inefficient and overpriced rail networks in Europe, and the pseudo-rationalism of unregulated capitalism had devastated economies around the world, the latest triumph of elfin ecology should come from that northern outpost of rugged landscapes and individuals, Iceland. Since 2007 Icelandic environmentalists the Friends of Lava had been protesting against plans for a new road out to the lava fields of the Álftanes peninsula, and by the time this story hit international headlines in 2013, hundreds of its members were regularly blocking the bulldozers. With the group arguing that the road would destroy existing elf habitat, and specifically a distinctive rock formation known as 'an elf church', a *Guardian* article cited a 2007 survey which found that 62 per cent of its 1,000 Icelandic respondents thought elves might exist. While writer and environmentalist Andri Snær Magnason was uncertain about the existence of elves, he nicely echoed both Lenihan and our learned author when he conceded that 'I got married in a church with a god just as invisible as the elves, so what might seem irrational is actually quite common [among Icelanders].'

Meanwhile, professor of Icelandic folklore Terry Gunnell saw the country's widespread openness to elves as an extension of their habitual experience of nature:

> this is a land where your house can be destroyed by something you can't see (earthquakes), where the wind can knock you off your feet, where the smell of sulphur from your taps tells you there is invisible fire not far below your feet, where the northern lights make the sky the biggest television screen in the world, and where hot springs and glaciers 'talk' ... In short, everyone is aware that the land is alive ...

Gunnell's further thoughts nicely bounce us back into the distinctive natural worlds of fairy believers, and the positively child-like relationship they might enjoy with nature. These Icelandic beliefs, he added, thrive 'because people remain in close contact with the land. Parents still let their children play out in the wilderness – often late into the night', with 'vast pristine areas' still common, even near the capital, Reykjavík. After a prolonged period of debate by the Icelandic supreme court, the road went ahead. But the elf church, like Lenihan's fairy tree, was safely moved to a new site nearby on 18 March 2015. Whatever the elves feel, it should certainly be impervious to vandals or iconoclasts.

In a period when eco-friendly 'hobbit houses' were beginning to be offered for holiday lets (and when I first marvelled at the impressive turf-covered example to be seen on the edge of St David's in west Wales), perhaps the most intriguing eco-creation to hit the mainstream was James Cameron's 2009 film *Avatar*. His nature spirits, the Na'vi, are blue rather than green, and unsurprisingly, come 2154, another planet is the only locale which can offer the mesmerizing combination of natural wonder and danger once lurking outside so many Celtic doorsteps. The Na'vi have a strikingly holistic relationship with nature, exemplified in the bond between riders and horses, and their powerful sense of the literal and minute interconnectedness of all life. We might also add that *Avatar* confounded distinctions between child and adult viewers with a success rarely seen since the first stagings of *Peter Pan*.

What also struck me when I first saw this film was how precisely it seems to mythicize an early encounter between the invading Christians of the sixteenth century, and the natives of Peru. For the central crux of *Avatar* is of course the destruction of the Na'vi's Tree of Souls, rooted above a deposit of unobtanium. Writing in 1590 of his personal experiences in South America, the Spanish Jesuit José de Acosta was dismayed at how intensely the Peruvians 'worshipped rivers, fountains, the mouths of rivers, entries of mountains, rocks or great stones, hills and the tops of mountains', in short, 'all things in nature, which seemed to them remarkable and different from the rest, as acknowledging some particular deity'. Acosta was probably happily oblivious of the ways that ordinary countryfolk did much the same in Spain, just as Christians would still be doing in much of the British and Irish countryside into the twentieth century. To Acosta and his peers this Peruvian stance was simple idolatry, just one more 'delusion of the Devil', and another sign of how badly these ignorant heathens needed to be saved. Such Christian beliefs must have contributed, in part, to the colossal genocide which the Spanish inflicted on native inhabitants from Central America southwards, detailed with horrific precision by fellow Spaniard Bartolomé de las Casas.

In another passage, Acosta is again struck by the way the Indians

> believed there was a certain divinity in any thing that was extraordinary and strange . . . attributing the like unto small stones and metals; yea unto roots and fruits of the earth . . . They did

likewise worship bears, lions, tigers and snakes, to the end they should not hurt them.

It hardly needs emphasizing what a cruel irony now overshadows these words, after avowedly Christian ideologies of progress and Enlightenment have brought the earth to one of the greatest natural crises in its history. Perhaps the sharpest irony of all, however, lies in Acosta's offhand admission that at one point in Lima, he and his peers 'cut down a great deformed tree, which for the greatness and antiquity thereof had been a long time the Oratory' or church 'of the Indians'. The reason they did so was to gain sufficient wood for a massive fire. And the fire was needed, in turn, to melt metal, to found a church bell.

It is all too likely that, if we had seen this 'deformed tree', we would have considered it beautiful rather than ugly, and perhaps not entirely unlike the Na'vi's Tree of Souls. Our own homegrown Celtic fairies, back here on Planet Earth, may have taken a more robustly earthy attitude to their trees and paths and forts – prizing them egotistically, perhaps, rather than as part of any systematic ecology. But it is certainly very clear that the world would not be in the state it now is, had it been left to the care of fairy believers.

What educated person in the twenty-first century could possibly believe in fairies? Yet if fairies exist, we can well imagine them wishing that they did not have to believe in humanity. The dangers of fairy scapegoating could be horrific and fatal, as could parallel beliefs about witchcraft. But it is very easy to sit at a bewildered distance from either these or the more comical habits of fairy believers. What is often more difficult is to be shocked at the ordinary madness of our own times. As the world simmers and floods and melts towards catastrophe, sales of SUVs surge, at times overtaking those of ordinary cars, while airfares compete with the price of a moderate supper for two. In another hundred years, will any fairy incident of the past look crazier than a remark such as 'there's never been a better time to buy an SUV' (*Daily Telegraph*, 18 May 2016)? Ordinary madness, extraordinary consequences . . . Let us hope it is not too late to avoid some of them. And, if it is? Then perhaps centuries from now, after the false clarity of utilitarianism has long crumbled into ashes, the green mist, one spring morning, might rise again.

SOURCES AND
FURTHER READING

IN THE AREA OF FOLKLORE I have been particularly indebted to
W. Y. Evans-Wentz's *The Fairy-faith*, as well as to the work of Katharine Briggs,
T. J. Westropp and Simon Young. Anyone who wants to buy just one book
on this subject would do well to choose either *The Fairy-faith* or Briggs's *The
Vanishing People*. Although a little more expensive, Peter Narváez's valuable
collection of essays is also recommended. While Westropp's numerous articles
are highly recommended to anyone who can access the scholarly database JSTOR,
Young's excellent articles are freely available via the website academia.edu.

In terms of literature, art and culture I would highly recommend Silver's
Strange and Secret Peoples, or Maas and Gere's *Victorian Fairy Paintings*. Both
Hanson's excellent *Peter Pan on Stage and Screen* and the Oxford World's
Classics edition of *Peter Pan* help clarify the complex and multi-layered
nature of Barrie's various Pan stories and stage scripts. Joe Cooper's book on
the Cottingley fairies and Angela Bourke's study of Bridget Cleary are also
thorough and engaging accounts of their respective subjects. A good deal of
primary and secondary material (including *The Fairy-faith*) is now available
online, as listed below.

As indicated, the divide between folklore and alleged fairy sightings may
not be as rigid as one would expect. Anyone wanting to look further at the
latter is advised to obtain Young's *Seeing Fairies* or Bord's *Fairies*. Both are
serious works, and Young's edition in particular offers an impressive range
of sightings from the widest possible spectrum of witnesses. As with people
who see ghosts or suffer poltergeists, fairy witnesses when taken as a whole
have nothing in common save their shared experiences. Even these vary
considerably in terms of what is seen, and responses to it. More on this subject
and on the history of the Fairy Investigation Society is available via Young's
excellent website. Where sources for stories or quotations are not evident in
my text, they have usually been sourced from original newspaper reports.

Books

Barrie, J. M., 'Peter Pan in Kensington Gardens' and 'Peter and Wendy'
(Oxford, 2008)

Bord, Janet, *Fairies: Real Encounters with Little People* (London, 1997)

Bottigheimer, Ruth, *Fairy Tales: A New History* (New York, 2009)

Bourke, Angela, *The Burning of Bridget Cleary: A True Story* (London, 2006)

Briggs, K. M., *The Vanishing People: A Study of Traditional Fairy Beliefs*
(London, 1978)

Cooper, Joe, *The Case of the Cottingley Fairies* (London, 1990)

Devereux, Paul, *Spirit Roads: An Exploration of Otherworldly Routes*
(London, 2007)

Evans-Wentz, W. Y., *The Fairy Faith in Celtic Countries* (Glastonbury, 2010)

Green, Richard Firth, *Elf Queens and Holy Friars: Fairy Beliefs and the
Medieval Church* (Philadephia, PA, 2016)

Hall, Alaric, *Elves in Anglo-Saxon England: Matters of Belief, Health, Gender
and Identity* (Woodbridge, 2007)

Hanson, Bruce K., *Peter Pan on Stage and Screen: 1904–2010*, 2nd edn
(New York, 2011)

Henderson, Lizanne, *Scottish Fairy Belief: A History* (Edinburgh, 2007)

Homer, *The Odyssey*, trans. Robert Fagles (London, 2001)

Johnson, Marjorie, and Simon Young, eds, *Seeing Fairies: From the Lost
Archives of the Fairy Investigation Society, Authentic Reports of Fairies
in Modern Times* (San Antonio, TX, 2014)

Kirk, Robert, *The Secret Commonwealth of Elves, Fauns and Fairies*, ed.
Andrew Lang (New York, 2008)

Larson, Jennifer, *Greek Nymphs: Myth, Cult, Lore* (Oxford, 2001)

Leavy, Barbara Fass, *In Search of the Swan Maiden: A Narrative on Folklore
and Gender* (New York, 1995)

Lenihan, Edmund, *In Search of Biddy Early* (Cork, 1982)

Maas, Jeremy, Charlotte Gere et al., *Victorian Fairy Painting* (London, 1997)

McManus, Diarmuid, *The Middle Kingdom: The Faerie World of Ireland*
(London, 1959)

Narváez, Peter, ed., *The Good People: New Fairylore Essays* (Lexington,
KY, 1997)

Parsons, Colin, *Encounters with the Unknown: True Accounts of Modern
Paranormal Experiences* (London, 1990)

Purkiss, Diane, *Troublesome Things: A History of Fairies and Fairy Stories*
(London, 2000)

Roberts, Kai, *Folklore of Yorkshire* (Stroud, 2013)

Ryan, Meda, *Biddy Early: The Wise Woman of Clare* (Cork, 2000)

Silver, Carole G., *Strange and Secret Peoples: Fairies and Victorian Consciousness* (Oxford, 1999)

Sitwell, Sacheverell, *Poltergeists: An Introduction and Examination* (New York, 1959)

Sneddon, Andrew, *Witchcraft and Magic in Ireland* (Basingstoke, 2015)

Sugg, Richard, *A Century of Supernatural Stories* (CreateSpace, 2015)

——, *A Century of Ghost Stories* (CreateSpace, 2017)

——, *Mummies, Cannibals and Vampires: The History of Corpse Medicine from the Renaissance to the Victorians*, 2nd edn (Abingdon, 2015)

Wade, James, *Fairies in Medieval Romance* (Basingstoke, 2011)

Articles and Dissertations

Chalmers, Robert, 'An Interview with Matthew Manning', GQ, 8 May 2014

Correll, Timothy Corrigan, 'Believers, Sceptics, and Charlatans: Evidential Rhetoric, the Fairies, and Fairy Healers in Irish Oral Narrative and Belief', *Folklore*, CXVI/1 (2005), pp. 1–18

Eberly, Susan Schoon, 'Fairies and the Folklore of Disability: Changelings, Hybrids and the Solitary Fairy', *Folklore*, XCIX/1 (1988), pp. 58–77

Gentile, John S., 'Stories of the Otherworld: An Interview with Eddie Lenihan', *Storytelling, Self, Society*, V/3 (2009), pp. 152–75

Ó Giolláin, Diarmuid, 'The Leipreachán and Fairies, Dwarfs and the Household Familiar: A Comparative Study' *Béaloideas*, LII (1984), pp. 75–150

Hayhurst, Yvonne, 'A Recent Find of a Horse Skull in a House at Ballaugh, Isle of Man', *Folklore*, C/1 (1989), pp. 105–9

Henderson, Lizanne, 'The Survival of Witchcraft Prosecutions and Witch Belief in South-West Scotland', *Scottish Historical Review*, LXXXV/219 (2006), pp. 52–74

Henningsen, Gustav, 'The Witches' Flying and the Spanish Inquisitors, or How to Explain (Away) the Impossible', *Folklore*, CXX (2009), pp. 57–74

Hooykaas, Jacoba, 'The Changeling in Balinese Folklore and Tradition', *Bijdragen tot de Taal*, CXVI (1960), pp. 424–36

Horn, Darwin, 'Tiddy Mun's Curse and the Ecological Consequences of Land Reclamation', *Folklore*, XCVIII/1 (1987), pp. 11–15

Huxley, Alice, 'Supernatural Selection: Shakespeare, the Victorians and the Competing Fairy Types', unpublished BA dissertation, Durham University, 2014

Letcher, Andy, 'The Scouring of the Shire: Fairies, Trolls and Pixies in Eco-Protest Culture', *Folklore*, CXII/2 (2001), pp. 147–61

O'Reilly, Barry, 'Hearth and Home: The Vernacular House in Ireland from c. 1800', *Proceedings of the Royal Irish Academy*, CXI (2011), pp. 193–215

Rabuzzi, Daniel Allen, 'In Pursuit of Norfolk's Hyter Sprites', *Folklore*, XCV (1984), pp. 74–89

Rudkin, E. H., 'Folklore of Lincolnshire: Especially the Low-lying Areas of Lindsey', *Folklore*, CXVI/4 (1955), pp. 385–400

Westropp, T. J., 'A Folklore Survey of County Clare', *Folklore*, XXI–XXIII (1910–12)

——, A Study of the Folklore on the Coast of Connacht, Ireland', *Folklore*, XXIX–XXXIV (1918–23)

Websites

A good deal of useful material on Manx fairies and popular culture can be found at:
www.asmanxasthehills.com

Evans-Wentz, W. Y., *The Fairy Faith*
www.sacred-texts.com/neu/celt/ffcc

The three volumes of W. W. Gill's *Manx Scrapbook* can be found here, along with many other valuable sources on Manx history and culture:
http://isle-of-man.com/manxnotebook/fulltext

Hewlett, Maurice, *The Lore of Proserpine* (New York, 1913)
https://archive.org/details/loreproserpine00hewlgoog

Hunt, Robert, *Popular Romances of the West of England*, 3rd edn (London, 1903)
www.sacred-texts.com

Woodyard, Chris, 'The Music of Fairy Recorded'
http://hauntedohiobooks.com/music-fairy-recorded

Young, Simon, 'Fairy Imposters in the Great Famine'; 'Irish Fairies and
    Fairy Food: the Mary Doheny Trial'. These and many other of Young's
    valuable articles are available at:
    https://umbra.academia.edu/simonyoung
——, 'The Fairy Investigation Society'
    www.fairyist.com/fairy-investigation-society

ACKNOWLEDGEMENTS

MANY THANKS TO BEN HAYES for his initial interest in my work and his enthusiasm for this project; and also to Michael Leaman, Rebecca Ratnayake, Amy Salter and Howard Trent at Reaktion Books for their help with the publication process. For generous reading, inside knowledge and comment, many thanks are due to Ann Alston, Michael Bell, Eiffel Gao, Sarah Lynch, Matthew Nisbet, Sara Robinson, Julie Sutherland and Simon Young. Thanks to Emily Velmans and the children of Wadhurst Primary School, Sussex for original and surprising fairy pictures. Special thanks to Sreemoyee Roy Chowdhury for her immensely patient, flexible and efficient help in researching fairy sightings and preparing images for the book. The colour printing in this book was paid for by the author.

PHOTO ACKNOWLEDGEMENTS

THE AUTHOR AND PUBLISHERS wish to express their thanks to the below sources of illustrative material and/or permission to reproduce it.

Collection of the author: p. 31; Bristol Museum and Art Gallery: p. 133 (top); from H. F. Feilberg, 'The Corpse-door: A Danish Survival', *Folklore*, XVIII/4 (December 1907): p. 146; photo Granger Historical Picture Archive/ Alamy Stock Photo: p. 225; Lady Lever Art Gallery, Liverpool: p. 135 (foot); Manchester Art Gallery: p. 133 (foot); private collections: pp. 130, 131 (foot), 132 (foot), 134, 135 (top); Scottish National Gallery, Edinburgh: p. 129 (foot); courtesy Faye Spencer: pp. 240 (reproduced by kind permission of Mrs Lisa Sewell, David Gourd's mother), 241 (reproduced by kind permission of Karen Weller); Tate, London: 131 (top), 132 (top); Victoria & Albert Museum, London: p. 129 (top).

Marie-Lan Nguyen, the copyright holder of the image at the top of p. 129, has published this online under conditions imposed by a Creative Commons Attribution 2.5 Generic license. Readers are free to share – to copy, distribute and transmit these works – or to remix – to adapt these works – under the following conditions: they must attribute the work(s) in the manner specified by the author or licensor (but not in any way that suggests that they endorse you or your use of the work(s)); and if they alter, transform, or build upon the work(s), they may distribute the resulting work(s) only under the same or similar licenses to those listed above.

Julian Paren, the copyright holder of the image on p. 137 (photo © Copyright Julian Paren), has published this online under conditions imposed by a Creative Commons Attribution-ShareAlike 2.0 Generic license. Readers are free to share – to copy and redistribute the material in any medium or format, or to adapt, to remix, transform, and build upon the material for any purpose, even commercially; the licensor cannot revoke these freedoms as long as you follow the license terms – under the following terms:

INDEX

Page numbers for illustrations are indicated by *italics*